Dao De Jing

Unfiltered Thoughts in Motion

道德經隨筆梳抄

Dear Barbara,

Though their words may vary and spin
Every great soul guides us
to the light within.

Nov 4 2024

Gordon Pang

ISBN: 9798343242065

Cover illustrated by: Marianne Nakamura

Copyright © 2024 by Gordon Pang

All rights reserved. No part of this publication may be reproduced, stored in a retrieval system, or transmitted in any form or by any means, electronic, mechanical, photocopying, recording, scanning, or otherwise, without the prior written permission of the author.

願此書能喚醒你的道心
May this Book Awaken the Dao within your Soul

Table of Contents

【緣起 How It All Began】 i

【Historical Background / Legend】 1

【第一章】Chapter 1 2

【第二章】Chapter 2 4

【第三章】Chapter 3 7

【第四章】Chapter 4 9

【第五章】Chapter 5 12

【第六章】Chapter 6 14

【第七章】Chapter 7 17

【第八章】Chapter 8 19

【第九章】Chapter 9 23

【第十章】Chapter 10 24

【第十一章】Chapter 11 33

【第十二章】Chapter 12 35

【第十三章】Chapter 13 37

【第十四章】Chapter 14 38

【第十五章】Chapter 15 43

【第十六章】Chapter 16 45

【第十七章】Chapter 17 50

【第十八章】Chapter 18 53

【第十九章】Chapter 19 54

【第二十章】Chapter 20 57

【第二十一章】Chapter 21 64

【第二十二章】Chapter 22 70

【第二十三章】Chapter 23 75

【第二十四章】Chapter 24 88

【第二十五章】Chapter 25 89

【第二十六章】Chapter 26 92

【第二十七章】Chapter 27 95

【第二十八章】Chapter 28 98

【第二十九章】Chapter 29 104

【 第三十章 】Chapter 30 105

【第三十一章】Chapter 31	107
【第三十二章】Chapter 32	113
【第三十三章】Chapter 33	114
【第三十四章】Chapter 34	116
【第三十五章】Chapter 35	117
【第三十六章】Chapter 36	124
【第三十七章】Chapter 37	126
【第三十八章】Chapter 38	127
【第三十九章】Chapter 39	137
【 第四十章 】Chapter 40	143
【第四十一章】Chapter 41	144
【第四十二章】Chapter 42	157
【第四十三章】Chapter 43	165
【第四十四章】Chapter 44	166
【第四十五章】Chapter 45	169
【第四十六章】Chapter 46	171
【第四十七章】Chapter 47	172
【第四十八章】Chapter 48	176
【第四十九章】Chapter 49	178
【 第五十章 】Chapter 50	180
【第五十一章】Chapter 51	190
【第五十二章】Chapter 52	192
【第五十三章】Chapter 53	201
【第五十四章】Chapter 54	203
【第五十五章】Chapter 55	209
【第五十六章】Chapter 56	216
【第五十七章】Chapter 57	218
【第五十八章】Chapter 58	220
【第五十九章】Chapter 59	222
【 第六十章 】Chapter 60	227
【第六十一章】Chapter 61	231
【第六十二章】Chapter 62	232
【第六十三章】Chapter 63	235
【第六十四章】Chapter 64	237

【第六十五章】Chapter 65 243

【第六十六章】Chapter 66 245

【第六十七章】Chapter 67 247

【第六十八章】Chapter 68 249

【第六十九章】Chapter 69 251

【Dao De Jing Side Note】 254

【 第七十章 】Chapter 70 258

【第七十一章】Chapter 71 260

【第七十二章】Chapter 72 261

【第七十三章】Chapter 73 262

【第七十四章】Chapter 74 264

【第七十五章】Chapter 75 266

【第七十六章】Chapter 76 267

【第七十七章】Chapter 77 269

【第七十八章】Chapter 78 271

【第七十九章】Chapter 79 273

【 第八十章 】Chapter 80 274

【第八十一章】Chapter 81 276

【Supplement and Ending Notes】 277

【Hundred-Character Monument】 281

【About Compassion】 284

緣起 How It All Began

In 2018, before my multi-year personal retreat, as I was conducting my final global teaching tour, several diligent students who had studied Daoist Neigong with me asked how they could continue to progress during my absence. I shared this concern with my master, Gordon, and inquired whether he could teach a group of dedicated students some more advanced Daoist practices. He graciously agreed. Consequently, in 2019, we organized two retreats—one lasting a week and the other three weeks.

To facilitate communication, we created a WhatsApp group for the retreat students. I never anticipated that, even after the retreats ended, Master Gordon would voluntarily continue teaching the group through this platform. He not only taught Daoist concepts but also summarized the core spiritual teachings of certain Buddhist sutras related to our practices, including the *Tibetan Book of Death*. His summaries unveiled esoteric teachings that cannot be found in either the English or Chinese versions of these texts. Alongside this, he shared lessons ranging from the basic principles of the Five Elements and Eight Trigrams to deeper classics found within the *Daoist Canon*. His explanations, even of the simplest concepts, differed significantly from what is commonly taught, reflecting the authenticity of the traditional Daoist lineage. Remarkably, he translated some *Daoist Canon* texts and their embedded practices and wisdom into accessible English—despite these texts never having been translated into any other language before.

At the end of 2023, I made a YouTube video titled, *The Untold History of Daoism: From its Origin to Lao Zi to the 5 Secret Gates to Daoist Religion*, where I introduced lesser-known aspects of Daoist history, tracing its development from pre-Laozi times to the present day. In it, I mentioned how a single Chinese character can have multiple meanings, leading to an exponentially greater number of interpretations for any given sentence. This complexity means that the *Dao De Jing* (as well as many other Daoist texts and Buddhist sutras) conceals numerous practical cultivation methods, which are often incomprehensible even to Chinese scholars unless they have attained a certain Qi or spiritual level through personal practice.

One student from the group after watching that video then asked Master Gordon if he could teach the *Dao De Jing*. Master Gordon, after meditative consultation with the lineage, agreed. Each week, he meditated to determine how much content was appropriate to reveal to the students at their current level. Over the course of about six months, he translated two or three chapters per week, leading to the creation of this unique version of the *Dao De Jing*.

A few months after the *Dao De Jing* teachings were completed, I casually asked Master Gordon if we could remove some of our lineage's practices from the text and make it publicly available. To my surprise, he said there was no need to remove anything; by sharing it with the group, it was already considered public. (On a side note, sometimes when I ask my master questions on WhatsApp, he insists on discussing them in person, and even then, he sets up protective boundaries before answering or teaching me.) Those practicing Tai Chi Neigong, Qigong Mode Level 3, and especially Daoist Neigong Foundation, will find that the cultivation aspects of the book resonate deeply with their experiences.

Throughout my more than two decades of teaching, students have often asked me to recommend a specific version of the *Dao De Jing*. Unfortunately, I rarely read English translations myself, as I found most to be heavily philosophical, focusing on just one aspect of the *Dao De Jing's* teachings. This made it difficult to recommend any particular version. Now, I'm excited to finally have an English version I can confidently recommend to everyone. *Dao De Jing: Unfiltered Thoughts in Motion* offers a style that feels like a conversation between a master and students, presented in a naturally evolving format.

Sifu Wing Cheung
Tai Chi, Qigong & Feng Shui Institute Founder
taichi18.com

Historical Background / Legend

Within a certain tradition of Daoism, there is a belief that Old Lord Taishang Laojun (太上老君), in the primordial void of emptiness, initially proclaimed the DDJ using cloud-seal script. Unfortunately, the majority of sentient beings were unable to comprehend it. Hence, he descended to our mortal realm and rewrote the DDJ in its physical forms. Before departing to the Western Regions, the original text was quite lengthy. After writing it, he showed it to his followers, asking if they understood. He deleted the comprehensible portions, while the rest was retained. (maybe using MS Word to do the editing, I don't think he needs to pay an annual fee to use 360 😊). After multiple revisions, this process resulted in the current popular version.

A cloud-seal script is an energy form, which appears as the smoky script in the skies…similar to the energy as said in the trigram (it is the energy, not the physical symbol). Please refer to the notes years ago.

In recent years, various archaeological discoveries from ancient tombs have revealed different versions of the Dao De Jing (DDJ). Some sentences have extra words or variations in certain characters, leading to distinct or divergent meanings. Moreover, in ancient China, writing was done on bamboo slips or with ink on surfaces, later bound together with a string, forming a sort of large scroll.

Legend has it that during the transportation of the DDJ's over 5000 characters back to the central lands, mishaps occurred. The bamboo slips scattered chaotically on the ground, as the laborers responsible for the transport were generally illiterate. Scholars took over and invested significant effort in piecing the bamboo slips back together, resulting in the present popular and coherent version over and after 2000 years.

The unearthed versions from ancient tombs require a similar process of integration, referencing the currently popular version and aligning the internal sequence. However, within the same sentence, there are occasional differences in individual characters or additional segments. The DDJ is a synthesis of the Dao and De sections, and in one tomb discovery, the De section was found to precede the Dao section, and so forth.

A similar fate befell the Śūraṅgama Sūtra (大佛頂首楞嚴經) during its transportation from India to China, resulting in the loss of a substantial portion. Through multiple efforts, the current volumes have been preserved.

【第一章】 Chapter 1

Most Common Translation

道可道，非常道。	The Dao that can be told is NOT the eternal (original) Dao.
名可名，非常名。	The name that can be named is not the eternal name.
無名天地之始；	The nameless is the origin of Heaven and Earth.
有名萬物之母。	The being named is the mother of myriad things.
故常無欲，以觀其妙；	Thus, constantly without desire, one observes its essence.
常有欲，以觀其徼。	Constantly with desire, one observes its manifestations.
此兩者，同出而異名，	These two emerge together but differ in name,
同謂之玄。	The unity is said to be the mystery.
玄之又玄，眾妙之門。	Mystery of mysteries, the door to all wonders.

My Literal translation

If the Dao can be described in ordinary language, it is not the true Dao. If anything can be named in ordinary language, it is not the true name. (Referring to a significant passage from the Diamond Sutra: 'The Tathagata says all XX are non-XX, that is called XX.' In other words, conventional designations are merely convenient linguistic tools, temporarily assigned to facilitate understanding for sentient beings.)

Take a simplified example: When I say 'apple,' this name cannot truly and completely describe the apple. The apple itself possesses numerous other beautiful qualities, both external and internal. Describing it as an 'apple' is just a convenient way for us to understand that it is not a pear. In childhood, teachers might say 'red' and 'round,' and the standard answer often becomes 'apple.' This is not entirely appropriate and is an imperfect logic ingrained through education.

The original substance, unnamed and imperceptible, is the origin of all things. What can be named, which we can perceive, gradually becomes the multitude of things in the world that we understand and apply. This process is established, organized, and built upon based on our desires, needs, and so on.

Therefore, if we can eliminate desires, prejudices, obstacles of inherent knowledge (karma), and preconceived perceptions (sense and organs), and observe everything as it truly is, we can directly perceive the subtle wonders and truths within the realms.

Conversely, if we habitually use the wisdom of our world to observe everything in this world, we can explore the edges of things. Existence and non-existence, named and nameless – these two may seem different and bear different names, mutually exclusive, but their origin is the same, from the Dao. Referring to the Yijing, the metaphysical is called Dao, and the physical is called vessels.

Understanding that these seemingly incompatible concepts originate from the same source (Dao), and although they appear different, they are mutually exclusive, one can peek into the gate of myriad wonders within the profound mysteries, the mysteries within mysteries.

We will return to discuss other aspects of 'name' as the later chapters unfold.

【第二章】 Chapter 2

Most Common Translation

天下皆知美之為美,斯惡已。	When the world knows beauty as beauty, ugliness arises.
皆知善之為善,斯不善已。	When it knows good as good, evil arises.
故有無相生,	Being and non-being mutually give rise to one another.
難易相成,	Difficult and easy bring about each other,
長短相較,	Long and short reveal each other,
高下相傾,	High and low leaning and supporting each other,
音聲相和,	Sound and voice harmonize with each other, (note 1)
前後相隨。	Front and back follow each other.
是以聖人處無為之事,	Therefore, the sages embrace the principle of wu wei in handling affairs. (note 2)
行不言之教;	Convey the wisdom through silent guidance.
萬物作焉而不辭,	Engage with countless elements but refrain from exerting control.
生而不有。	Create but do not possess.
為而不恃,	Act but do not presume,
功成而弗居。	Succeed but do not dwell on.
夫唯弗居,	Indeed, since and only if they do not dwell on,
是以不去。	Loss is of no consequence.

My Literal translation

This is the first chapter, extending towards the concept of (名). (名) is not merely a designation for things or sentient beings; it also names the principles and concepts used in the world, thereby exerting a valuable influence. The original text states that the world recognizes beauty and strives to achieve it, which is a commonly accepted concept. It refers to the idea that certain names or behavioral norms are established through shared recognition or common habits.

We are given a defined concept, such as what is considered beautiful in the text. Anything that does not conform to these criteria is deemed not beautiful and may even be considered undesirable. The same applies to good and bad. In addition to conceptual definitions, there are relative aspects, such as long and short, high and low, and so on. These are generally binary oppositions. When we say something is good, there must be a standard for what is not good in our minds. Unconsciously, this gradually develops into an inherent awareness of loving beauty and disliking filth.

Surprisingly, the worldly definition of beauty is not necessarily universally accepted. Your idea of beauty may differ drastically from mine, changing with geography and evolving over time. Contradictions lead to disputes.

This does not align with the Dao. As described in the first chapter, the Dao is not a binary opposition; it is harmonious. We know that the Dao manifests in the world as a vessel or tool (refer to Chapter 1). It follows people like a shadow, with a constant interplay of yin and yang, forming shadows in unity. Furthermore, the interdependence of yin and yang does not imply incompatibility; often, they support each other, as seen in the example of long and short in the original text. Therefore, the sage cannot be fixed in one perspective, not choosing between likes and dislikes, only doing what aligns with the Dao. When success is achieved, they do not cling to power or fame, and thus, they do not lose the way. (Note: The "not losing" or "lost" in the Dao De Jing does not exclusively refer to worldly power, positions, and fame but rather not losing the way of Dao.)

As we conclude, I am reminded of a poem by the poetic immortal Li Bai (a Daoist swordsman): "The deeds are done, I brush my robe and leave, deeply hidden both in person and name." Let's conclude with this line from his poem.

Note 1: The term "音聲" (yīn shēng) in the context of the passage from the Dao De Jing refers to sound and voice. Here's a breakdown of the two components:

    a. 音 (yīn): Sound

This character refers to sound in a broad sense, including any audible vibrations or noises, in raw form

It encompasses the idea of acoustic elements and vibrations that can be perceived by the ear.

    b. 聲 (shēng): Voice

This character specifically refers to the human voice or vocal sound.

It is the sound produced by vocal cords and resonating in the human throat.

In the context of the passage, it represents the more intentional and expressive aspect of sound, particularly the harmonization of voices.

PS: please remember this, because it contributes an integral part of the later chapter.

Note 2: "無為" (wú wéi) is a concept from Daoism (Taoism) and is often translated as "non-action" or "effortless action". It is a key principle in the philosophy of Daoism, particularly as presented in the Dao De Jing, attributed to Laozi.

Here's a deeper exploration of the concept:

1. Non-action or Inaction: wú wéi "無為" emphasizes the idea of acting in harmony with the natural order, without unnecessary or forced effort. It does not imply complete inactivity but suggests that actions should be spontaneous, by the flow of the Dao (the Way).
2. Effortless Action: Actions taken in accordance with wú wéi "無為" are considered to be without struggle or unnecessary exertion. It's about allowing things to unfold naturally, rather than imposing one's will forcefully.
3. Alignment with the Dao: wú wéi "無為" encourages individuals to align their actions with the Dao, the fundamental principle that underlies and unites the universe. By doing so, one is in tune with the inherent order of things.
4. Letting Go of Ego: It involves letting go of personal desires and ego-driven motives, allowing the natural course of events to unfold without interference. It's about transcending the self and surrendering to the wisdom of the Dao.
5. Spontaneity and Intuition: Actions arising from wú wéi "無為" are spontaneous and intuitive, emerging from a deep understanding of the present moment and a profound connection with the natural flow of life.

The concept of wú wéi "無為" is central to Daoist philosophy, emphasizing a way of living that is attuned to the rhythms of nature, avoiding unnecessary striving, and allowing things to develop organically. It doesn't advocate complete passivity but rather a kind of aligned and purposeful action that arises naturally from a deep understanding of the Dao.

The above said is the most common textbook explanatory, a deeper concept of wú wéi "無為, is: 無為乃是有為極至，如種花。 Inaction (wú wéi) is the ultimate form of action (yǒu wéi), just like planting flowers.

【第三章】 Chapter 3

Most Common Translation

不尚賢，使民不爭；	Not esteeming the talented prevents people from competing.
不貴難得之貨，使民不為盜；	Not valuing rare treasures prevents theft among the people.
不見可欲，使民心不亂。	Not displaying desirable things prevents the hearts of the people from being disturbed.
是以聖人之治，	Therefore, the sage rules by:
虛其心，	Emptying the mind,
實其腹；	Filling up the abdomen,
弱其志，	Weakening the ambition,
強其骨。	Strengthening the bones.
常使民無知無欲，	Fading the civilian thirst for glory and desire for gain,
使夫智者不敢為也。	So that those with wisdom dare not act.
為無為，	Acting without acting,
則無不治。	Then, everything is subject to governance.

My literal translation

The most usual explanation of this chapter/verse is:

Not promoting individuals of talent prevents people from striving for empty fame; not valuing rare possessions prevents people from resorting to theft and robbery; not showcasing things that stimulate desires prevents the hearts of the people from becoming confused. Therefore, the sage's method of governing the world is to purify the minds of the people, satisfy their material needs, weaken the desire of the people for fame and gain, and strengthen the physical bodies of the people, so that they have no cunning and unfulfilled desires. This makes even those with cunning thoughts hesitant to act recklessly. By adhering to the principle of "non-action", the sage can bring about great order in the world.

However, this passage delves into the concept of nurturing the internal energy (Qi) within our bodies, drawing parallels to governing a nation. It follows an explanation of the reasons for steering clear of superfluous desires. (you need the key to unlock it), and also please refer to the 5 Kitchens Scripture, which we had discussed around a year ago.

Note: The original Chinese phrase "實其腹" encompasses a range of meanings owing to the nuanced use of its constituent characters. "實" conveys notions of solidity, firmness, and filling, while "腹" refers to the region between the mid and lower Dāntián, encompassing the expanse of the abdominal area. Consequently, this expression can be interpreted in various contexts, such as nourishing the populace or addressing hunger, fortifying the core muscles for physical fitness, and delving into the realm of Qi and vital energy. This exemplifies how the Chinese language, particularly in its ancient forms, often unfolds in multiple directions, capturing diverse layers of meaning and interpretation.

【第四章】 Chapter 4

Most Common Translation

道沖而用之或不盈，	The Way flows and is utilized but never filled to maximum capacity.
淵兮似萬物之宗。	Profound, it resembles the origin of myriad things.
挫其銳，	Blunt its sharpness,
解其紛，	Untangle its confusion,
和其光，	Harmonize its light,
同其塵。	Synchronize with the dust.
湛兮似或存 (note 1)，	Clear and calm, it seems to endure,
吾不知誰之子，	I do not know whose offspring it is,
象帝之先。	It seems to precede the Lord.

Note 1: 湛兮似或存, should be translated as Deep (with blue/purple tints) and clear, seemingly existing and present. It describes the inner vision of qi and the sources.

Before the translation, here is a reference regarding the chapter from a document known as 老子想爾注, (If using English word-to-word translation it is translated as "Laozi thinks about you, make a note of it")

The Way flows and its utilization is never complete. The Way values moderation (中和, note 2), and one should follow the path of moderation. One's aspirations and intentions should not overflow, as it goes against the teachings of the Way. 'Profound, it resembles the origin of myriad things.' This is the Way. When people follow the Way without deviation, their depth is akin to the Way. 'Blunt its sharpness, untangle its fury.' Sharpness refers to the inclination of the heart towards wickedness, and fury is anger. Both are not pleasing to the Way. When the heart desires to do wrong, it should be blunted, and when anger wants to erupt, one should pacify and resolve it, preventing the internal organs from becoming angry. Self-discipline adheres to the principles of the Way, self-encouragement leads to longevity, and in this, one attains correctness. Furious contention leads to harsh discord, akin to the tense sound of a taut string, causing harm and swiftness in death, affecting the internal organs. The Way is unable to heal, hence the emphasis on the weight of the Way's teachings and gentle guidance. The harm to the internal organs is due to the disharmony of the metal, wood, water, fire, and earth elements. When they are in harmony, they support each other; when in conflict, they overcome one another, leading to various issues when anger arises. If one organ is affected, it will overcome what it dominates, causing illness and endangering life. When encountering external stimuli, if one releases the shackles and suppresses the urges, even if anger is present, it will not cause harm, and death will be averted. However, if one is weakened, allowing the impulses to rule, disaster will follow. 'Harmonize its light, merge with the dust.' When emotions and nature are calm, and joy and anger do not erupt, all internal organs harmonize and support each other, aligning with the radiance of the Way and dust of the world. 'Clear and calm, it seems to endure.' In this serene state, it seems to persist without fading. 'I do not know whose offspring it is, resembling the ancient ruler.' My actions are the Way. The ancient ruler is also the Way, as it aligns with the nameless origin of all things. I do not know whose child can follow this path. Those who can resemble the Way, akin to the ancient ruler.

老子想爾注 -「道沖而用之不盈。」道貴中和，當中和行之，志意不可盈溢違道誡。「淵似萬物之宗。」道也。人行道不違誡，淵深似道。「挫其銳，解其忿。」銳者，心方欲圖惡。忿者，怒也。皆非道所喜。心欲為惡，挫還之，怒欲發寬解之，勿使五藏忿怒也。自威以道誡，自勸以長生，於此致當。忿爭激，急弦聲，所以者過。積死遲怒，傷死以疾，五藏以傷，道不能治，故道誡之重，教之丁寧。五藏所以傷者，皆金木水火土氣不和也。和則相生，戰則相剋，隨怒事情，輒有所發。發一藏則故克所勝，成病煞人。人遇陽者，發囚刻王，怒而無傷，雖爾去死如發耳。如人衰者，發王刻囚，禍成矣。「和其光，同其塵。」情性不動，喜怒不發，五藏皆和同相生，與道同光塵也。「湛似常存。」如此湛然常在不亡。「吾不知誰子，像帝之先。」吾事，道也。帝先者，亦道也，與無名萬物始同一耳。未知誰家子能行此道，能行者便像道也，似帝先矣。

Note 2: "中和" can be translated as "center harmonization". It's like the central line dividing the yin and yang fish in the Tai Chi/Ji diagram. It's also akin to the blade in Zhuangzi's "庖丁解牛. páo dīng jiě niú. Chef cutting Up an Ox" chapter.

My literal translation

From the perspective of the people, society, and philosophical norms, this chapter is quite simple. It's akin to driving on the road - don't over speed, adhere to the rules of the road (In Chinese, the character Dao and Road are the same 道), stay within the lanes, obey traffic lights, always turn on your headlights when you are traveling at dark, and maintain vigilance and composure. It embodies the unity of people and vehicles and the way of Dao/Road.

In the realm of Dao's internal practice, emphasis is placed on regulating heat with precision—avoiding overcooking and maintaining a singular focus on the foundational/primordial source while disregarding peripheral distractions (refer to note 2). Furthermore, aligning oneself with the inner light is encouraged, if attainable (see note 1). The concept of "dust" holds multifaceted significance; envision it as visible particles on a brilliantly sunny day, observable to the naked eye. This symbolism extends to the vibrations inherent in the energy of light. Moreover, the term "dust" is also associated with neidan, commonly referred to as the yellow medicine or yellow spouts. It is essential to establish a connection between this concept and our neigong and BXQ (Bu Xing Qi) practices.

PS: I can not disclose too much in this area, otherwise it will be deemed as 洩露天機 which translates to "disclose heavenly secrets" or "reveal celestial secrets" in English. Unless we are at the right heavenly "crucial point". (契機)

【第五章】 Chapter 5

Most Common Translation

天地不仁，	Heaven and Earth are not benevolent,
以萬物為芻狗；(Note 1)	Treating all things as straw dogs;
聖人不仁，	The sage is not benevolent,
以百姓為芻狗。	Treating the people as straw dogs.
天地之間，	Between Heaven and Earth, (Note 2)
其猶橐籥(Note 3)乎？	Is it not like a bellows and pipes?
虛而不屈，	Empty, yet not collapsing,
動而愈出。	Moving, yet producing more.
多言數窮，	Excessive words (Note 4) result in exhaustion,
不如守中。	Better to hold moderation. (中和 Note 5)

Note 1: "芻狗 Straw dog" refers to an ancient practice of crafting animal-shaped objects using dry straw, specifically for ritual purposes, such as offerings to the heavens.

Note 2: Between Heaven and Earth, please refer to what I taught in our retreat. It is the two specific locations (energy centers) within our body.

Note 3: The term "橐籥" in Chinese, pronounced as "tuó yuè", refers to a device from ancient times used to blow air and kindle fire (Bellows). Metaphorically, it represents the function of governing respiration and regulating the flow of vital energy (The heat). (We had purposely discussed this before, 2 years ago?) The "橐籥" played a role in advancing the development of metal smelting too. In the context of music, it describes bamboo pipes with three holes, used to harmonize various sounds. (please remember this).

Note 4: In this chapter, the term "多言" (talkative, or over speech) is used. Consider the analogy of speaking akin to exhaling air (qi), connecting it to the previous lines about the bellows. It implies not merely speaking too much, but rather an overflow or loss of vital energy, akin to the release of air from a bellows, or pushing too harsh with the bellows.

Note 5: "守中" literally meaning guarding the center, involves guiding oneself to align with the "中和之氣" or the energy of balance. The term "中和" (zhōng hé) denotes center or balance, while "之氣" (zhī qì) signifies the energy or qi. Together, it emphasizes the pursuit of balance and harmony in aspects like emotions, actions, and the overall environment.

My 5 cents

In the dance of heaven and earth, the sages, adorned with wisdom's grace, wear not the cloak of partiality. Their benevolence unfolds not as a selective embrace, but as a boundless symphony of impartial love. Amidst the celestial ballet, they harbor no bias, no prejudice in their hearts.

As the poets of existence, they pen verses of compassion that cascade like gentle rain upon all living things. Each soul, each blossom, finds solace in the embrace of their impartial gaze. In the tender tapestry of their regard, every note of creation, every echo of existence, is a melody cherished in equal measure.

Amidst the battlefield of nations, where the clash of swords echoes the fervor of strife, the mothers' pleas ascend to the divine ear. Yet, in the celestial realm, God remains impartial, a guardian to all children, irrespective of borders and banners. The sages, like ethereal troubadours, embody this divine refrain, singing a song of unity that transcends the ephemeral divisions of the mortal realm.

【第六章】 Chapter 6

Most Common Translation

谷神不死，	The valley spirit never dies, (Note 1)
是谓玄牝，	It is called the mysterious female, (Note 2)
玄牝之门，	The entrance of the enigmatic feminine, (Note 3)
是谓天地根。	Is called the root of heaven and earth.
绵绵若存，	Continuous, seemingly existing,
用之不勤。	Use it without exhaustion.

Note 1: 谷神, The spirit (God) of the valley, often referred to as the divine essence within, doesn't pertain to a literal valley. Instead, it signifies an inner space where our primordial spirit is stored as an energy form within our body, manifesting a valley-like essence. Imagine how the wind (energy) blows/flows within, inside, and out of the valley, and it also symbolizes a sacred reservoir within.

Lots of scholars tried to find an explanation for this term, 谷神, The spirit (God) of the valley, over decades, and unfortunately without success.

Note 2: 玄牝, the term 玄 means mysterious, or scared, if used as an adjective, it means black. While it does not really mean black, it means something dark and mysterious, the yin side. 牝, means female, usually used to describe a female animal. It is yin. So, putting two words together, it means mysterious yin, double yin, pure yin.

Same as the spirit of God, over decades, scholars tried very hard to determine what does it means.

Note 3: Drawing from both notes 1 and 2, the third line of the verse alludes to the entrance of a distinct realm within the body. Various Daoist schools and systems feature numerous interpretations, with the most widely recognized understanding being:

會蔭 (Huì Yìn), 百會 (Bǎi Huì), 智慧眼 (Zhì Huì Yǎn) - Wisdom Eye

In addition, we have 梵穴 (Fàn Xué) - Brahma's chakra within our lineage too.

Laozi think about you and make note:

'The valley spirit does not die; it is called the mysterious feminine.'

The valley refers to desire. The essence condensed becomes spirit, desiring to make the spirit eternal, one should guard and preserve the essence. The feminine refers to the earth. The body is at peace, resembling a woman, hence it is not violated. When a man desires to guard the essence, the mind should resemble the earth, like a woman, and avoid engaging in activities prematurely.

'The mysterious feminine is the root of heaven and earth.'

The feminine, representing the earth, is likened to a woman. The opening of the yin is the gateway, the official of life and death, crucially named the root. The male, also called the root, desires to guard the essence.

'Softly, softly it seems to exist.'

The way of yin and yang is to softly guard the essence for life, understanding destiny through the years, and thus naming it self-restraint. In one's youth, even though there may be moments of indulgence, one should be mindful and restrained. 'Softly, softly' implies a subtle existence. By following this subtlety, longevity is attained, much like the eternal nature of youth. However, what is presented now is a great harm. How does one cultivate the way? By placing importance on ancestral rites, ensuring the continuation of one's lineage. Desiring to unite essence and produce life, hence teaching the young to be mindful and not to cease, for without teaching, it becomes a toil.

The plan of toil stems from the foolishness of the human heart; how can one blame the way? Those of supreme virtue possess firm and strong aspirations, capable of not being attached to desires and producing life. In their youth, they cut off indulgence, and their spirits mature early. This statement pertains to the essence of the way, therefore allowing heaven and earth to be without sacrifice, dragons without descendants, immortals without spouses, and celestial maidens without husbands. Such is the great truth.

'Using it, you are not worn out.'

Those who can utilize this way should attain immortality. The matters of men and women cannot be neglected; they must be diligent.

PS: The above serves as a useful external reference, though it doesn't explicitly elucidate the meaning of Chapter 6. Nevertheless, the concepts presented offer valuable mental nourishment, contributing to a deeper understanding and providing food for thought. For some extreme Daoists or scholars, the interpretation leans towards viewing it as sexual activities, given the close resemblance to descriptions of female and male organs and the concept of giving birth to life.

"谷神不死，是謂玄牝。"谷者，欲也。精結為神，欲令神不死，當結精自守。牝者，地也。體性安，女像之，故不擊。男欲結精，心當像地似女，勿為事先。"玄牝門，天地根。"牝，地也，女像之。陰孔為門，死生之官也，最要故名根。男茶亦名根。"綿綿若存。"陰陽之道，以若結精為生，年以知命，當名自止。年少之時，雖有當閉省之。綿綿者，微也。從其微少，若少年則長存矣。今此乃為大害。道造之何？道重繼祠，種類不絕。欲令合精產生，故教之年少微省不絕，不教之勤力也。勤力之計，出愚人之心耳，豈可怨道乎！上德之人，志操堅強，能不戀結產生，少時便絕，又善神早成。言此者，道精也，故令天地無祠，龍無子，仙人無妻，玉女無夫，其大信也。"用之不勤。"能用此道，應得仙壽，男女之事，不可不勤也。

My literal translation

Our body harbors numerous energy gates that establish a connection with the cosmic universe, essentially representing pure yin energy. Once we attain awareness of these gates, their existence becomes palpable. Given their link to the eternal energy source, utilizing them doesn't lead to exhaustion.

At a later opportune moment, we delve into the river diagram together, offering additional insights into and comprehending this chapter. Furthermore, as mentioned previously (over two years ago), there's a connection with the Genesis narrative in the Bible.

【第七章】 Chapter 7

Most Common Translation

天長地久。	Eternal are heaven and earth.
天地所以能長且久者，	The reason why heaven and earth can be long-lasting.
以其不自生，	Is that they are not self-born. (They do not come into existence on their own.)
故能長生。	Hence, they can long endure.
是以聖人	Therefore, those Sages
后其身而身先，	Prioritize others over ONE self, yet stand at the forefront;
外其身而身存。	Transcending self, one finds enduring presence.
非以其無私邪？	Isn't it that through selflessness?
故能成其私。	one can achieve their aspirational goals and fulfill their ideals?

My literal translation

A literal translation may not be necessary for this chapter. Once we grasp the initial verses, the rest become self-explanatory. If it does not, please let me know.

My 5 cents

Re: Eternal are heaven and earth. The reason why heaven and earth can be long-lasting, is that they are not self-born.

This passage presents a profound challenge, prompting many scholars to retain the enigmatic language even in its original Chinese form and swiftly transition to subsequent concepts. The key lies in unraveling why heaven and earth endure, characterized by their non-self-born nature. However, nuanced interpretations often deviate from the concept of Oneness.

"Dao" is an enduring entity, unaffected by the cycle of birth and death, neither arising nor ceasing. Serving as the vessel of "Dao", heaven and earth embody and express its essence. Their functionality arises from the eternal and intricate dance of Yin and Yang, rather than being self-generated or self-operating, rooted in the cyclic nature. The term "non-self-born" encapsulates this essence of mutual cyclical operation – the (sacred dance), as reflected in the familiar principle of "lone Yin does not prosper, sole Yang does not generate".

Furthermore, the enduring phenomena of heaven and earth, depicted as "long-lasting", is portrayed from the perspective of human cognition and perception. This description is filtered through the lens of our limited understanding, emphasizing temporality rather than the eternal transcendence of "Dao" or the fundamental unity (Oneness). In other words, heaven and earth are not inherently long-lasting; they merely serve as vessels for Dao.

P.S. The details of this chapter will be unveiled in the upcoming chapters.

【第八章】 Chapter 8

Most Common Translation

上善若水。	The highest virtue is like water.
水善利萬物而不爭，	Water is good at benefiting all things without contending.
處眾人之所惡，	It stays in places that people dislike,
故幾於道。	Thus, close to the Dao.
居善地，	Dwell in a good place,
心善淵，	Kind-hearted and profound,
與善仁，	Share in harmony and compassion,
言善信，	Speech is good and trustworthy,
正善治，	Govern with virtuous deed,
事善能，	Capable of virtuous actions,
動善時。	Acting at the right time.
夫唯不爭，	Because it does not contend,
故無尤。	Hence, free from blame and lame.

Extract from Laozi He Shang Gong Zhang Ju (Laozi DDJ commented by He Shang Gong):

"The highest virtue is like water. A person of the highest virtue is like the nature of water. Water is good at benefiting all things without contending. In the heavens, it becomes mist and dew; on the earth, it becomes the source of springs. It dwells in places that people dislike, as people dislike the low, damp, dirty places, yet water alone nurtures and sustains them. Thus, it is close to the Dao.

Reside in a good place; the nature of water is pleased with the earth. It flows down wherever there is grass and trees, resembling the way a mysterious female descends (please refer to note 2, chapter 6). A good-hearted person has a profound mind, just as water is deep and clear. Being kind and benevolent, water nourishes all things. All living things thrive through the gift of water. When giving, giving those in need without bestowing upon those with abundance.

Words are trustworthy, water reflects inner images without losing its true essence. Governance is effective and fair, leaving nothing untouched, clean, clear, and fair. Skillful in action, it can be square or round, bending and straightening according to its form. It moves at the right time, dispersing in summer and congealing in winter, responding to the seasons.

Thus, it does not contend; when blocked, it stops; when opened, it flows. It follows the way of nature, listening to others. Therefore, it is without fault. The nature of water is like this, hence under heaven, there is nothing that can blame or criticize water."

(Note: When delving into He Shang Gong's remarks on the Dao De Jing, it is advised to interpret and comprehend with a focus on nurturing and fostering Qi. However, it is important to note that the authenticity of these commentaries, attributed to He Shang Gong, remains a subject of ongoing debate among scholars.)

老子河上公章句

上善若水。上善之人，如水之性。水善利萬物而不爭，水在天為霧露，在地為源泉也。處眾人之所惡，眾人惡卑濕垢濁，水獨靜流居之也。故幾於道。水性幾於道同。居善地，水性善喜於地，草木之上即流而下，有似於牝動而下人也。心善淵，水深空虛，淵深清明。與善仁，萬物得水以生。與，虛不與盈也。言善信，水內影照形，不失其情也。正善治，無有不洗，清且平也。事善能，能方能圓，曲直隨形。動善時。夏散冬凝，應期而動，不失天時。夫唯不爭，壅之則止，決之則流，聽從人也。故無尤。水性如是，故天下無有怨尤水者也。

Some Background for He Shang Gong (河上公)

He Shang Gong is a hermit in history. His "He Shang Gong Zhang Ju " annotated by Laozi was the earliest, most widely circulated, and most influential, but no one knows his name and birthplace. "The Legend of Immortals" records: "The name of the prince on the river is unknown".

He Shang Gong is also known as "He Shang's father-in-law", a real person on He Shang, an alchemist in Langya 琅琊, the master of Huang Lao's philosophy, and the founder of Fangxian Tao (方仙道)

One of the disciples of Master He Shang Gong once discussed the Dao and the concept of immortality with Emperor Qin Shi Huang (The first emperor who united China in history). It is said that from that time on, Qin Shi Huang began his quest to find the way to immortality.

PS: Qin Shi Huang (259 BC to July 12, 210 BC) was the founder of the Qin dynasty and the first emperor of China. Rather than maintain the title of "king" borne by the previous Shang and Zhou rulers, he assumed the invented title of "emperor".

Laozi think about you and make note:

"The highest virtue is like water, which is good at benefiting all things and yet does not contend. Water excels in being gentle and weak, flowing to lower places and avoiding the solid to return to the empty. It constantly nourishes and benefits all things without striving. Thus, it is desired to emulate its way.

Dwell in the places that people dislike, and thus be close to the Dao. Water is able to accept and endure impurity and filth, resembling the Dao in this way.

Live in good places and have a kind heart. Water is good at dwelling in lowly places and is deep. 'Deep' here implies being profound.

Associate with those who are virtuous. People should follow the example of water and always delight in kindness and benevolence.

Speak truthfully. People should constantly teach and advise each other to be truthful and have sincere integrity.

Govern with good policies. Rulers should govern their countries in accordance with the Tao to achieve harmony.

Perform tasks skillfully. People, when seeking teachers or mentors, should seek those who are skillful and knowledgeable about the true path, not pursuing deceit or cunning.

Act at the right time. When engaging in actions, do not violate the principles of the Tao, and do not harm the spiritual essence.

Only by not contending can one be free from blame. By being alone, one can emulate water's ability to avoid great harm."

"上善若水，水善利萬物又不爭。"水善能柔弱，像道去高就下，避實歸虛。常潤利萬物，終不爭，故欲令人法則之也。"處眾人之所惡。故幾于道。"水能受垢辱不潔之物，幾像道也。"居善地，心善淵。"水善得窐空，便居止為淵。淵，深也。"與善仁。"人當法水，心常樂善仁。"言善信。"人當常相教為善有誠信。"政善治。"人君理國，常當法道為政則致治。"事善能。"人等當欲事師，當求善能知真道者，不當事耶偽伎巧耶知驕奢也。"動善時。"人欲舉動，勿違道誡，不可得傷工氣。"夫唯不爭，故無尤。"唯，獨也。尤，大也。人獨能放水不爭，終不遇大害。

My 5 cents

In the realm of attributes:

Water descends from above, like sweet dew upon the crown,
As Li Bai's verses proclaim: "Descending in a cascade flying down of three thousand feet,
As if the Milky Way from the ninth heaven did fleet. (Nine Skies)"
(Note: BXQ3)

As for water's self-reflection:
Within, its image mirrors the form, not losing its essence.
Reflection within is an effortless art,
Yet, preserving essence, a formidable part.
To achieve this essence, to remain true,
The heart must be tranquil, desireless, seeking nothing,
Only then can the heart be still like placid water,
Water deep in boundless emptiness, profound and clear.
Its surface mirrors, like a tranquil mirror.
Reflecting reality, as in Li Bai's verse: "afar, the waterfall in front of the river it shows."

In terms of functionality:

Water benefits all, above as mist and dew,
Below is the wellspring,
(Ref. The "Yellow River Chart" (Heto, 河圖): "Heavenly ONE generates water, earth SIX embraced and borne.")

(Note: Neigong 2 and 3. The Qi of the heart condensed as dew falling from heaven)

Water dwells in places despised by man,
Cleansing impurities, purifying the soul.
Whitening the spirit, refining the divine.

【第九章】Chapter 9

Most Common Translation

持而盈之，	Holding and keep filling it up,
不如其已。	Is not as good as stopping in time.
揣而銳之，	Pounding and make it sharp,
不可長保。	Cannot be maintained for long.
金玉滿堂，	A hall filled with gold and jade,
莫之能守。	None can be retained.
富貴而驕，	Wealth and glory, and arrogant,
自遺其咎。	One brings upon their fault.
功成身退，	Achieve success, then gracefully retreat,
天之道。	The way of heavenly Dao

My literal translation

Holding a cup to fill with water requires knowing when to stop; otherwise, it spills over. Sharpening a tool to an extreme razor edge makes it prone to breaking. Accumulating too much worldly treasure is unsustainable. Pursuing pride and glory leads to self-inflicted faults and blame, both physically and in terms of mentality or attitude.

This is a response that reiterates concepts from the preceding chapters. Its primary purpose is to emphasize the control of qi and the mastery of internal energy.

【第十章】Chapter 10

Most Common Translation

載營魄抱一，	Carrying the vital (Húnpò (魂魄)) energy and embracing oneness,
能無離乎？	Is it possible to avoid separation?
專氣致柔，	The aim of gathering and concentrating Qi is to attain the utmost softness,
能嬰兒乎？	Can your Qi flow like an infant? (Can you bring forth an infant?)
滌除玄覽，	To cleanse and eliminate profound observations and perceptions,
能無疵乎？	Can you be without flaws?
愛民治國，	To love the people and govern the country,
能無知乎？	Can it be done without knowledge?
天門開闔，	As Heaven's gate opens and closes,
能無雌乎？	Can it be without femininity?
明白四達，	Understanding in all directions,
能無為乎？	Can it be Wuwei?
生之、畜之，	Give birth to it, nurture it. (Give birth to it, without obstructing its source. Nurture it, without suppressing its nature.)
生而不有，	Giving Birth yet not possessing,
為而不恃，	To act without relying,
長而不宰，	To nurture without dominating,
是謂玄德。	This is called the mysterious virtue.

Note: This passage predominantly employs archaic inverted rhetorical questions, encompassing both affirmative and negative nuances. (Inversion).

I have not delved into how to govern a country, build a society focused on personal growth, or discuss moral perspectives here. You can easily find more about these topics in other articles.

My literal translation

When we engage in the practice of carrying our soul's energy, encompassing both Hún and Pò (魂魄), and strive to return to Oneness, it is essential to minimize distractions and maintain a balanced focus. The goal is to avoid separation, ensuring that our attention is neither overly scattered nor excessively concentrated during the practice.

Forcing and practicing our Qi flows as soft and gentle as possible, like an infant. In other words, at one point, we may have an infant. That is the internal embodiment (Qi embryo), which contrasts with another practice involving external embodiments, the separation of yang spirit and yin spirit, and out-of-body experiences.

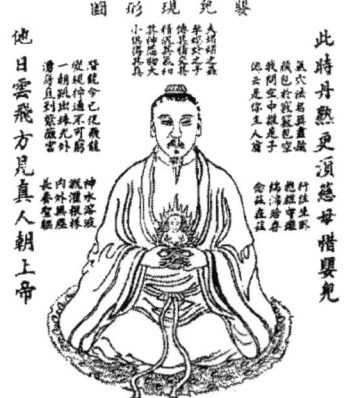

The diagram of Qi baby appears

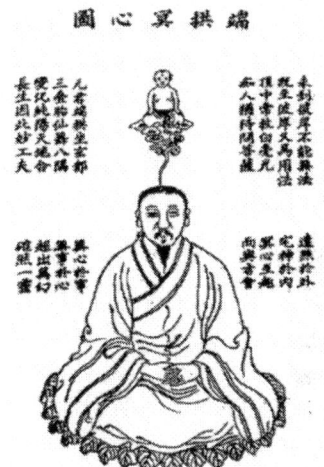

The diagram of the Primordial Soul arises

When encountering the Qi embryo, observe it without the influence of perceptions or interruptions, utilizing your profound wisdom, often referred to as the third eye.

When the Gate of Heaven, also known as the Brahma Chakra or the thousand lotus petals (a bit lower at Bǎi huì 百會) opens, is it possible for it to occur without any Yin energy? In simpler terms, is it necessary to commence with pure Yang energy, but transform it from a state of pure Yin as started? The intricacies of this process highlight its complexity. (For the avoidance of doubt, some lineages use the pure Yin energy).

明白四達, Comprehend in all directions - where "明" signifies bright light and "白" represents white or realization. In this context, it goes beyond conventional understanding to embody the idea of radiant light penetrating through the entire body, reaching the core (central Meridian and or the core body), and extending to all four limbs. This achievement reflects a profound level of mastery. In this occurrence, it is essential to embody the state of Wuwei (無為) consciousness.

Birth the Qi embryo, and nurture it without obstruction or suppression. Give rise without possession, devoid of reliance and expectations from repeated experiences, all without asserting dominance. Through this, attain immortality and the enigmatic virtue and may also be close to the Dao.

PS: since you guys learned the BXQ 3 and our neiqong 1, (2 and 3). I am allowed to explain this chapter in more detail and deep, otherwise, it will still be based on the common scenario.

Laozi think about you and make notes:

"Carry the essence, embrace the spirit as one, and there will be no separation. The Yin spirit Pò (魄), luminous and pure, shares the same essence (white). The body serves as the vessel for the essence, and when the essence is depleted, it must be replenished. As the spirit matures, it becomes the vital force within the human form. To achieve complete mastery, one must be in harmony with the Dao, the unifying principle. Where does this unity reside within the human form? How does one guard and cultivate it? The unity is not confined to the human body alone; it transcends the various attachments to the physical form. Many in the world often engage in deceptive practices, deviating from the true path. The unity exists beyond the realms of heaven and earth, while humans traverse within these realms. It permeates the entirety of existence, not confined to a singular place. The unity disperses to become the essence, coalescing to form the Supreme Old Lord (Note: the realm of Tai Ching), eternally presiding over Kunlun (Bǎi huì (百會)). Some call it emptiness/Void (Xūwú 虛無), others refer to it as nature, or the nameless — all expressions converge into the same essence. Today, the teachings are disseminated, instructing people to abide by the precepts without deviation, which is tantamount to guarding the unity. Failure to adhere to these precepts results in losing the unity. The world often engages in deceptive practices, labeling the five organs as unity (It implies engaging in practices for the sake of health and physical longevity, as this chapter predominantly emphasizes spiritual aspects.). Closing one's eyes (when 2 eyes become 1, it means the wisdom eye) and contemplating, and desiring blessings (it means worldly or material blessing), is not the way; it distances one from the true essence. 'Focus the energy to attain flexibility, and one can become like an infant.' The infant, devoid of deliberate action, naturally aligns with the Dao, but many are unaware of their own creation."

"載營魄抱一，能無離。"魄，白也，故精白與元同色。身為精車，精落故當載營之。神成氣來，載營人身。欲全此功，無離一。一者，道也。今在人身何許？守之雲何？一不在人身也，諸附身者。悉世間常偽伎，非真道也。一在天地外，人在天地間，但往來人身中耳。都皮裏悉是，非獨一處。一散形為氣，聚形為太上老君，常治崑崙。或言虛無，或言自然，或言無名，皆同一耳。今布道誡，教人守誡不違，即為守一矣。不行其誡，即為失一也。世間常偽伎，指五藏以名一。瞑目思想，欲從求福，非也，去生遂遠矣。"專氣致柔，能嬰兒。"嬰兒無為，故合道，但不知自制。

Extract from Laozi He Shang Gong Zhang Ju (Laozi DDJ Commented by He Shang Gong)

Carry the essence, the essence of the soul. Human existence relies on the presence of the soul, and it should be cherished and nurtured. Joy and anger can cause the soul to dissipate, and sudden shock can harm the soul. The Hún (魂) soul resides in the liver, and the pò (魄) 's essence in the lungs. Indulging in rich wines and sweet dishes can damage the liver and lungs. Therefore, a calm soul devoted to the Dao ensures a peaceful and extended life.

Embrace the unity, to be without separation, signifies the ability to embrace the unity within oneself and not let it depart. This longevity is attained by aligning with the Dao, which is the essence of supreme harmony. Thus, it is said: that by spreading the concept of unity throughout the world, heaven attains clarity, earth attains tranquility, and rulers achieve righteousness and peace. (Author quote from Chapter 39 of DDJ), It enters as the heart, manifests as action, practices generosity as virtue, and consolidates its name as one. The concept of unity implies having an undivided will. Focusing energy to attain flexibility, safeguarding the essence and preventing disorder, allows the body to respond and be supple. This is akin to embodying the qualities of an infant who lacks internal thoughts and external concerns, ensuring that the spirit remains undisturbed.

Purify the mysterious vision, wash the heart, and make it pristine. The heart resides in the profound darkness, observing and understanding all things, hence the term "mysterious vision". Being without blemish implies avoiding impurities and maintaining purity (original wording: sexual impropriety or moral corruption). Love the people, govern the country, and in managing the self, love the vital energy to ensure bodily well-being. In governing the country, love the people to ensure national security.

Be without action, in managing the self, breathe in the essence without letting the ears hear. In governing the country, bestow benevolent deeds without allowing the subjects to be aware. The Gate of Heaven opens and closes, referring to the North Pole, the Purple Palace (In the sky, it is the Polaris area, Ziwei_enclosure - 北極紫微宮 (original text in the scripture), see diagram). Opening and closing indicate the beginning and end of the five seasons. In managing the self, the Gate of Heaven implies the nostrils opening, the breath inhaled and exhaled.

Be feminine, in managing the self, one should be like a female, calm, gentle, and receptive. In governing the country, be adaptable and harmonious, combining without discord. Understand in all directions, signifying clarity and understanding radiating in all directions, like the sun and moon illuminating the entire world. Therefore, it is said: not seen when looked at, not heard when listened to, spreading across the ten directions, shining brightly and magnificently.

Be without knowledge, as there is no one who can fully comprehend the Dao throughout the world. Give birth to it and nurture it; the Dao brings forth and nurtures all things. It gives birth without possessing, as the Dao gives birth to all things without acquiring anything. Act without reliance, as the Dao acts without expecting anything in return. Grow without domination, as the Dao nurtures all things without dominating or controlling them. This is called profound virtue, signifying the Dao's way of acting and nurturing, which is mysterious and cannot be seen. The intention is to make people emulate the Dao.

PS: The lineage of G. Master He Shang Gong focusing the practice of Anapanasati (安那般那), nose and mouth breathing technique. That is why, most of his guidelines in DDJ are based on their school of practice.

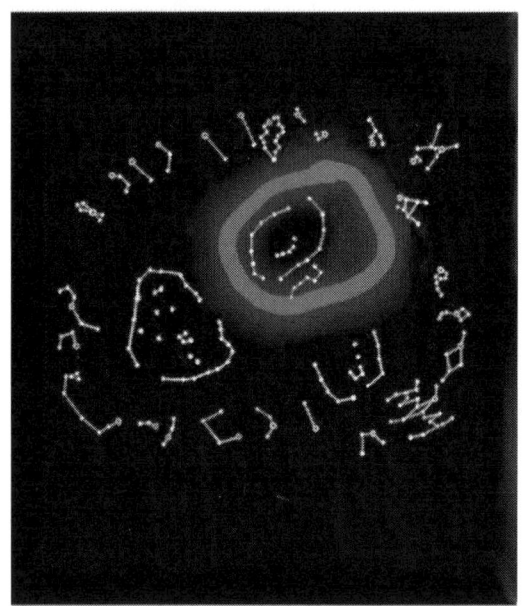

紫微垣 (Zǐ Wēi Yuán) – Circled One: Purple Forbidden Enclosure ...... governing the cultural and related stuff

太微垣 (Tài Wēi Yuán): Supreme Palace Enclosure ..... governing the political

天布垣 (Tiān Bù Yuán): Heavenly Market Enclosure .... governing the social and economic

載營魄，營魄，魂魄也。人載魂魄之上得以生，當愛養之。喜怒亡魂，卒驚傷魄。魂在肝，魄在肺。美酒甘肴，腐人肝肺。故魂靜志道不亂，魄安得壽延年也。抱一，能無離乎，言人能抱一，使不離於身，則長存。一者，道始所生，太和之精氣也。故曰：一布名於天下，天得一以清，地得一以寧，侯王得一以為正平，入為心，出為行，布施為德，摠名為一。一之為言，志一無二也。專氣致柔，專守精氣使不亂，則形體能應之而柔順。能嬰兒。能如嬰兒內無思慮，外無政事，則精神不去也。滌除玄覽，當洗其心，使潔淨也。心居玄冥之處，覽知萬事，故謂之玄覽也。能無疵。

不淫邪也，淨能無疵病乎。愛民治國，治身者，愛氣則身全；治國者，愛民則國安。能無為。治身者呼吸精氣，無令耳聞；治國者，佈施惠德，無令下知也。天門開闔，天門謂北極紫微宮。開闔謂終始五際也。治身：天門，謂鼻孔開，謂喘息闔，謂呼吸也。能為雌。治身當如雌牝，安靜柔弱，治國應變，合而不唱也。明白四達，言達明白，如日月四通，滿於天下八極之外。故曰：視之不見，聽之不聞，彰布之於十方，煥煥煌煌也。能無知。無有能知道滿於天下者。生之、畜之。道生萬物而畜養之。生而不有，道生萬物，無所取有。為而不恃，道所施為，不恃望其報也。長而不宰，道長養萬物，不宰割以為器用。是謂玄德。言道行德，玄冥不可得見，欲使人如道也。

Su Zhe (苏辙) notes and interpretation of DDJ:

Personal Background: Su Zhe (1039–1112) was a prominent scholar and poet during the Song Dynasty in China.

Carrying the vital (Húnpò (魂魄)) energy and embracing oneness

The reason why the spirit (魂) is different from the corporeal soul (魄) is that the soul is material, while the spirit is divine. The "Yi Jing / I Ching" (易經, Book of Changes) states: "Essence and energy constitute the material, while wandering spirits undergo transformations." Hence, we understand the nature and state of ghosts and spirits. The soul being material is mixed and stationary, while the spirit being divine is unified and transformative. When referring to "carrying the essence and embracing the spirit as one", it speaks of their unity. Indeed, the Dao is omnipresent, inherent in human nature, and the marvelous aspect of nature is the divine spirit. When described as pure and unadulterated, it is called unity; when described as concentrated and not dispersed, it is called simplicity. Their return is all in accordance with the Dao, each expressing its reality.

Sages have a stable nature and a concentrated spirit, not moved by material things. Even though the corporeal soul serves as a dwelling, the spirit desires to move. With the soul unopposed, the spirit follows willingly, and thus, the spirit constantly carries the soul. Ordinary people, being enslaved by material desires, have dimmed spirits and lack self-discipline. In such cases, the spirit obeys the soul; the senses are clouded by sounds and colors, and the nose and mouth are fatigued by smells and tastes. With the soul desiring to act, the spirit follows, and thus, the soul constantly carries the spirit. Therefore, they are taught to embrace the spirit and carry the soul, ensuring that the two are inseparable. This is indeed the essential aspect of the sage's self-cultivation. As for the ancient true individuals, deeply rooted and firmly established, living long lives and seeing far, their Dao also follows these principles.

The aim of gathering and concentrating Qi is to attain the utmost softness

Can your Qi flow like an infant?

When the spirit is not regulated, the breath becomes chaotic. The strong are fond of conflict, and the weak are prone to joy and fear, lacking self-awareness. When the spirit is regulated, the breath behaves appropriately; joy and anger are expressed according to their nature. This is what is meant by concentrating the breath. It is the pinnacle of spiritual emptiness and the beginning of vital energy being substantial.

Emptiness, taken to the extreme, results in flexibility; substance, taken to the extreme, results in rigidity. Being pure in nature and free from excessive breath, this is what is meant by attaining flexibility. An infant is unaware of preferences and dislikes, thus maintaining a complete nature. With a complete nature and subtle breath, the body becomes supple. By concentrating the breath to attain flexibility, one can be like an infant in the utmost sense.

To cleanse and eliminate profound observations and perceptions, can you be without flaws?

The sage, externally, is not carried away by the corporeal soul, and internally, is not controlled by the breath. Thus, the cleansing of impurities and dust is complete. At this point, their spirit is clear and expansive, perceiving all things with profound insight. They understand that everything originates from nature, impartially observing purity and impurity without finding any flaws or blemishes.

To love the people and govern the country, Can it be done without knowledge?

Having regulated oneself, extend the same principles to others, even in the governance of the people and the country. Even when it comes to loving the people and governing the nation, approach it with a mind free from personal desires. If one governs with personal desires, the act of loving the people may unintentionally harm them, and governing the country may inadvertently cause disorder.

As Heaven's gate opens and closes, can it be without femininity?

The Gate of Heaven is the source of order, chaos, decline, and prosperity. When one assumes responsibility for the world, at the juncture of its opening and closing, where changes and events unfold, ordinary individuals value gains and fear losses. They take proactive measures to seek blessings. However, the sage adheres to the natural order, understanding the mandate of Heaven, and harmonizes in due time.

The "Yi Jing" says: 'Anticipate Heaven and Heaven will not defy you; it is not anticipation alone. Observe the timing of Heaven after it has been established; it is not solely dependent on timing.' This means that being in harmony with the mandate of Heaven is a constant consideration. Otherwise, those who act prematurely will face failure, and those who act too late will also miss the opportunity. Hence, what is referred to as being able to be feminine does not deviate from the timing.

Understanding in all directions, Can it be Wuwei?

Internally, one governs oneself; externally, one governs the country. When facing changes, there is nothing that is not governed by the Dao. Is it not achieved through understanding in all directions? Understanding in all directions refers to the mind; it is a mind that knows everything. However, there has never been a mind capable of knowing itself. The mind is singular, and if there were another knowing mind, that would make it dual. From unity to duality, confusion arises, and ignorance begins.

Consider a mirror reflecting objects; it merely responds to whatever comes before it. How can it possess knowledge of the objects it reflects? In its essence, it has none, and it is the imposition of thought that leads to the source of delusion.

Give birth to it, nurture it. Giving Birth yet not possessing. To act without relying. To nurture without dominating is called the mysterious virtue.

Its Dao is sufficient to give birth to and nurture all things. It is also able to act without possessing, without relying on, and without dominating. Even with great virtue, things do not recognize it. Hence, it is called profound virtue.

苏辙《老子解》

載營魄，抱一能無離乎？

魄之所以異於魂者，魄為物，魂為神也。《易》曰：精氣為物，遊魂為變，是故知鬼神之情狀。魄為物，故雜而止；魂為神，故一而變。謂之營魄，言其止也。蓋道無所不在，其於人為性，而性之妙為神。言其純而未雜則謂之一，言其聚而未散則謂之樸，其歸皆道也，各從其實言之耳。聖人性定而神凝，不為物遷，雖以魄為舍，而神所欲行，魄無不從，則神常載魄矣。眾人以物役性，神昏而不治，則神聽於魄，耳目困以聲色，鼻口勞以臭味，魄所欲行而神從之，則魄常載神矣。故教之以抱神載魄，使兩者不相離，此固聖人所以修身之要。至於古之真人，深根固蒂，長生久視，其道亦由是也。

專氣致柔，能如嬰兒乎？

神不治則氣亂，強者好鬥，弱者喜畏，不自知也。神治則氣不妄作，喜怒各以其類，是之謂專氣，神虛之至也，氣實之始也。虛之極為柔，實之極為剛，純性而亡氣，是之謂致柔。嬰兒不知好惡，是以性全。性全而氣微，氣微而體柔，專氣致柔，能如嬰兒極矣。

滌除玄覽，能無疵乎？

聖人外不為魄所載，內不為氣所使，則其滌除塵垢盡矣。於是其神廓然，玄覽萬物，知其皆出於性，等觀淨穢，而無所瑕疵矣。

愛民治國，能無為乎？

既以治身，又推其餘以及人。雖至於愛民治國，一以無心遇之。苟其有心，則愛民者適所以害之，治國者適所以亂之也。

天門開闔，能為雌乎？

天門者，治亂廢興所從出也。既以身任天下，方其開闔變會之間，眾人貴得而患失，則先事以徼福；聖人循理而知天命，則待唱而後和。《易》曰：先天而天弗違，非先天也；後天而奉天時，非後天也。言其先後常與天命會耳。不然先者必蚤，後者必莫，皆失之矣。故所謂能為雌者，亦不失時而已。

明白四達，能無知乎？

內以治身，外以治國，至於臨變，莫不有道也，非明白四達而能之乎？明白四達，心也，是心無所不知，然而未嘗有能知之心也。夫心一而已，苟又有知之者，則是二也。自一而二，蔽之所自生，而愚之所自始也。今夫鏡之於物，來而應之則已，矣，又安得知應物者乎？本則無有，而以意加之，此妄之源也。

生之畜之，生而不有，為而不恃，長而不宰，是謂玄德。

其道既足以生畜萬物，又能不有不恃不宰，雖有大德，而物莫之知也，故曰玄德。

【第十一章】 Chapter 11

Most Common Translation

三十輻共一轂，	Thirty spokes share one hub,
當其無，	In their emptiness,
有車之用。	Carriage can be used.
埏埴以為器，	Mold clay into a vessel,
當其無，	In their emptiness,
有器之用。	A vessel can be used.
鑿戶牖以為室，	Cut out doors and windows to make a room,
當其無，	In their emptiness,
有室之用。	The room can be used.
故有之以為利，	Thus, existence contributes to facilitate,
無之以為用。	Utilizing the non-existent to for usefulness.

My literal translation

Thirty spokes converge at the hub to create a wheel, and it is within the void that the wheel fulfills its purpose. Shaping vessels with blended clay, the utility of the vessel arises from the emptiness within. Carving doors and windows to construct a house, the functionality of the house emerges from the void within the walls. Hence, the "existence" that offers convenience does so because the crafted emptiness" serves a role.

The inherent emptiness within a tool, aligning with the principles outlined in Chapter 6, mirrors the essence of the valley spirit. The formation of a valley unfolds in a manner consistent with this concept. Consequently, all instances of resonance, echoes and the thriving of life find their foundation in this shared condition, underscoring the interconnected relationship between emptiness and manifestation in the natural order.

Therefore, the tangible benefits to people are inseparable from the intangible functionality.

My 5 Cents

We can interpret this chapter in relation to the 30-day lunar cycle, aligning it with our internal practice. It can also be connected to the Cultivation Chart (修真圖, Xiūzhēn tú). Here, the void corresponds to the Yellow Court, which ties into our Neigong Set #2.

PS: 9+6=15, 15 x 2 = 30 (2 cycles)

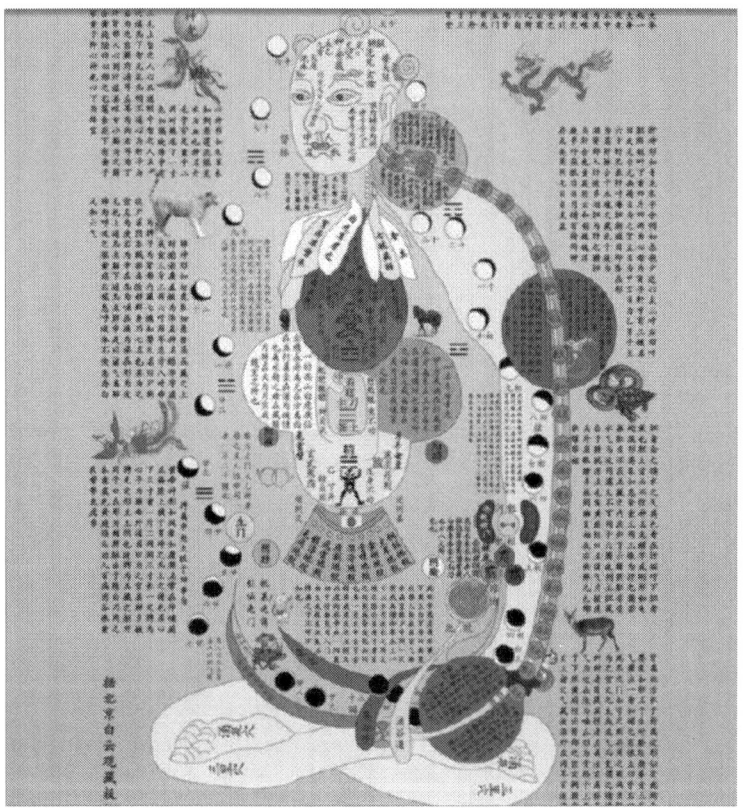

Cultivation Chart (修真圖, Xiūzhēn tú).

【第十二章】Chapter 12

Most Common Translation

五色令人目盲，	The sight of five colors blinds people,
五音令人耳聾，	The sounds of five tones deafen their ears,
五味令人口爽，	The taste of five flavors dulls their palate,
馳騁畋獵令人心發狂，	Engaging in hunting and chasing drives the heart to madness,
難得之貨令人行妨。	Rare goods possession obstructs their path.
是以聖人為腹不為目，	Therefore, the sage cares for the inner essence, not the outer, (The sage attends to their abdomen, not to the visual.)
故去彼取此。	Choosing release over attachment. (Therefore, abandon the former and embrace the latter.)

Usual translation

Coveting the five colors confuses distinctions between right and wrong.
Delighting in the five sounds makes one resist honest advice.
Craving the five flavors leads to neglecting the experience of hardship.
Pursuing field and game hunting drives one's mind and intentions to madness.
Rare possessions lead people to plan devious schemes.
Therefore, the governance of the wise focuses on enriching the inner self, not on superficial appearances.
Hence, decisions are made based on this principle.

My 5 cents

This chapter reinstates and emphasizes the perspective that in our journey of practice, external elements like visuals, sounds, and tastes (which are perceived by our senses—eyes, ears, and tongue) can disturb the tranquility of our hearts. Furthermore, the pursuit of external recognition or the chase for desired objects can also divert our hearts from a state of peace. Therefore, sages live solely on fulfilling fundamental daily needs, without pursuing anything unnecessary.

Supplement:

Five Elements (Five Eternal Energy, Pinyin = Wǔháng):
金 (Jin) – Metal,
水 (Shui) - Water
木 (Mu) - Wood
火 (Huo) - Fire
土 (Tu) – Earth

Five Colors:
青 (Qing) - Green/Blue (Associated with Wood)
赤 (Chi) - Red (Associated with Fire)
黄 (Huang) - Yellow (Associated with Earth)
白 (Bai) - White (Associated with Metal)
黑 (Hei) - Black (Associated with Water)

Five Sounds:
宫 (Gong) - Gong (1st note, Do, associated with Earth)
商 (Shang) - Shang (2nd note, Re, associated with Metal)
角 (Jue) - Jue (3rd note, Mi, associated with Wood)
徵 (Zhi) - Zhi (5th note, So, associated with Fire)
羽 (Yu) - Yu (6th note, La, associated with Water)

Five Tastes:
酸 (Suan) - Sour (Associated with Wood, affecting the liver)
苦 (Ku) - Bitter (Associated with Fire, affecting the heart)
甘 (Gan) - Sweet (Associated with Earth, affecting the spleen)
辛 (Xin) - Pungent/Spicy (Associated with Metal, affecting the lungs)
鹹 (Xian) - Salty (Associated with Water, affecting the kidneys)

Order of the Five Elements:

The general sequence is "Earth, Metal, Water, Wood, Fire" with Earth being the first and generating the others, creating a cycle. The Daoist idiom says, "Middle Earth gives rise to the other's four symbols."

The order of "(Gold) Metal, Water, Wood, Fire, Earth" is based on my personal preference. This is because my practice is rooted in Gold and Water. You do not need to follow it.

Additionally, the common convention in the public domain is to use the order (Metal, Wood, Water, Fire, Earth).

【第十三章】Chapter 13

Most Common Translation

寵辱若驚，	To be favored and to be disgraced are like startling events,
貴大患若身。	To be greatly esteemed is like a great peril to the self.
何謂寵辱若驚？	What is meant by 'to be favored and to be disgraced are like startling events'?
寵為下，	Being favored as inferior,
得之若驚，	To obtain it is like being startled,
失之若驚，	To lose it is like being startled,
是謂寵辱若驚。	This is what is meant by 'to be favored and to be disgraced are like startling events.
何謂貴大患若身？	What is meant by 'to be greatly esteemed is like a great peril to the self?
吾所以有大患者，	I have great peril,
為吾有身，	Because I have the self,
及吾無身，	and, If I do not have the self,
吾有何患！	what peril do I have?
故貴以身為天下，	Thus, one who values the self as the world,
若可寄天下；	May place the wish to the world,
愛以身為天下，	One who loves the self as the world,
若可托天下。	Maybe entrusted with the world.

My Literal Translation

When unexpected favor descends, the favored rejoices ecstatically, while those who fall out of favor are gripped with fear and dismay; this phenomenon is described as being equally surprised by both favor and disgrace.

My susceptibility to joy and sorrow arises from my inability to break free from the confines of my own limitations, our mental prison. If I were to achieve freedom of both body and mind, what troubles would remain for me?

Hence, what people highly value is an individual capable of harmonizing with the world, as such a person can entrust themselves to the world. Similarly, what people hold dear is someone who can seamlessly integrate with the world, as such an individual can be entrusted to the world.

【第十四章】 Chapter 14

Most Common Translation

視之不見名曰夷，	To see (to regard) it without seeing, and call it 'Yi (夷)',
聽之不聞名曰希，	To listen to it without hearing, and call it 'Xi (希)',
搏之不得名曰微。	To grasp (or capture) it without obtaining and call it 'Wei (微)'.
此三者不可致詰，	These three cannot be thoroughly fathomed and examined. (deduce the truth)
故混而為一。	Therefore, they merge into one.
其上不皦，	Its upper part is not bright.
其下不昧。	its lower part is not obscure.
繩繩不可名，	Consistently, it defies precise naming,
復歸於無物，	Reverting to a state of nothingness.
是謂無狀之狀，	This is known as the formless form,
無物之象。	An embodiment symbol of a state of nothingness.
是謂惚恍。	This is identified as obscure and elusive. (Trance or absentminded).
迎之不見其首，	Confront it, and its head remains unseen;
隨之不見其后。	Pursue it, and its tail eludes perception.
執古之道，	Adhere to the ancient path,
以御今之有，	Guiding the present existence.
能知古始，	Understanding the origins of antiquity,
是謂道紀。	This is denoted as the chronicle of the Dao. Or, this is denoted as the discipline of the Dao.

My literal translation

Unable to see an image, it is called Yi (夷);

Unable to hear the sound, it is called Xi (希);

Unable to touch a physical form, it is called Wei (微).

Recalling the teachings of the Dao De Jing, specifically Chapter 1, verses 3 and 4, which emphasize the limitations of naming and the recognition that the named is the source of myriad things, we can interpret Yi, Xi, Wei as symbolic representations or words denoting particular stages in our spiritual practice. Attempting to articulate the essence of Yi, Xi, Wei through mere words seems inadequate and irrelevant in my perspective, despite the common inclination of many to do so.

Yi, Xi, and Wei all symbolize aspects of our inner experiences—vision, hearing, and sensible perception—especially during a stage meditation (NOT samadhi). In these states, we may encounter situations where we seem to perceive something indistinct, beyond our normal physical senses: seeing the uncertain, hearing the subtle, and sensing the intangible. A parallel can be drawn to Paramahansa Yogananda's experience of heightened awareness before meeting his master (if my memory is correct, even before his initiation), where he felt the nuances of the entire village over a mile in diameter, seemingly sensible yet beyond touch. Furthermore, a particular sect of Sikhism, with a mythical perspective, delves into the intricacies of inner vision and sound.

In the context of inner vision, Daoist scriptures describe a situation where one can see without using the physical eyes, particularly in a completely dark enclosed room—a milestone in spiritual achievement.

Inner sound holds significant importance, representing energy. Analogies such as Lord Krishna's high-pitched flute or Shiva's drum offer glimpses into this concept. References to the WORD in the Bible, Genesis, align with these profound energy vibrations. The Dao De Jing, later in Chapter 41, will further connect these ancient teachings.

This colorless, soundless, and formless entity defies linguistic description, representing the undifferentiated primal energy before the emergence of Yin and Yang. (In Chinese it is called as 陰陽未判的混元一氣). Above, there is no visible brightness; below, no visible darkness. Unable to be precisely defined, it is likened to a return to a state of nothingness, a stage often encountered in meditation and echoed in the early verses of Genesis, before GOD made everything. (we have discussed this before way at the beginning over 2 years ago). Many practitioners may struggle or give up at this stage, especially if breakthroughs are not achieved within a certain timeframe.

This state embodies a form of formlessness, seemingly nonexistent yet existent, characterized by ambiguity, flickering, and uncertainty. Tracing back, its origin is unknown; moving forward, its end is equally elusive. This brings to my mind the story of Brahma seeking to comprehend the essence of time through deep meditation.

To grasp the ancient Dao of nature for governing today's existence and to perceive the ancient origins and developments constitute the discipline and chronicle of the Dao. (In other words, follow your lineage).

In conclusion: It is essentially describing a manifestation of profound inner consciousness, or we may categorize it as a stage in the art of meditation.

Laozi think about you and make notes:

Not seeing it, yet called YI (profound); Not hearing it, yet called Xi (rare); Not grasping it, yet called Wei (subtle). The unseeable, the unhearable, the untouchable – these three cannot be examined, hence they fuse into {one}.

This {one} is pure and clear. It is the embodiment of Dao's virtue and beauty. The profound (Yi) means flat and expansive; the rare (Xi) is broad and encompassing; the subtle (Wei) is the pure essence of Dao. (The literal meaning of the wording). These three aspects express the beauty of Dao.

These three cannot be probed or questioned; therefore, they merge into one. It is not harmed by multiplicity; simplicity, dispersion, purity, and thinness enter into it. Therefore, it cannot be probed.

Above, it is not bright; below, it is not obscured. Dao's vital energy constantly moves upward and downward, managing the inner and outer realms of heaven and earth. It is not visible because of its clarity and subtlety. It is neither bright above nor obscured (忽) below; the obscured (in here, 忽 the word obscure means extremely subtle), produces sound.

Endlessly nameless, it returns to nothingness. Dao is like this, unnameable, as if it doesn't exist. It is the formless form, the image of nothingness. Dao is the highest, subtle and concealed, without a distinct appearance. It can only be followed in its guidance; it cannot be seen or known.

In the present world, there are false arts that point to form and name them as Dao, making them conform to various appearances and characteristics, but this is not correct. This is nothing but deception.

This is called confused and perplexed. Facing it, you cannot see its front; following it, you cannot see its rear. Dao is clear but cannot be seen or known; it is formless and imageless.

Adhering to the ancient Dao to deal with present situations. How do we know that the Dao of the present is still intact? Observe those who attained longevity in the past, all followed this path to confirm that the present customs are not broken.

Therefore, the ancient beginning is called Dao's record. By using the longevity of ancient sages as an analogy, one can understand the current existence of Dao. Thus, diligently strive to guard the true Dao, and you will then obtain the fundamental principles and guidelines of Dao.

"視之不見，名曰夷；聽之不聞，名曰希；搏之不得，名曰微。"夷者，平且廣；希者，大度形；微者，道⬚清：此三事欲嘆道之德美耳。"此三者不可致詰，故混而為一。"此三者淳說道之美。道者天下萬事之本，詰之者所況多，竹素不能勝載也，故還歸一。多者何傷，樸散淳薄更入耶！故不可詰也。"其上不皦，其下不忽。"道炁常上下，經營天地內外，所以不見，清微故也。上則不皦，下則不忽，忽有聲也。"繩繩不可名，復歸於無物。"道如是不可見名，如無所有也。"是無狀之狀，無物之像。"道至尊，微而隱，無狀貌形像也。但可從其誡，不可見知也。今世間偽伎，指形名道，令有服色名字狀貌長短，非也。悉耶偽耳。"是謂惚恍，迎不見其首，隨不見其後。"道明不可見知，無形像也。"執古之道，以禦今之有。"何以知此道今端有，觀古得仙壽者悉行之，以得知今俗有不絕也。"以故古始，是謂道紀。"能以古仙壽若喻，今自勉厲守道真，即得道綱紀也。

Extract from Laozi He Shang Gong Zhang Ju (Laozi DDJ Commented by He Shang Gong):

Not seeing and calling it 'Yi'; colorless and called 'obscure'. Saying it is formless and colorless, not possible to see with the eyes.

Not hearing and calling it 'Xi'; soundless and called 'rare'. Saying it is without sound, not possible to hear with the ears.

Not grasping and calling it 'Wei'; formless and called 'subtle'. Saying it is without a tangible form, not possible to touch or hold.

Describing it as one without a definite form, not possible to shape or hold.

These three cannot be probed or questioned; the three, referred to as 'Yi,' 'Xi,' 'Wei.'

The reason they cannot be probed is because they are without color, sound, and form. Words cannot express them; writings cannot transmit them. They are to be embraced in stillness, sought through spirit, and cannot be obtained by questioning.

Therefore, they merge into one. Merging, combining. Thus, they unite as one.

Above, it is not bright; stating that the one is in the heavens, not bright. Bright, radiant.

Below, it is not obscured; stating that the one is in the world, not obscured. Obscured, having some darkness or mystery.

Endlessly nameless, 'endlessly' means movement without limit or level. 'Endlessly' refers to infinite motion.

Nameless, it is not one color, it cannot be distinguished as blue, red, yellow, white, or black (the five colors); it is not one sound, it cannot be heard as do, re, mi, so; la (the five Sounds), it is not one form, it cannot be measured in terms of length, size, or degree. (please refer to Chapter 12 of DDJ)

Returning again to nothing. '物' refers to substance or essence, and it is to return to non-substance or non-essence.

This is called the formless form; stating that the one is without a specific form, yet it can give form to all things.

The image of non-substance; one without substance, yet providing form and image to all things.

This is called trance, absentminded, elusive, and perplexed; one is neither clearly present nor completely absent, making it imperceptible.

Facing it, you cannot see its front; it has no beginning or end, making it unpredictable.

Following it, you cannot see its rear; stating that the one leaves no trace, not possible to be observed.

Holding on to the ancient Dao, to govern the present existence. Sages adhere to the ancient path, giving birth to the one to govern all things, knowing that the present will have the one.

Able to know the beginning of antiquity, this is called the chronicle of the Dao. Those who can understand the ancient origin of the one, this is called knowing the fundamental principles and guidelines of Dao. (the discipline of the Dao)

老子河上公章句 -> 道經 -> 贊玄

視之不見名曰夷，無色曰夷。言一無采色，不可得視而見之。聽之不見名曰希，無聲曰希。言一無音聲，不可得聽而聞之。搏之不得名曰微。無形曰微。言一無形體，不可搏持而得之。此三者不可致詰，三者，謂夷、希、微也。不可致詰者，夫無色、無聲、無形，口不能言，書不能傳，當受之以靜，求之以神，不可問詰而得之也。故混而為一。混，合也。故合於三名之為一。其上不皦，言一在天上，不皦。皦，光明。其下不昧。言一在天下，不昧。昧，有所闇冥。繩繩不可名，繩繩者，動行無窮極也。不可名者，非一色也，不可以青黃白黑別，非一聲也，不可以宮商角徵羽聽，非一形也，不可以長短大小度之也。復歸於無物。物，質也。復當歸之於無質。是謂無狀之狀，言一無形狀，而能為萬物作形狀也。無物之象，一無物質，而為萬物設形象也。是謂惚恍。一忽忽恍恍者，若存若亡，不可見之也。迎之不見其首，一無端末，不可預待也。除情去欲，一自歸之也。隨之不見其後，言一無影跡，不可得而看。執古之道，以御今之有，聖人執守古道，生一以御物，知今當有一也。能知古始，是謂道紀。人能知上古本始有一，是謂知道綱紀也。

【第十五章】 Chapter 15

Most Common Translation

古之善為士者，	The ancient virtuous ones,
微妙玄通，	Subtle, mysterious, and profound,
深不可識。	Their depths cannot be fathomed.
夫唯不可識，	Because they cannot be fathomed,
故強為之容。	One can only describe them vaguely.
豫焉若冬涉川，	Hesitant, as if crossing a winter river,
猶兮若畏四鄰，	Cautious, as if fearing their neighbors on all sides,
儼兮其若容，	Reserved, as if they are guests,
渙兮若冰之將釋，	Yielding, like ice about to melt,
敦兮其若樸，	Simple, like uncarved wood,
曠兮其若谷，	Open, like a vast valley,
混兮其若濁。	Opaque, like muddy water.
孰能濁以靜之徐清？	Who can be calm and gradually clear, while stirring up the mud?
孰能安以久動之徐生？	Who can be tranquil and allow the still to slowly become lively?
保此道者不欲盈，	Those who follow this Way do not seek fullness,
夫唯不盈，	Only by not seeking fullness,
故能蔽不,新成。	Hence, capable of shielding and emerging anew. (Ability to draw new energy (life) from the consumption of decline.)

My literal translation

In ancient times, practitioners who embraced goodness as their path possessed subtle profundity derived from the mysterious cultivation, too profound to be fathomed.

Due to its profound nature, one can only reluctantly attempt to describe it.

Be cautious, as if walking on thin ice; be vigilant, fearing disturbance to the neighbors; be devout, showing reverence like a guest; be gentle, like the melting of ice; be honest, resembling simplicity; be open-minded, with a mind as vast as a valley (DDJ Chapter 6); be chaotic, like turbidity yet unclear.

Who can gradually clarify the murky and make it clear? Who can initiate the lifelessness and bring about slow rebirth?

Those who uphold this virtuous path have no desire to display the fullness of their spiritual journey of their own.

Only by not flaunting one's fullness can one draw new energy from the consumption of decline.

My 5 cents

This chapter elucidates the approach to navigating and overcoming the challenges presented in the preceding section. It emphasizes the importance of mindfulness, discourages stirring up unnecessary disturbances (stirring mud over water), and advocates for a demeanor akin to a serene valley, as discussed in Chapter 6.

【第十六章】 Chapter 16

Most Common Translation

致虛極，	To attain utmost emptiness,
守靜篤，	Adhere steadfastly to quietude.
萬物並作，	All things flourish,
吾以觀復。	I repeatedly observe their recurring cycles.
夫物芸芸，	The countless entities in existence,
各復歸其根。	Each return to its source.
歸根曰靜，	Returning to the source is tranquility,
是謂復命。	Is called returning to one's destiny and life.
復命曰常，	To return to one's destiny is called the constant,
知常曰明，	To understand the constant is called wisdom,
不知常，妄作，凶。	Not understanding the constant, one acts recklessly and brings calamity.
知常容，	Understanding the constant leads to extreme tolerance；generosity, forgiveness, and hold.
容乃公，	Tolerance brings impartiality,
公乃王，	Impartiality leads to nobility,
王乃天，	Nobility leads to the heavenly,
天乃道，	Heavenly leads (is) to the Dao,
道乃久，	Dao endures,
沒身不殆。	Throughout one's entire life, there will be no sense of unease. (nearly exhausted)

My literal translation

Cultivating the Tao leads to the realm of ultimate emptiness, where one peacefully maintains tranquility and a serene composure.

All things progress through the tunnel of time and space; I can repeatedly observe their cycles.

The myriad beings in the universe, each destined to return to their outcomes.

Witnessing these outcomes can be described as the effect of stillness. Only through stillness can one comprehend the true essence of life, which is the rhythm of development. Understanding the rhythm of development is true enlightenment.

45

Without knowledge of the laws of development, reckless actions naturally bring danger.

Understanding the laws of development allows for embracing everything; embracing everything leads to impartiality. Impartiality results in justice and magnanimity. Justice and magnanimity bring completeness and thoroughness. Being complete and thorough aligns with nature, which is following the Great Dao. Following the Great Dao ensures enduring peace, and throughout one's life, there will be no sense of unease.

Note:

<u>RE: verse 2: Adhere steadfastly to quietude</u>

Guarding stillness to the utmost, guarding stillness with great earnestness. Zhuangzi (369-286BC), may call it "sitting in forgetfulness", exchanging with the qi of heaven and earth. (守靜至極，守靜至篤。莊子或稱之為座忘。與天地之氣互相往還。)

Within some schools of Daoist practices, there is a quest to locate the actual location of quietude within the human body. Some assert it lies at the lowest point of the Tai Qi/Chi Diagram, while others engaged in primordial soul training may point to the wisdom eye. Both perspectives hold validity, contingent on the specific focus of one's practice.

Laozi think about you and make notes:

"To attain the utmost emptiness, guard tranquility with utmost sincerity." The true Dao possesses a constant standard, beyond human comprehension. Yet, people often, in their ignorance, seek artificial means and worldly tricks. They teach and prescribe, defining forms and names for the Dao, assigning specific places, clothing, and appearances, imposing limitations on length and size, all within the realm of worldly thoughts. Such endeavors lead to extreme suffering and lack genuine blessings; they are mere deceptions. Striving to make these deceptions appear real is even more misguided. It is better to guard tranquility with sincerity.

"All things flourish, and I observe their return. All things, as they are, return to their roots." All things contain the essence of the Dao and flourish when they first arise. I, representing the Dao, observe their essence returning in due time, as everything ultimately returns to its roots, prompting people to be cautious and regretful.

"Returning to the roots brings tranquility." The Qi of the Dao returns to its roots, signifying purity and tranquility.

"Tranquility is called returning to one's destiny, and returning to one's destiny is called the constant." Knowing the treasure of one's roots and maintaining tranquility is the constant way of returning to one's destiny.

"To know the constant is clarity." Understanding this constant way is true enlightenment.

"Not knowing the constant leads to reckless actions and calamities." The world is filled with deceitful arts, and those who do not understand the constant engage in misguided activities, leading to calamities.

"To know the constant is to be tolerant." Understanding the constant way allows one to maintain composure and tolerance.

"Tolerance leads to impartiality." Adhering to the Dao maintains one's appearance, aligning with the harmony of heaven and earth. Dwelling in the midst of heaven and earth without fearing death is impartiality.

"Impartiality leads to nobility." Following the righteous path of the Dao leads to nobility.

"Nobility leads to longevity." Practicing the Dao's principles leads to a long and healthy life.

"Longevity leads to emulating heaven." Achieving longevity is akin to emulating the ways of heaven.

"Heaven emulates the Dao." Heaven's enduring nature is based on the principles of the Dao.

"The Dao endures." When people follow the Dao's principles, they too can endure.

"Throughout one's life, there is no peril." The path of the Tai Yin accumulates and refines the essence of form. Some places in the world are unsuitable for dwelling, and wise individuals avoid them and seek refuge in death. Passing through the Tai Yin and returning to one side, life appears again, and one passes away without danger. Common people who cannot accumulate virtuous deeds truly die when they die, and their earthly officials depart.

Note: The portions highlighted in RED may also depict the experience of observing the inner flow of Qi within the body. I presume that some individuals in our group have had or currently have this profound experience, recognizing the tranquility it brings. (The INNER VISION, refer to my extra note in a separate cover)

"致虛極，守靜篤。"道真自有常度，人不能明之，必復企暮（慕）凹間常為伎，因出教授，指形名道，令有處所服色，長短有分數，而思想之。苦極無福報，此虛詐耳。強欲令虛詐為真，甚極。不如守靜自篤也。"萬物並作，吾以觀其復。夫物云云，各歸其根。"萬物含道精，並作，初生起時也。吾，道也。觀其精復時，皆歸其根，故令人寶慎恨也。"歸根曰靜。"道氣歸根，愈當清淨也。"靜曰復命，復命曰常。"知寶根清靜，復命之常法也。"知常明。"知此常法，乃為明耳。"不知常，妄作兇。"世間常偽伎，不知常意，妄有指畫，故悉兇。"知常容。"知常法意，常保形容。"容能公。"以道保形容，為天地上容。處天地間，不畏死，故公也。"公能生。"能行道公政，故常生也。"生能天。"能致長生，則副天也。"天能道。"天能久生，法道故也。"道能久。"人法道意，便能長久也。"沒身不殆。"太陰道積練形之宮也。世有不可處，賢者避去託死。過太陰中，而復一邊生像，沒而不殆也。俗人不能積善行，死便真死，屬地官去也。

Extract from Laozi He Shang Gong Zhang Ju (Laozi DDJ Commented by He Shang Gong):

To the utmost emptiness, those who attain the Dao abandon emotions and desires. The inner aspects become pure and tranquil, reaching the pinnacle of emptiness. Guarding stillness earnestly and preserving clarity and tranquility requires sincere and profound practice. All things simultaneously come into existence, signifying birth. I observe the return, expressing the idea that everything ultimately returns to its origin. Humans should reflect on the significance of returning to their roots.

In the myriad of living things, their abundance is like flourishing leaves. Each return to its root, indicating that everything withers and falls, only to return to its root and be reborn. Returning to the root is called tranquility, signifying the essence. The root is calm, gentle, and humble, situated below, thus avoiding decay. This is called returning to one's destiny, suggesting that tranquility ensures the return of one's nature and prevents death. The continuity of this return is called the constant. To continuously return is the constant way of the Dao.

Understanding the constant is called enlightenment. Those who comprehend the consistent path of the Dao achieve enlightenment. Not understanding the constant and engaging in misguided actions result in calamity. Ignorance of the Dao's consistent path leads to deceitful actions, causing a loss of spiritual clarity and resulting in calamity.

Understanding the constant allows for tolerance. Those who comprehend the consistent path of the Dao can let go of emotions and desires, embracing everything. Tolerance leads to impartiality, as one can embrace all without bias, thwarting any evil influence. Impartiality leads to kingship, representing a ruler who governs justly and impartially, becoming a king of the world.

When the self is well-governed, the body becomes harmonious, and the spirit shines brightly, contributing to one's well-being. The king becomes akin to heaven, ruling with virtue that aligns with spiritual clarity, thus connecting with heaven. Heaven, in turn, aligns with the Dao, merging with the consistent way. The Dao, being enduring, ensures longevity. By aligning with the Dao, one can achieve lasting endurance.

Without danger, one can be public-spirited and kingly, harmonize with heaven, and unite with the Dao. Possessing these qualities, along with pure virtue, leads to an expansive and far-reaching moral path. Without calamities or faults, one can peacefully join the realms of heaven and earth, without peril or danger.

Where is the root of this Tai Chi/Ji Diagram? Everything will return to its starting point and re-born, that is the cycle. (9+6=15, 15X2=30)

老子河上公章句 -> 道經 -> 歸根

致虛極，得道之人，捐情去欲，五內清靜，至於虛極。守靜篤，守清靜，行篤厚。萬物並作，作，生也。萬物並生也。吾以觀復。言吾以觀見萬物無不皆歸其本也。人當念重其本也。夫物芸芸，芸芸者，華葉盛也。各復歸其根，言萬物無不枯落，各復反其根而更生也。歸根曰靜，靜謂根也。根安靜柔弱，謙卑處下，故不復死也。是謂復命。言安靜者是為復還性命，使不死也。復命曰常。復命使不死，乃道之所常行也。知常曰明；能知道之所常行，則為明。不知常，妄作凶。不知道之所常行，妄作巧詐，則失神明，故凶也。知常容，能知道之所常行，去情忘欲，無所不包容也。容乃公，無所不包容，則公正無私，眾邪莫當。公乃王，公正無私，可以為天下王。治身正則形一，神明千萬，共湊其躬也。王乃天，能王，德合神明，乃與天通。天乃道，德與天通，則與道合同也。道乃久。與道合同，乃能長久。沒身不殆。能公能王，通天合道，四者純備，道德弘遠，無殃無咎，乃與天地俱沒，不危殆也．

【第十七章】 Chapter 17

Most Common Translation

太上，不知有之。	The highest, act without a sense of self.
其次，親而譽之。	The next, act through charisma and praise.
	(The next, act with a sense of self and yet be praised.) (Make people follow you with the affinity of a good reputation.)
其次，畏之。	The next, act with a sense of fear.
其次，侮之。	The lowest, act with a sense of disdain.
	(Through education, make them repent, regret, thus guiding them towards goodness)
信不足焉，	If trust is not sufficient, (lack of credibility)
有不信焉。	Then there is no trust. (face skepticism)
悠兮其貴言。	Especially from those who place excessive importance on the power of language.
	(original wording: expensive word/speech)
功成事遂，	With the success achieved and goals accomplished,
百姓皆謂我自然。	The populace believes, 'It unfolded naturally.

My literal translation

The most enlightened rely on intangible mental power to induce compliance.

The next level utilizes the attractive influence of a positive reputation to secure obedience.

Following that, it uses a wielded deterrent force to compel submission.

The next tier employs lower-level control to force compliance.

Those lacking credibility naturally face skepticism, especially from those who overemphasize the power of language.

After achieving significant accomplishments for the world, the people will say, 'The emergence of such a person is a natural outcome.

Laozi think about you and make notes:

The highest virtue is knowing the existence of the Dao. Knowledgeable is the topmost understanding. Knowing the Dao, one dislikes wrongdoing, which is the higher knowledge. Even with this higher knowledge, one should recognize the nature of wrongdoing and strive not to engage in it.

The next step is to be close to and praise those who seek goodness. When encountering individuals seeking virtue, understanding their intentions, and befriending them is appropriate. Encountering those learning virtues with diligence, it is fitting to praise and encourage them, diligently assisting in spreading the teachings.

Following that is to instill fear. When facing evildoers, admonish and persuade them towards goodness. If they hear and understand righteousness, they may submit, allowing for teaching and transformation. Reinforce these teachings with moral authority, urging them to change.

Regret is necessary. If speaking goodness to evildoers does not bring about change and they scoff, they belong to the category of weeds and thorns, not true human beings. (Sometimes we use the word Corpse, not Zombie, Zombie is Western kinds of stuff? No Umbrella Corp yet.) They can be deceived and scorned, and it's best not to engage in conversation with them.

Insufficient trust leads to disbelief. Weeds and thorns lack internal trust; hence they distrust the words of virtuous individuals. Despite this, the Dao's teachings are highly esteemed. The words of the Dao are invaluable, leading to success in endeavors.

The people, thinking it happened naturally, refer to me as an immortal. The common people do not learn about my esteemed and trustworthy teachings, which lead to these accomplishments. Instead, they attribute it to a natural state, indicating their unwillingness to strive and emulate my efforts.

"太上下知有之。"知道，上知也。知也惡事，下知也。雖有上知，當具識惡事，改之不敢為也。"其次親之譽之。"見求善之人，曉道意，可親也。見學善之人，勤勤者，可就譽也，復教勸之，勉力助道宣教。"其次畏之。"見惡人，誠為說善，其人聞義即服，可教改也。就申道誡示之，畏以天威，令自改也。"悔之。"為惡人說善，不化而甫笑之者，此即芻茍之徒耳，非人也。可欺侮也，勿與語也。"信不足，有不信。"芻茍之徒，內信不足，故不信善人之言也。"猶其貴言，成功事遂。"道之所言，無一可棄者。得仙之士，但貴道言，故輒成功事遂也。"百姓謂我自然。"我，仙士也。百姓不學我有貴信道言，以致此功，而意我自然，當示不肯企及效我也。

Extract from Laozi He Shang Gong Zhang Ju (Laozi DDJ Commented by He Shang Gong):

The Supreme, known below but not acknowledged. The Supreme refers to the ancient unnamed ruler. Those below who know acknowledge the existence but do not submit; they possess simplicity and sincerity. Next is to be close to and praise. The virtue is apparent, and the grace is commendable, hence the closeness and praise. Following that is to instill fear. Establish laws and penalties to govern. After that is to disdain. Implement numerous restrictions and burdens, making it impossible to turn sincerely, hence subjecting them to disdain.

With insufficient trust, there is mistrust. If the ruler's trust is lacking, the subjects respond with distrust, deceiving their ruler. Yet, the words are esteemed. Advising the Supreme ruler, actions carry weight, valuing deeds more than words, fearing deviation from the natural way. Accomplish goals and things follow suit, signifying peace in the world. The people all say, 'It happened naturally.' The people do not recognize the ruler's profound virtues but attribute the state of affairs to their own natural order

老子河上公章句 -> 道經 -> 淳風

太上，下知有之。太上，謂太古無名之君。下知有之者，下知上有君，而不臣事，質朴也。其次，親之譽之。其德可見，恩惠可稱，故親愛而譽之。其次畏之。設刑法以治之。其次侮之。禁多令煩，不可歸誠，故欺侮之。信不足焉，〔有不信焉〕。君信不足於下，下則應之以不信，而欺其君也。猶兮其貴言。說太上之君，舉事猶貴重於言，恐離道失自然也。功成事遂，謂天下太平也。百姓皆謂我自然。百姓不知君上之德淳厚，反以為己自當然也。

Note:

In Verse 1, "太上", as mentioned earlier, "太" implies something slightly larger than the largest, and "上" denotes above, akin to the alternate name for Laozi, 太上老君. It conveys the idea of being a little larger than the largest, while "老君" translates to an old and respectable figure. Nevertheless, 太上老君 is commonly rendered as the Supreme Venerable Lord.

In this context, the same Chinese phrase yields diverse meanings and interpretations. This discrepancy is evident in the three translations provided above.

【第十八章】Chapter 18

Most Common Translation

大道廢，	The grand way of Dao may be abandoned,
有仁義；	Yet benevolence and righteousness endure;
慧智出，	Wisdom and intelligence emerge,
有大偽；	Yet there is great deception, amidst the rise of cunning deceit,
六親不和，	Family relations are discordant,
有孝慈；	Yet filial piety and kindness arise;
國家昏亂，	The nation is in turmoil,
有忠臣。	Yet loyal ministers arise.

Note: The chapter speaks for itself, no need for elaboration.

【第十九章】 Chapter 19

Most Common Translation

絕聖棄智，	Abandon sacredness and discard wisdom,
	(The lofty sage and virtuous scholar, ruling a nation without resorting to deceit and worldly wisdom),
民利百倍；	People's benefits increase a hundredfold;
絕仁棄義，	Abandon benevolence and discard righteousness,
民復孝慈；	People will return to filial piety and kindness;
絕巧棄利，	Abandon cunning and discard profit,
盜賊無有。	There will be no thieves or bandits.
此三者，	These three virtues,
以為文不足，	Deem them insufficient in culture, (in governing)
	(are insufficient in cultivating one's character,)
故令有所屬，	Therefore, establish something (additional) to rely upon,
見素抱朴，	See simplicity, embrace the uncarved,
少私寡欲。	Reduce selfishness and diminish desires.

My 5 cents

In a realm untouched by the schemes of the mundane,
The sage abstains from the ordinary's gain.
No tools, no treasures to rule the land,
Hand in hand, guiding the nation, like guiding oneself.

In the tapestry of life woven by the sage,
Lines of virtue pursue the sacred spirit's Totem.
In the practice of qi, a harmonious the softness flow,
Harmonizing with nature, a mutual embrace.
Poetry of a tranquil soul, untouched by greed's excess,
A sacred land, unspoiled, and pristine.
Untouched, a profound silence,
The path of the sacred, the key to harmony.

In the realm of the nation, non-interference,
In the dance of qi, the art innate.
Balancing the self with the grace of enlightened love,
Is the journey of the sage, a divine embrace.
Laozi think about you and make notes:

Laozi think about you and make notes:

"Reject the holy and abandon knowledge, and the people will benefit a hundredfold." This refers to those who falsely claim to possess holy knowledge. The truly holy individuals are supported by heaven, and their existence naturally manifests. The fame of rivers and mountains is evident, yet they consistently proclaim the truth and are not misled. Those who follow the path of skepticism towards the teachings of the sages cause the great sages to demonstrate the truth over thousands of years, gradually purifying false doctrines. Present-day individuals lack proper conduct, are immersed in various studies without grasping the true path, and hastily proclaim themselves as holy. Without understanding the fundamental principles and scrutinizing their own actions, they cannot attain the true path. They speak of benefiting oneself without advising the people on the achievable path to immortality, neglecting self-cultivation and instead claiming that immortality comes naturally. They have not reached the essence of the practice, falsely asserting that the Daoist scriptures deceive people, committing grave sins and becoming great evildoers. This leads future learners to lose faith in the Dao. They do not follow the ancient ways, do not remember to provide for their ancestors, neglect farming, and only pursue superficial Daoist teachings. Exhausted by reciting scriptures, they end up in poverty throughout their lives. They cannot sincerely practice filial piety and loyalty, cannot achieve longevity through self-discipline, and fail to contribute to the peace of the nation. The people, following such practices, abandon cities, leaving them empty. Therefore, reject false claims of holy knowledge but do not abandon true knowledge of the Dao.

"Reject benevolence and abandon righteousness, and the people will return to filial piety and kindness." In governing a country, follow the Dao and allow the people to practice benevolence and righteousness without forcing rewards upon them. By honoring and promoting virtue, spreading the teachings of the Dao, and allowing people to cultivate benevolence and righteousness sincerely, they will naturally be rewarded by heaven. Those who are not sincere will be naturally punished by heaven. Heaven observes and judges everyone, knowing who respects the Dao and fears heaven, and benevolence and righteousness will naturally be sincere. However, if rulers force rewards, the people will not return to heaven. When people see that deception is rewarded, they pretend to be benevolent and righteous to seek wealth and rewards. Even if others know their deceit, seeing the material benefits, they also imitate it, pretending to be benevolent and righteous, but ultimately not achieving sincerity. People may not fully understand, so it is necessary to reject rewards and the people will naturally return to kindness and filial piety. This approach may clash with popular opinions, but it will eventually be understood and align with the Dao. Rulers should deeply understand and implement it.

"Reject cleverness and abandon profit, and there will be no thieves and bandits." Cleverness refers to the acquisition of wealth. If the world does not pursue it, thieves and bandits will have no incentive. These three principles are the roots of great chaos in the world, and their dispersal is desired. The text may not be sufficient, and the simple bamboo slips may not be enough. Following the order, I have attached this Dao text, not for external recognition but to explain the general idea. This is the essence of resolving chaos. "Be content with little and have few desires." The Dao teaches to be free from personal desires in worldly matters.

"絕聖棄知，民利百倍。"謂詐聖知耶文者。夫聖人天所挺，生必有表，河雒著名，然常宣真，不至受有誤。耶道不信明聖人之言，故令千百歲大聖演真，滌徐耶文。今人無狀，載通經藝，未貫道真，便自稱聖。不因本而章篇自揆，不能得道，言先為身；不勸民真道可得仙壽，修善自勤，反言仙自有骨錄；非行所臻，雲無生道，道書欺人，此乃罪盈三千，為大惡人。至令後學者不復信道。元元不旋，子不念供養，民不念田，但逐耶學，傾側師門，盡氣誦病，到于窮年。會不能忠孝至誠感天，民治身不能仙壽，佐君不能致太平，民用此不息，倍城邑虛空，是故絕詐聖耶知，不絕真聖道知也。

"絕仁棄義，民復孝慈。"治國法道，聽任天下仁義之人，勿得強賞也。所以者，尊大其化，廣聞道心，人為仁義，自當至誠，天自賞之；不至誠者，天自罰之。天察必審於人，皆知尊道畏天，仁義便至誠矣。今王政強賞之，民不復歸天。見人可欺，便詐為仁義，欲求祿賞。旁人雖知其都交，見得官祿，便復慕之，詐為仁義，終不相及也。世人察之不審，故絕之勿賞，民悉自復慈孝矣。此義平忤俗夫心，久久自解，與道合矣。人君深當明之也。"絕巧棄利，盜賊無有。"耶巧也，所得財寶也。世不用之，盜賊亦不利也。"此三言為文未足，故令有所屬，見素抱樸。"三事天下大亂之源，欲演散之。億文復不足，竹素不勝矣，受故令屬此道文，不在外書也，撲說其大略，可知之為亂原。"少私寡欲。"道之所說，無私少欲於世俗耳。

【第二十章】 Chapter 20

Most Common Translation

絕學無憂。	Mastering knowledge, one is free from worry. Abandon knowledge, one is free from worry. (Note 1)
唯之與阿，	Only with 'it' and 'what', "this" and "that" [do we know it exists], (Note 2)
相去幾何？	How much is the difference between them?
善之與惡，	Good and bad,
相去若何？	how far apart are they?
人之所畏，	What people fear from,
不可不畏。	Cannot not be feared.
荒兮其未央哉！	Chaotic and endless it seems!
眾人熙熙，	Everybody bustling and busy,
如享太牢，	Like enjoying a feast in a prison,
如春登台。	Like ascending to a terrace in spring.
我獨泊兮其未兆，	I alone drift, not yet having found a sign,
如嬰兒之未孩。	Like an infant not yet a child.
儽儽兮若無所歸。	Listless and aimless, as if with nowhere to return.
眾人皆有余，	The multitude all have more than enough,
而我獨若遺。	And I am all alone like being abandoned.
我愚人之心也哉！	I have the mind of a fool, indeed! (Note 3)
沌沌兮！	Chaos....... (Vague and elusive)!
俗人昭昭，	Laity (ordinary people) are bright and clear,
我獨昏昏；	I alone am muddled and confused.
俗人察察，	Laity are perceptive and alert,
我獨悶悶。	I alone am dull and inert.
澹兮其若海，	Tranquil and peacefully like the ocean,
飂兮若無止。	Drifting, like there is no end.
眾人皆有以，	Everybody has something similar,
而我獨頑似鄙。	And I alone am stubborn and lowly (humble).
我獨異於人，而貴	I alone am different from people and hold a cherished worth. (I am unique among people, precious, and esteemed.)
食母。	Nourishing from the mother of (Dao).

Note 1 - The term 絕學 can be understood in two ways. First, it conveys the idea of reaching the pinnacle or absolute mastery in learning (學) or knowledge (學). In this sense, 絕學 means attaining the highest level of understanding in a particular field. Similarly, 絕聖 (Chapter 19, verse 1) suggests achieving the highest standard of saintliness (聖) or sage (聖)-like qualities.

The second interpretation of 絕 involves complete abandonment or letting go to the extreme. In this context, 絕學 signifies letting go of all acquired knowledge, and 絕聖 implies abandoning all saintly qualities without any attachment or lingering sentiments.

This concept is reflected in verses 3 and 5 of chapter 19, where abandoning benevolence means reaching the highest level of benevolence. When one truly embodies benevolence and compassion towards others, the guidelines of righteousness become secondary tools. This perspective is highlighted in chapter 18, where righteousness and benevolence are emphasized due to the loss of the grand way of Dao. These examples showcase the use of inverted sentences, or inversion paragraphs, conveying dual or multiple meanings.

Note 2 - 唯之與阿. 唯 and 阿 encompass multiple meanings, including "sincerely accepted", "cater to", "just nod" and "giving". There are many other ways of usage in these two words too. To capture their versatility, I utilized "this" and "that" in my translation above.

I recall a joke which was shared some time ago......

Interviewer: "What can you contribute to the company?"

Candidate: "I can handle everything for the company, except two things."

Intrigued, the interviewer asks, "What are those two things?"

Candidate: "I can't do 'this,' and I can't do 'that.'"

Interviewer: "You're dismissed. Please leave my office."

Note 3 - **Great wisdom seems like foolishness (大智若愚)**

When posing the question "What is 1 plus 1?" to a kindergarten child, the response is often a confident and unequivocal "2". However, if the same question is directed toward a world-class mathematician or professor, their reaction may be one of uncertainty or hesitation, seemingly unaware of the straightforward answer. This disparity arises from the fact that the child's understanding is rooted in simple knowledge of addition, while the mathematician may grapple with the need to clarify the specific context or underlying assumptions, considering various scenarios or bases before providing a nuanced response.

I have a practice partner for push hand exercises, who used to work as a chef in a renowned Italian banquet hall. His expertise lies in preparing specialized dishes for individuals with specific health or religious requirements, such as Kosher, Halal, Buddhism, and various types of vegetarian options. One day, his wife requested him to make breakfast for their youngest son the next morning. When he asked his son about his breakfast preferences, the response was "egg and sausage". This seemingly simple request left my friend in a state of bewilderment, resembling a frozen computer. His wife, irritated, wondered why he found it so challenging. However, my friend explained that it's not as simple as it appears. There are numerous ways to cook an egg, prepare sausage, and even consider the presentation of the dishes. The culinary choices and nuances involved make it a more intricate task than meets the eye.

The following day, he returned to his workplace and approached the reception secretary, requesting assistance in creating a breakfast menu for his son. Similar to reviewing an order, the options included scrambled eggs, stir-fried eggs, and sunny-side-up eggs (one side or two sides fried). Additionally, various types of sausages were considered, with details on their preparation methods such as butterfly cuts, slices, and so on.

In recent years, there's been a popular Japanese dining style in Hong Kong called "omakase", which means 'I leave it up to you.' This is commonly experienced at Japanese restaurants, where customers trust the chef to choose and serve seasonal specialties, usually at a higher cost.

Our mother also frequently prepares meals for us. Similarly, without a fixed menu or planned ingredients, she goes to the market daily. Whatever is affordable, she buys and cooks, or whatever is left in the fridge. (Similar to our Neiqong retreat or Tai Chi Camp). It can be said that she doesn't have any specific cooking techniques; it's just the taste of her dishes. This has been our daily special from childhood to adulthood – our mother's version of omakase, just acted within the boundaries of "this" and "that".

Now, the question is, which one truly captures the essence?

My Literal Translation

Mastering knowledge and we are free from worry.

What is the difference between sincere acceptance and catering to others? Where do good and evil begin, and where do negative consequences and sentiment emerge, between "this "and "that"?

Many people enjoy the outward appearance of grandeur, like elaborate ritual ceremonies or taking the stage in joyful performances as if riding the spring breeze.

We seem to be like a clear, undisturbed pool of water, with a mindset as innocent as a newborn baby. We go with the flow, seemingly indifferent to our destination, while seemingly pursuing something within.

While others are eager to chase excessive desires, we seem to have lost the burden of greed. Our simple and guileless hearts are chaotic yet unblemished.

The worldly-wise appear enlightened, but we seem befuddled and ignorant. The perceptive notices the smallest details, while we remain dull and muddled.

Tranquility is like the vast, boundless sea, and elegance is like the unrestrained and never-ending wind.

Everyone has their strengths, but we seem obstinate and miserly.

Our qualities are precious and esteem, which lies in absorbing the great energy from maternity that sustains all things.

Laozi think about you and make notes:

The abandonment of learning brings no worries, only to what extent, how far is it apart. Those who do not know inquire again, to abandon learning, is it to follow the Way? How close or distant is it from the Way? To abandon learning and adhere to the Way, the Way must surely accompany it. Is it distant from learning, guarding the Way alone? The Way must surely be with it. Is it distant from the Way and learning? The Way gives birth, learning leads to death; death belongs to the earth, life belongs to heaven, hence extremely distant.

The difference between beauty and ugliness, how is it compared? Those who do not know inquire again, wanting to know how close or distant beauty and ugliness are, also the closeness or distance between the Way and learning. At present, they are considered equivalent. Beauty is goodness. Born, it belongs to heaven; ugliness, in death, also belongs to the earth.

What people fear, it is unavoidable not to fear; reckless and endless. The Way establishes life to reward the good, establishes death to awe the wicked; death is what people fear. Immortal kings and ordinary people both know to fear death and love life, but their actions differ. Ordinary people are reckless and endless, avoiding death limitlessly. Although ordinary people fear death, they fundamentally do not believe in the Way, delighting in wicked deeds. How can they escape death limitlessly? Immortal scholars fear death, believe in the Way, and adhere to its teachings, thus harmonizing with life.

"絕學無憂，唯之與何，相去幾何。"未知者復怪問之，絕耶學，道與之何？耶與道相去近遠？絕耶學，獨守道，道必與之。耶道與耶學甚遠，道生耶死，死屬地，生屬天，故極遠。"美之與惡，相去何若。"未知者復怪問之，欲知美惡相去近遠何如，道與耶學近遠也，今等耳。美，善也。生故屬天，惡死亦屬地也。"人之所畏，不可不畏，莽其未央。"道設生以賞善，設死以威惡，死是人之所畏也。仙王士與俗人，同知畏死樂生，但所行異耳。俗人莽莽，未央脫死也。俗人雖畏死，端不信道，好為惡事，奈何未央脫死乎！仙士畏死，信道守誡，故與生合也。

The multitude is bustling as if enjoying a grand feast or ascending a springtime platform. The common people do not believe in the Way, delighting in wicked deeds as if indulging in food and drink, ascending a high platform in the spring.

I, my spirit not yet manifested, like an infant not yet grown, have no place to return. I, an immortal scholar, only delight in believing in the Way and adhering to its teachings, not finding joy in wicked deeds. Amidst wickedness, I have no intention, like an unborn infant.

All people have excess, I alone am like a remnant. The hearts of the common people are always full of intentions, thoughts, and considerations. In the mind of an immortal scholar, everything is forgotten, with nothing possessed.

I, simple-hearted like a foolish person. The immortal scholar tastes the Way, ignorant of worldly affairs, pure and simple, as if infatuated.

Common people, observant. Common people do not believe in the Way, only seeing the benefits of wickedness. Observant, very discerning.

I alone, as if in a state of confusion. The immortal scholar closes the mind, not pondering the benefits of wickedness, as if in a state of confusion.

Common people, clear-sighted. Knowledgeable about worldly matters.

I alone, in a state of melancholy. Unaware of worldly matters.

"眾人熙熙，若亨大牢，若春登臺。"眾俗之人不信道，樂為惡事，若飲食之，春登高臺也。"我魄未兆，若嬰兒未孩，魑無所歸。"我，仙士也。但榮信道守誡，不樂惡事。至惡事之間，無心意，如嬰兒未生時也。"眾人皆有餘，我獨遺。"眾俗之懷惡，常有餘意，計念思慮。仙士意中，都遺忘之，無所有也。"我愚人之心純純。"仙士味道，不知俗事。純純，若癡也。"俗人照照。"俗人不信道，但見耶惡利得。照照，甚明也。"我獨若昏。"仙士閉心，不思慮耶惡利得，若昏昏冥也。"俗人察察。"知俗事審明也。"我獨悶悶。"不知俗事也。

Suddenly, as if obscured, with no place for the mind to rest. The immortal scholar's will is like obscurity, thinking of lying down on a peaceful bed, no longer entangled in worldly matters. The focused thoughts rest on the Way, not on worldly affairs.

All people have achieved; I alone remain stubborn and humble. Common people have attained wealth, honor, and fame in the world, while the immortal scholar remains stubborn and humble in the worldly sense.

I desire to be different from others, yet I value nourishing the body. The immortal scholar is different from ordinary people, not valuing fame, wealth, or treasures but valuing nourishing the body. To nourish the body is to care for oneself internally, focusing on the stomach, which governs the qi of the five organs. Ordinary people eat grains, and without grains, they die. The immortal scholar has grains for sustenance or else consumes qi. The qi returns to the stomach, making the intestines heavy and the abdomen full, as discussed in the previous section. (refer to the 5 Kitchen Scripture)

"忽若晦，家無所止。"仙士意志道如晦，思臥安床，不複雜俗事也。精思止于道，不止于俗事也。"眾人皆有已，我獨頑以鄙。"俗人於世間自有財寶功名，仙士于俗如頑鄙也。"我欲異於人，而貴食母。"仙士與俗人異，不貴榮祿財寶，但貴食母。食母者，身也，于內為胃，主五藏氣。俗人食穀，穀絕便死。仙士有穀食之，無則食氣。氣歸胃，即腸重囊也。腹之為寶，前章已說之矣。

Extract from Laozi He Shang Gong Zhang Ju (Laozi DDJ Commented by He Shang Gong) – Different Custom:

Abandon learning, abandon learning, not true; does not conform to the Way and literature. No worries. Except for superficiality, there are no worries and troubles. Only with what and A, how far apart are they? Both are responsive, yet how far apart are they? Despise swift times and cheapen substance, but value literature. How different are goodness and evil? Goodness receives praise; evil receives reproach. How can they be so different? Despise swift times and embrace loyalty and straightforwardness, instead of using deceit and cunning. What people fear, it is unavoidable not to fear. People refer to those following the Way. What people fear is the fear of rulers who do not abandon learning. It is unavoidable not to fear, approaching with allure, killing benevolence and virtue. Chaotic, it is boundless! Describing the disorderliness of worldly people, desiring to advance learning through literature, with no limit.

The multitude is bustling, bustling, indulging in excessive desires and passions. Like enjoying a grand feast, like hungering for the details of a grand feast, the mind never satisfied. Like ascending a platform in spring. Spring, the exchange between yin and yang, all things in motion, observing from the platform, the mind immersed in lustful thoughts. I alone fear, there is no sign yet. I alone fear and remain tranquil, showing no signs of carnal desires. Like an infant not yet grown. Like a child who cannot respond to others. Drifting along as if with no place to return. I drift along in poverty and obscurity, with nowhere to turn. All people have excess; they indulge in wealth for extravagance, use excess intelligence for deceit. But I alone am like a remnant. I alone appear abandoned, seemingly lacking.

The heart of a foolish person, not following the common people, steadfast and unchanging, like the heart of a foolish person. Confused and undifferentiated. The common people are clear and knowledgeable. But I alone am as if in darkness. Like obscurity. The common people are sharp and swift. But I alone am melancholic. Melancholic, without any division or separation. Suddenly, as if vast as the sea. I alone am suddenly flowing, like the rivers and seas, no one knows my ultimate destination. Drifting along as if with no place to rest. I alone drift along, like flying or soaring, with no place to stop; my aspirations lie in the realm of the divine.

All people have motives and actions, and I alone am stubborn, seemingly lowly. I alone am different from others, and I value the nourishment of the Dao.

老子河上公章句 -> 道經 -> 異俗

絕學絕學不真，不合道文。無憂。除浮華則無憂患也。唯之與阿，相去幾何。同為應對而相去幾何。疾時賤質而貴文。善之與惡，相去若何。善者稱譽，惡者諫諍，能相去何如。疾時惡忠直，用邪佞也。人之所畏，不可不畏。人謂道人也。人所畏者，畏不絕學之君也。不可不畏，近令色，殺仁賢。荒兮其未央哉！言世俗人荒亂，欲進學為文，未央止也。眾人熙熙，熙熙，放淫多情欲也。如享太牢，如飢思太牢之具，意無足時也。如春登臺。春，陰陽交通，萬物感動，登台觀之，意志淫淫然。我獨怕兮其未兆，我獨怕然安靜，未有情欲之形兆也。如嬰兒之未孩。如小兒未能答偶人時也。乘乘兮若無所歸。我乘乘如窮鄙，無所歸就。眾人皆有餘，眾人餘財以為奢，餘智以為詐。而我獨若遺。我獨如遺棄，似於不足也。我愚人之心也哉，不與俗人相隨，守一不移，如愚人之心也。沌沌兮。無所分別。俗人昭昭，明且達也。我獨若昏。如闇昧也。俗人察察，察察，急且疾也。我獨悶悶。悶悶，無所割截。忽兮若海，我獨忽忽，如江海之流，莫知其所窮極也。漂兮若無所止。我獨漂漂，若飛若揚，無所止也，志意在神域也。眾人皆有以，以，有為也。而我獨頑我獨無為。似鄙。鄙，似若不逮也。我獨異於人我獨與人異也。而貴食母。食，用也。母，道也。我獨貴用道也。

【第二十一章】 Chapter 21

Most Common Translation

孔德之容，	Peering through a pinhole to glimpse the countenance of virtue (De 德, the 2nd D of DDJ). (Note 1)
惟道是從。	Is shaped and determined by the Dao.
道之為物，	If one contemplates the Dao as an entity, (an object, or a substance)
惟恍惟惚。	Its appearance is only elusive and vague. (absented mind and unclear)
惚兮恍兮，	Vague eh, and yet elusive eh,
其中有象；	Yet within and between, there is an image.
恍兮惚兮，	Elusive eh, and yet Vague eh,
其中有物。	Yet within and between, there is substance.
窈兮冥兮，	Dim eh, and yet dark eh, (Note 2)
其中有精；	Yet within and between, there is essence;
其精甚真，	This essence is very real,
其中有信。	Yet within and between, there is assurance and message.
自古及今，	Throughout the ages,
其名不去，	Its name remains unvanquished and timeless.
以閱眾甫。	Examining the essence of the beginning and signifying its inception. (Note 3)
吾何以知眾甫之狀哉？	How do I know the essence of the beginning?
以此。	By this.

PS: please read this chapter with Chapter 14

Note 1 - 孔德 (Kǒng dé).

Kǒng (孔) means a hole. Spiritually, we often express the concept of peering into the entire universe through a hole. In Buddhism, it is said, "A mustard seed (芥子) can enter into Mount Sumeru (須彌山), and Mount Sumeru (須彌山), can fit into a mustard seed. [芥子入須彌，須彌入芥子] " (PS: reversion structured sentence again). How do we glimpse or encompass the entirety of Mount Sumeru within a mustard seed(芥子)? It is through this aperture, the hole of our wisdom eye.

Kǒng (孔), Kong Qiu (孔丘，孔子), Confucius.

In later generations, some interpretations identified Kong De (孔德) with Confucius (551-479BC), which meant the virtues suggested by Kong Qiu, making Kong De synonymous with the virtues espoused by Confucius. However, although there is a legend that Confucius once sought the Way (Dao) from Laozi (571-471BC), this legend is first recorded over a hundred years later in the writings of Zhuangzi (369-286BC). The reason for interpreting the Dao De Jing through the virtues articulated by Confucius might be that Confucianism flourished in China centuries later, gaining wide acceptance among subsequent rulers. (Note: Confucius's teachings were not widely accepted by rulers during his lifetime.)

According to legend, Confucius, also known as Kong Zi or Kong Qiu, sought guidance on the Dao from Laozi. Following this, it is said that he secluded himself for three months, maintaining silence for three consecutive days.

Another good reference:

Kǒng (孔), a hole, inside the hole is emptiness. Only by embracing emptiness as virtue, can one then be able to move and act by the Dao.

德 (dé), the dé of the main title Dao De Jing.

Warm Reminder: Translating "De" as the term virtue, it serves as the vessel for the Dao, unveiling its journey into the fabric of our tangible reality (Physical world).

PS: Another saying or common interpretation of this verse is that trying to observe true virtue through a narrow perspective is insufficient and incomplete, meaning we do not get the whole picture. However, it is not in line with the later verses.

Note 2

窈: Deep, Dark, profound, obscure and mysterious. (I used Dim to conclude that)

冥: Refer to the world one enters after death, which is gloomy, obscure, and murkiness. (I used dark to conclude that, to maintain the tone of the verse)

Note 3 - 眾甫：甫與父通，引伸为始": Zhòng fǔ (眾甫): Fu shares a common pronunciation with 'fu' (father), extended to signify the beginning of everything.

My 5 cents

In the depths of meditation's sacred trance,
A journey unfolds a cosmic traveling chance.
Witness the genesis, where shadows play and block the way,
In the realm of beginnings, where mysteries sway.

(YCHYD) whispers, a guiding mapping light,
Through the unclear, glimpses take flight.
Seemingly hidden, yet something is nearby,
A mystical journey, drawing us near.

On the brink of surrender, practitioners stand,
Confronting the juncture, as destiny is planned.
A mystical stage, demands commitment true,
Seer delves within, consciousness to pursue.

Navigate realms elusive, before all things begin,
A dance of intricacies, where secrets spin.
A pivotal moment in the Odyssey Divine,
Seeker unlocks existence, in sacred design.

Primordial essence orchestrates the cosmic HUM and OM,
Before the SOUND of GOD, where light and dark succumb.
Daunting is the task, aspiring hearts may sway,
Yet, for those who persist, mysteries unveil on their way.

Laozi think about you and make notes:

The countenance of virtuous virtue, only the Tao follows. The Dao is profound and great, instructing Confucius to attain wisdom. In later generations, some do not believe in the Dao but uphold the Confucian classics, considering them supreme. The Dao enlightens them, guiding the later sages. 'The Dao as a thing is only vague and elusive.' The Dao is subtle, alone able to be vague and elusive, not visible. Within the vagueness and elusiveness, there are things; within the elusiveness and vagueness, there are images. It should not be dismissed as the Dao (in here, it means the spirit of Qi) is not visible and therefore insignificant. Within it, there is a great spiritual essence, hence the metaphor of a bagpipe. (the bellows, in here, it does not mean the control of the heat, it means the spirit of God flows through the valley ref. to chapter 6).

In the profound darkness, there is essence. This refers to the elimination within the great void. The Dao separates and shares essence with all things; all things share a common origin of essence, incredibly genuine, serving as the official of life and death. Refining this essence is akin to cherishing a treasure. 'Within it, there is trust.' Ancient immortals cherished essence for vitality; nowadays, people lose essence leading to death—a great trust. Now, if one only retains essence, can one attain life? Not necessarily.

All various deeds must be prepared, so essence can be the distinct vital force of the Dao. Entering the human body as the root, and preserving its half is the initial step. To desire the essence, a hundred deeds should be prepared, myriad virtues should be embraced, harmonizing the five elements, and eliminating joy and anger completely. The Heavenly Court (天曹左契) (Note 4, from the Daoist religion, 天曹 the God official, 左契, good deeds are recorded on the left side, cherish life, while bad deeds are recorded on the right, death. Or good people are lining up on the left side after death.) has the mandate, and if there is a surplus in the {bamboo grove} (Note 5, words are marked or crafted on bamboo in the old days, no paper yet. Or, in here, it also means the Qi of life, liver, wood); essence must be guarded. If an evil person cherishes essence, from the Tang Dynasty to the present, hardship will persist and not cease, inevitably leading to leakage. The mind should regulate all matters, hence the name Bright Hall (note 6: forehead area). The three paths (Central meridian lines) spread, avoiding the harm of excess and deficiency, and maintaining balance to measure the vital energy of the Dao (Qi of Water or the spiritual sound energy). Essence is metaphorically compared to a pool of water; the body is the dam that encloses it, and virtuous deeds are the source of water. If these three preparations are made, the pool will be solid. (Solid the abdominals)

If the mind is not solely focused on goodness, without a dam to enclose it, water will inevitably escape. If virtuous deeds are not accumulated, the water will diminish. If the source is not unobstructed, the water will dry up. If the water overflows and irrigates the fields, it will become streams and rivers. Even with a dam, if the source is not regulated, it will inevitably become empty and cracked, and numerous illnesses will arise. If these three precautions are not taken, the pool becomes an empty pit. 'From ancient times to the present, its name does not depart.' Throughout the ages, this same Dao has been consistently followed, not departing from humanity. 'By examining the multitude of beginnings,' the Dao has existed and will continue to exist, not being one.

"Why do I know that the end and the beginning are so? Because of this". I, the Dao, know the past and present, the end and the beginning, all follow this one Dao. Such is the nature of things.

PS 1: Remember, legendary said, this enclosure/or guidance was written by the founder of one of the most major schools of Daoism (Religious side). Although, some debate about this point of view is still on its way.

PS 2: This concept of left and right aligns with the arrangement of officials during the daily court sessions of ancient Chinese emperors. Civil officials stood on the left, and military officials on the right. The emperor's throne faced south from the north, so civil officials stood in the east, and military officials in the west. However, in pure spiritual practice, this arrangement is reversed, yet this reversal does not imply opposition or conflict.

"孔德之容，唯道是從。"道甚大，教孔丘為知。後世不信道文，但上孔書，以為無上，道故明之，告後賢。"道之為物，唯慌唯惚。"道微，獨能慌惚不可見也。慌惚中有物，惚慌中有像，不可以道不見故輕也。中有大神氣，故喻囊龠。"窈冥中有精。"大除中也。有道精分之與萬物，萬物精共一本，其精甚真，生死之官也，精其真，當寶之也。"其中有信。"古仙士寶精以生，今人失精以死，大信也。今但結精，便可得生乎？不也。

要諸行當備，所以精者道之別氣也。入人身中為根本，持其半，乃先言之。夫欲寶精，百行當備，萬善當著，調和五行，喜怒悉去。天曹左契，{竹下}有餘數，精乃守之。惡人寶精，唐自苦終不居，必自泄漏也。心應規制萬事，故號明堂。三道布陽耶陰害，以中正度道氣。精並喻像池水，身為池堤封，善行為水源。若斯三備，池乃全堅。心不專善，無堤封；水必去，行善不積；源不通，水必燥幹；決水溉野，渠如溪江。雖堤在，源氵不泄，必亦空。{山行}燥炘裂，百病並生。斯三不慎，池為空坑也。"自古及今，其名不去。"古今常共此一道，不去離人也。"以閱眾甫。"道有以來，更閱終始，非一也。甫者，始也。"吾何以知終甫之然，以此。"吾，道也，所以知古今終始共此一道。其事如此也。

Extract from Laozi He Shang Gong Zhang Ju (Laozi DDJ Commented by He Shang Gong) - "Void your Heart"

The countenance of virtuous virtue, 'Kong,' signifies greatness. A person of great virtue embraces all, tolerating impurities, and dwelling in humility. Only by following the Dao. 'Wei,' (惟, 唯) means solely or alone. A person of great virtue does not conform to the ways of the world but solely follows the Dao. The Dao, as a thing, is only vague and elusive. Regarding all things, the Dao is alone vague and elusive, not fixed in any particular place. Elusive and vague, within it, there are images. The Dao is only elusive and vague, within it, having myriad patterns of the laws of all things. Elusive and vague, within it, there are things. The Dao is only elusive and vague, within it, having unity, managing birth and transformation, and establishing substance through the blending of energies.

Profound and dark, within it, there is essence. The Dao is only profound and dark, formless within it, having substantial essence. Spirits and brightness intermingle, the convergence of yin and yang. Its essence is extremely genuine, speaking of preserving essence and energy. Its subtlety is exceedingly real, without any embellishment. Within it, there is trust. The Dao conceals achievements and hides its name; its trust lies within.

From ancient times to the present, its name does not depart. 'Zi,' (自) means from. From ancient times to the present, the Dao has always been present and does not depart. By examining the multitude of beginnings, 'Yue,' (閱) means inherit. 'Fu,' (甫) means beginning. It is said that the Dao is inherited, and all things begin, receiving energy from the Dao. Why do I know that the multitude of beginnings is so? Why do I know that all things receive energy from the Dao? Because of this. 'Ci,' (此) means now. Because now, all things receive the essence and energy of the Dao, giving rise to movement and activity. Without the Dao, it is not so.

老子河上公章句 -> 道經 -> 虛心

孔德之容，孔，大也。有大德之人，無所不容，能受垢濁，處謙卑也。唯道是從。唯，獨也。大德之人，不隨世俗所行，獨從於道也。道之為物，唯怳唯忽。道之於萬物，獨怳忽往來，於其無所定也。忽兮怳兮，其中有象；道唯忽怳無形，之中獨有萬物法象。怳兮忽兮，其中有物。道唯怳忽，其中有一，經營生化，因氣立質。窈兮冥兮，其中有精，道唯窈冥無形，其中有精實，神明相薄，陰陽交會也。其精甚真，言存精氣，其妙甚真，非有飾也。其中有信。道匿功藏名，其信在中也。自古及今，其名不去，自，從也。自古至今，道常在不去。以閱眾甫，閱，稟也。甫，始也。言道稟與，萬物始生，從道受氣。吾何以知眾甫之然哉。吾何以知萬物從道受氣。以此。此，今也。以今萬物皆得道精氣而生，動作起居，非道不然。

【第二十二章】Chapter 22

Most Common Translation

曲則全，	Curve leads to wholeness, (Being able to be flexible and adapt enables self-completion) (Note 1)
枉則直，	Crook leads to straightness, (The ones who often endure injustice are usually the most upright.)
窪則盈，	Hollow leads to fullness,
敝則新，	Worn out leads to renewal,
少則得，	Having less leads to obtaining.
多則惑。	Too many leads to doubt and worry.
是以聖人抱一，	Therefore, the sage embraces oneness,
為天下式。	As a protocol for the world.
不自見故明，	Not displaying oneself, one shines,
不自是故彰，	Not asserting oneself, one stands out;
不自伐故有功，	Not boasting oneself, one achieves,
不自矜故長。	Not bragging about oneself, one endures.
夫唯不爭，	Indeed, by only not contending,
故天下莫能與之爭。	No one in the world can contend with them.
古之所謂曲則全者，	What the ancients meant by 'Curved leads the path to wholeness,
豈虛言哉！	How could it be empty words?
誠全而歸之。	Embrace it wholeheartedly and return to completeness.

Note 1 - There is a growing trend in suggesting that the original wording of the first two verses of this chapter should be interpreted as "曲則直，枉則全", leading to a different meaning: "Curve and you will make it straightened, deviate and you will correct it and make it perfected". This perspective aligns with modern attitudes or perceptions and is gaining popularity, emphasizing the importance of staying on the right path and acting with integrity to achieve a just and complete outcome.

My literal translation

In the pursuit of perfection, it is emphasized to avoid extremes, as excessively correcting a situation may result in overcompensation. The key is to maintain a balanced and harmonious state, much like the fluidity of tai chi forms, where one's shape remains an arc, never too rigid, storing energy and allowing for adaptability in the face of potential challenges, like shooting an arrow.

Simplicity fosters understanding, while excessive pondering can lead to confusion and illusions, draining mental energy. Therefore, aligning oneself with the principles of Dao, exemplified by sages, serves as a model for all. Clear perception arises from letting go of personal biases, and benevolence becomes evident in the absence of rigid judgments. Achievements flourish when one seeks no personal glory and remains modest about their abilities, fostering continuous and flexible growth.

The sage, uninvolved in worldly conflicts, finds that the world, in turn, has no one to contend with. The ancient saying, "Curve leads to wholeness " (曲則全), is not mere rhetoric; those who follow this path with integrity will find their place in the world.

Laozi think about you and make notes:

Curve and you will be complete. This is humility. Just as the moon humbly takes a curved path before becoming fully illuminated, learning the Dao involves going against common practices. Initially, one may seem insufficiently flexible, but later one becomes enlightened. 'Deviate and you will be upright.' Deviation is also a form of curvature. When the path curves, it eventually leads to correctness. Learning the Dao involves going against societal norms, diligently pursuing one's path, even if at the time it may seem like a deviation; in the end, it leads to righteousness.

"Bend and you will be filled." This embodies the spirit of humility and modesty. By acting without malice, one's presence becomes empty. The Dao, like water, prefers to dwell in empty places and shun those filled with negativity, choosing goodness and becoming fulfilled.

"Weaken and you will be renewed." Just as worn-out things are replaced with new, learning the Dao involves shedding weaknesses, and later, attaining new blessings.

"Less leads to gain, more leads to excess." Cultivating one's strength judiciously ensures self-sufficiency. Heaven provides; accordingly, seeking excessive prosperity beyond one's needs may lead to unnecessary burdens or challenges.

"Therefore, the sage embraces unity as the model for the world." Unity refers to the Dao. The sage follows these principles as a model for all, teaching and setting an example for the world.

"Not asserting oneself, therefore one shines." The wise rejoice in these teachings and willingly follow them, while those who do not find joy in them are discreetly advised without forcing it upon them.

"Not promoting oneself, therefore one achieves." The malicious boast about their own achievements as if wielding a destructive weapon. The sage, adhering to the Dao and avoiding evil, does not boast, thus ensuring the continuation of their achievements.

"Not glorifying oneself, therefore one endures." The sage, following the Dao, focuses on accumulating positive deeds, leading to a long and enduring life. By not boasting or indulging in luxury, the sage retains their virtue.

"In not contending, therefore no one can contend with them." The sage does not engage in disputes with ordinary people. If a conflict arises, the sage gracefully avoids it, making it impossible for ordinary people to compete.

"Of old, those who were called 'Curve and you will be complete,' were not uttering empty words; thus, they achieved completeness and returned to it." The notion of being humble and flexible before achieving completeness is not mere rhetoric. To ensure understanding, it is reiterated.

"Not asserting oneself, hence one is illuminated." The sage follows the Dao, achieving significant deeds without much self-promotion, emphasizing virtue over personal abilities.

"Not promoting oneself, hence one succeeds." Boasting is a weapon used by the wicked against themselves. The sage, adhering to the Dao and avoiding evil, does not indulge in self-promotion, ensuring the continuation of their success.

"Not glorifying oneself, hence one perseveres." The sage, following the Dao, accumulates virtuous deeds, leading to longevity. By not boasting or indulging in luxury, the sage maintains a flourishing and enduring life.

"In not contending, therefore no one can contend with them." The sage does not engage in conflicts with ordinary people. If a dispute arises, the sage gracefully avoids it, making it impossible for ordinary people to compete.

"In ancient times, what was called 'Curve and you will be complete' was not mere empty words; hence, they achieved completeness and returned to it." Humility and flexibility followed by completeness were not mere rhetoric. To dispel any doubts, this idea is reiterated."

"曲則全。謙也。月謙先曲後全明，學道反俗，當時如曲不足也，後亦令明。"枉則正。"枉亦曲也，曲變則正。學道反俗，獨自勤苦，當時如相侵枉也，後致正。"窪則盈。"謙虛意也。行無惡，其處空。道喻水喜歸空居惡處，便為善，◌◌歸滿故盈。"弊則新。"物弊變更新，學道贏弊，後更致新福也。"少則得，多則或。"陳力殖穀，裁令自足。天與之，無基考可得福，多望不止則或，或耶歸之也。"是以聖人抱一為天下式。"一，道也。設誠，聖人行之為抱一也，常教天下為法式也。"不自是故章。"明者樂之，就誠教之，不樂者墨以不言。我是若非，勿與之爭也。

"不自見故明。"聖人法道，有功不多，不見德能也。"不自伐故有功。"惡者伐身之斧也。聖人法道不為惡，故不伐身，常全其功也。"不自矜故長。"聖人法道，但念積行，令身長生。生之行，垢辱貧贏，不矜傷身，以好衣美食與之也。"夫唯不爭，故莫能與爭。"聖人不與俗人爭，有爭避之高逝，俗人如何能與之共爭乎？"古之所謂曲則全，豈虛語，故成全而歸之。"謙曲後全，明非虛語也。恐人不解，故重申示之也。

Extract from Laozi He Shang Gong Zhang Ju - "Embrace Humility"

"Bend and you will be complete." By bending oneself to align with others, avoiding self-centeredness, one ensures the completeness of their own being. Deviate and you will be upright. Deviation involves bending oneself to accommodate others, and in the long run, one attains uprightness through this selfless approach. Embrace humility and you will be filled. Like water filling a low place, when a person humbly lowers themselves, virtue flows towards them. Embrace modesty and you will be renewed. By willingly accepting shortcomings and putting others before oneself, the world respects and renews such an individual continuously. Gain by being moderate. Receiving modestly leads to abundant gains; the celestial way favors humility, and spiritual clarity resides in emptiness. Excess leads to confusion. Those with abundant wealth may be confused by what they possess, and extensive learning may lead to confusion through diverse teachings. Therefore, the sage embraces unity as the model for the world. Embrace refers to safeguarding, and model signifies the principles. The sage guards the unity and principles of Dao, understanding myriad things, thus becoming a model for the world.

"Not asserting oneself, hence one shines." The sage does not rely solely on their own vision to see a thousand miles away. Instead, they utilize the vision of the world to gain clarity.

"Not promoting oneself, hence one achieves." The sage's virtues and influence spread naturally, without actively seeking attention. By not pursuing personal gain, the sage achieves success throughout the world.

"Not glorifying oneself, hence one endures." The sage does not boast of their greatness, allowing for a lasting and secure existence.

"Only by not contending, therefore no one can contend with them." This statement applies to the virtuous and the unworthy in the world; none can contend with those who do not engage in conflict.

"Of old, those who were called 'Bend and you will be complete' were not uttering empty words." The ancient wisdom of bending to completeness is not mere rhetoric. It is a sincere practice that leads to fulfillment. Those who sincerely follow this path return to the origin without harm, embodying truth and reality. By embodying flexibility, one secures their essence and returns to the source, ensuring no harm to oneself or others."

老子河上公章句 -> 道經 -> 益謙

曲則全，曲己從眾，不自專，則全其身也。枉則直，枉，屈己而伸人，久久自得直也。窪則盈，地窪下，水流之；人謙下，德歸之。敝則新，自受弊薄，後己先人，天下敬之，久久自新也。少則得，自受取少則得多也，天道祐謙，神明託虛。多則惑。財多者，惑於所守，學多者，惑於所聞。是以聖人抱一為天下式。抱，守也。式，法也。聖人守一，乃知萬事，故能為天下法式也。不自見故明，聖人不以其目視千里之外也，乃因天下之目以視，故能明達也。不自是故彰，聖人不自以為是而非人，故能彰顯於世。不自伐故有功，伐，取也。聖人德化流行，不自取其美，故有功於天下。不自矜故長。矜，大也。聖人不自貴大，故能久不危。夫惟不爭，故天下莫能與之爭。此言天下賢與不肖，無能與不爭者爭也。古之所謂曲則全者，豈虛言哉。傳古言，曲從則全身，此言非虛妄也。誠全而歸之。誠，實也。能行曲從者，實其肌體，歸之於父母，無有傷害也。

【第二十三章】 Chapter 23

Most Common Translation

希言自然。(note 1)
1. Abstaining from speech marks him who is obeying the spontaneity of his nature.
2. Sacred words, self arise from within. Or; Sacred sound (chapter 14, Inner hearing sound (Xi), arises from within. Or the sound we can not hear)
3. Wishful blessing words are natural.
4. Nature rarely talks. (most common)
5. Express yourself completely, then keep quiet, and be like the forces of nature.
6. To be of few words is natural.

故飄風不終朝，	Hence, the drifting wind does not last all morning.
驟雨不終日。	Sudden showers do not last all day.
孰為此者？	By whom is this done?
天地。	Heaven and Earth.
天地尚不能久，	Not even Heaven and Earth can endure eternally,
而況於人乎？	How much can humans go/do?
	How much less can humans?
故從事於道者，	Thus, those who align with the principles of Dao,
道者同於道，	Are the ones with Dao.
德者同於德，	Those who possess virtue are one with virtue,
失者同於失。	Those who lose are the ones with lose.
同於道者，	Those who are one with the Dao,
道亦樂得之；	Dao is also delighted to have them;
同於德者，	Those who are one with virtue,
德亦樂得之；	Virtue is also delighted to have them;
同於失者，	Those who are one with loss,
失亦樂得之。	Loss is also delighted to have them.
信不足焉，	Those lacking in belief naturally,
	Insufficient trust leads to disbelief,
有不信焉。	Some lack trust. Have a deficiency in confidence.

Note 1 - 希言自然

Translating this verse presents a unique challenge due to the complexity of the character 希. On its own, 希 signifies hope, rarity, and scarcity. In Chapter 14, 希 is associated with the term (Xi), conveying a sense of sacredness. It's noteworthy that in this context, it is paired with the character for sound (音) rather than voice (言), as seen in the current chapter. Chapter 41 further deepens the understanding, stating that the grandest sound resembles 希 (大音希声), suggesting a sacred resonance. Therefore, a comprehensive interpretation of this verse could be that 希 represents not just hope or rarity but a sacred sound (or word, the word energy, or in some religious lineage, it is the word from GOD), emphasizing the profound significance of the interconnected characters and their contextual variations.

In the ancient era of Laozi, the concept of nature as we understand it today did not exist. In Chinese, each character typically carries a single meaning, either on its own or in combination with others. Therefore, the term 自然, often translated as "nature" or "natural" in modern times, should be separated into 自 and 然 for a more nuanced understanding.

希言自然 can be reinterpreted as 希言, 自, 然. This literal breakdown suggests that the sacred word originates from within, and 然 serves as an emphatic particle, conveying a sense of certainty or indeed. In this context, the phrase could be translated as "The sacred word arises from within, indeed." This conveys a deeper sense of the source and certainty associated with the sacred utterance, aligning more closely with the nuances of the ancient Chinese philosophical perspective.

In light of the challenges posed by various interpretations in the quoted text, I choose to concentrate on the second explanation (my interpretation), emphasizing the notion of the sacred word. This approach aims to maintain coherence with subsequent verses, ensuring a more harmonious flow of meaning. Consequently, my translation centers around the concept that the sacred word, symbolized by 希言, is of paramount importance, allowing for a more seamless integration with the surrounding verses.

Most Common Translate (an example)

Saying less is natural, (or wishful blessing words are natural..etc., you may fill in the others as wish)

The drifting wind does not last through the early morning, and torrential rain cannot persist throughout the day.

Who stirs up the wind and rain? It is the heavens and the earth.

If even the heavens and the earth cannot remain constant, how much more so for humans?

Therefore, those aspiring to the Dao must embrace the significance of the Dao, those aspiring to virtue must embrace the meaning of virtue.

Those who embrace the meaning of the Dao and Dao are also delighted to have them.

Those who embrace the meaning of virtue and virtue are also delighted to have them.

O people of insufficient faith, naturally, skeptics arise.

PS: Numerous alternative translations are readily available online, and I won't duplicate them here.

My version of the translation

Sacred words and self arise from within, indeed.
Hence, the drifting wind does not last all morning.
Sudden showers do not last all day.
By whom is this done? Heaven and Earth.
Not even Heaven and Earth can endure eternally,
How much can humans go/do?
Thus, those who align with the principles of Dao,
Are the ones with Dao.
Those who possess virtue are one with virtue,
Those who lose are the ones with lose.
Those who are one with the Dao,
Dao is also delighted to have them;
Those who are one with virtue,
Virtue is also delighted to have them;
Those who are one with loss,
Loss is also delighted to have them.
Those lacking in belief naturally,
Insufficient trust leads to disbelief,
Some lack trust.
Have a deficiency in confidence.

My 5 cents

Sacred WORD and SOUND emerge from within, indeed, (when we go into a certain stage of deep meditation. Also note 2)
Therefore, the drifting winds don't endure the entire morning. (note 3, the unconquerable/uncontrollable qi flows stop because of the SOUND)
Sudden showers cease before the day concludes. (note 4)
By whom is this orchestrated? It is the collaboration of Heaven and Earth. (note 5)
Not even the enduring forces of Heaven and Earth persist indefinitely, (note 6)
How much less can mortals?
Hence, those attuned to the principles of Dao, truly embody Dao.
Those embodying virtue are synonymous with virtue,
Those embodying loss find themselves in the realm of loss.
Those in harmony with Dao, find Dao delighted to have them;
Those in harmony with virtue, find virtue equally pleased to have them;
Those in harmony with loss, find loss also welcomes them.

For those lacking conviction, insufficient trust naturally leads to disbelief, some harbor a deficiency in confidence.

Note 2 - When contemplating the Lu Dongbin 100 Characters Monument (hereafter referred to as 100 words for convenience), it also points to the verse: Transforming and spreading in thunderous sound (The Word, an inner sound, embodies the most potent form of energy, sometimes manifesting in the harmonious resonance of musical tunes.)

Hence, in the 100 words, it says: sitting, listening to the soundless music. The original expression suggests listening to music produced by an instrument without strings. I will delve into a more detailed explanation when the situation permits and as our understanding progresses to that level.

For more details, kindly consult my notes on inner vision and sound in a separate document.

Note 3 - Wind, a term commonly employed in Daoism, signifies 風息, representing the flow of qi. The concept of drifting wind implies uncontrolled or wandering qi within our body (真氣散亂).

In the practice of Qi, the gentle murmurs of the wind, referred to as 風的消息, typically convey internal messages or signals from the body. These sensations indicate that something is actively unfolding as the qi courses through our being.

Note 4 - Sudden showers, referenced as sweet dew showers on Mount Sumeru, are also indicated in the 100 words. (Mount Sumeru, means the crown of our head, in here)

The inquiry arises: why do the showers do not last all day? The original wording of the verse attributes this phenomenon to the setting sun (日 means, a day, and means the SUN either), signifying the retreat of yang energy—a natural cycle.

Note 5 - Where is Heaven and Earth, and the cycle of energy. you guys should know that. In the 100 words, refers to: In the vessel (a vase), harmonize the kan (water) and li (fire).

Note 6 - Why can't even Heaven and Earth endure eternally? This is attributed to the natural cycle of "nine retreats/turn and seven returns" 九轉七還. I've previously elaborated on this in our group chat; please refer to the notes for details, as I won't reiterate them here

Laozi think about you and make notes:

To be a few words arise naturally. Nature is the Dao. Be joyful and serene, less talk enter serenity; harmonize with nature, and it can last long. 'Wandering winds do not last the morning, chasing rain does not last the day.' If one does not conform to the serenity of nature, it will not last until the end of the day. 'Who is responsible for this heaven and earth?' 'Who' refers to who. Heaven and earth produce wandering winds and chasing rain, serving as a warning to humanity. If one does not conform to the Dao, it will not last long.

'Heaven and earth cannot last long, how much less can humans?' If heaven and earth cannot endure for long, how can humans, who engage in restless and anxious affairs, with thoughts and plans, endure for long? 'Therefore, one who follows the Dao achieves it.' 'Achieves it' means acting like the Dao. When people engage in affairs under the Dao, the Dao desires to obtain them, thus it is said to be natural.

'Those who share virtues obtain virtue.' When people engage in affairs in harmony with virtues, virtues desire to obtain them. 'Those who share faults lose the Dao.' When people engage in affairs without fearing the warnings of the Dao, losing the intention of the Dao, the Dao will naturally depart. It is as simple as that.

'Insufficient trust leads to lack of trust.' This has been explained in the previous passages".

希言自然。自然，道也。樂清靜，希言入清靜；合自然，可久也。"飄風不終朝，趨雨不終日。"不合清靜自然，故不久竟日也。"孰為此天地。"孰，誰也。天地為飄風趨雨，為人為誡，不合道，故令不久也。"天地尚不能久，而況於人。"天地尚不能久，人欲為煩躁之事，思慮耶計，安能得久乎？"故從事而道得之。"而，如也。人舉事令如道，道善欲得之，曰自然也。"同於德者，德得之。"人舉事與德合，德欲得之也。"同於失者，道失之。"人舉事不懼畏道誡。失道意，道即去之，自然如此。"信不足，有不信。"前章已說之也。

Extract from Laozi He Shang Gong Zhang Ju - Xūwú (虛無)

Hopeful words arise naturally. The term 'hopeful words' refers to words of love. Words of love represent the way of nature. Hence, swift winds do not last the morning, and sudden rain does not last the day. Swift winds refer to strong winds, and sudden rain refers to heavy rain. Words of haste cannot endure, just as the violent cannot persist for long. Who is responsible for this? Heaven and earth. (same here, heaven and earth, fire and water) 'Who' means who. Who is responsible for these strong winds and heavy rain? It is what heaven and earth bring about (the cycle of fire and water). If even heaven and earth cannot endure for long, unable to persist from morning to evening, how much less can humans endure? Heaven and earth, in their divine essence, combine to create strong winds and heavy rain, yet even they cannot make it last from morning to evening. How then can humans, who desire sudden and violent actions, achieve longevity?

Therefore, those who engage in the way should align their actions with the Dao. 'Align' here means to act. People should engage in affairs in a manner that reflects the tranquility of the Tao, not in the manner of swift winds and sudden rain. The Dao is the same as the way, referring to those who love the Dao. Those who are the same as the Dao are those who align with the Dao. Virtuous individuals are the same as virtue, referring to those who love virtue. Those who are the same as virtue are those who align with virtue. Those who are lost are the same as loss. Loss here means disregarding others for one's own desires. Those who are the same as loss are those who align with loss. Those who align with the Dao find joy in it. Those who are aligned with the Dao also find joy in it. Those who align with virtue find joy in it. Those who are aligned with virtue also find joy in it. Those who align with loss find joy in it. Those who are aligned with loss also find joy in it. If trust is insufficient, the ruler's lack of trust in those below will lead to a lack of trust in the ruler. This lack of trust is mutual.

This is saying that things of similar nature attract each other, sounds resonate together, and spirits seek each other.

Clouds follow the dragon (liver qi), wind follows the tiger (lung qi), water flows towards wetness, fire seeks dryness—these are natural phenomena. (note 8)

老子河上公章句 -> 道經 -> 虛無

希言自然。希言者，謂愛言也。愛言者，自然之道。故飄風不終朝，驟雨不終日。飄風，疾風也。驟雨，暴雨也。言疾不能長，暴不能久也。孰為此者？天地。孰，誰也。誰為此飄風暴雨者乎？天地所為。天地尚不能久，不能終於朝暮也。而況於人乎？天地至神合為飄風暴雨，尚不能使終朝至暮，何況人欲為暴卒乎。故從事於道者，從，為也。人為事當如道安靜，不當如飄風驟雨也。道者同於道，道者，謂好道人也。同於道者，所謂與道同也。德者同於德，德者，謂好德之人也。同於德者，所謂與德同也。失者同於失。失，謂任己而失人也。同於失者，所謂與失同也。同於道者，道亦樂得之。與道同者，道亦樂得之也。同於德者，德亦樂得之，與德同者，德亦樂得之也。同於失者，失亦樂得之。與失同者，失亦樂失之也。信不足焉，君信不足於下，下則應君以不信也。有不信焉。此言物類相歸，同聲相應，同氣相求。雲從龍，風從虎，水流濕，火就燥，自然之類也。

Note 8 (PS: no note 7 😊)

The Discourse on Cultivation and Transmission of Dao - Chapter Eight: On Dragon and Tiger

For those unfamiliar with the lineage, Zhong Zu (Zhōnglí quán) serves as the Master to Lü Zu (Lu Dongbin), and together, they are the founders of Den Dao, an internal alchemical tradition. According to legend, their ultimate teacher is Emperor Donghua (東華帝君, Dōnghuá dìjūn), the sovereign ruling over both heaven and earth. Recently, a Chinese television series titled "Three Lives, Three Worlds, The Pillow Book" (三生三世枕上書) has gained popularity. The main male character in the series is Emperor Donghua, and it portrays a romantic story between Emperor Donghua and a nine-tailed fox. My wife is a big fan of this drama. 😊

Lü Zu (Lu Dongbin) said: The dragon is originally the symbol of the liver, and the tiger is the spirit of the lungs. Within the fire of this heart, the essence is produced; this essence becomes true water. Within the water, there is a profound and mysterious presence, hiding the true dragon. Why does the dragon emerge not from the liver but from the LI (fire) palace? This is because, within the kidney's water, the qi is born. This qi becomes true fire. Within the fire, there is a state of haziness, and in this state, the true tiger is concealed. Why does the tiger not arise from the lungs but is born in the position of Kan? This is the question.

Zhong Zu (Zhōnglí quán) said: The dragon is a yang entity, soaring in the sky, its roar causing clouds to rise. It receives nourishment and benefits all beings. In symbolism, it is the Azure Dragon (we have discussed the relationship between purple, blue and green, please refer to the previous note), in the directional aspect it represents the first two Heavenly Stems (Jia and Yi), in the material world it corresponds to wood, in the season it is associated with spring, in the Dao it embodies benevolence, in the hexagram it is linked to Thunder (Zhen), and within the human body, it is the liver.

The tiger, on the other hand, is a yin entity, swiftly moving on the ground, its roar generating winds. It dominates all creatures (original wording controls all hundreds of worms, hundreds of worms mean sickness of all kinds) upon reaching the mountain. In symbolism, it is the White Tiger, in the directional aspect it corresponds to the seventh and eighth Heavenly Stems (Geng and Xin), in the material world it represents metal, in the season it is associated with autumn, in the Dao it embodies righteousness, in the hexagram it is linked to Lake (Dui), and within the human body, it is the lungs.

The liver is yang, yet it resides in a yin position. This is why the qi of the kidneys transfers to the liver, as qi moves from parent to child, with water giving rise to wood. When the qi of the kidneys is abundant, the qi of the liver is generated. Once the qi of the liver is generated, it cuts off the excess yin of the kidneys, allowing the pure yang qi to rise.

The lungs are yin, yet they reside in a yang position. This is why the fluid of the heart transfers to the lungs, as fluid moves between husband and wife, with fire controlling metal. When the fluid reaches the lungs, the fluid of the lungs is generated. Once the fluid of the lungs is generated, it cuts off the excess yang of the heart, allowing the pure yin fluid to descend.

As the liver belongs to yang, cutting off the excess yin of the kidneys, it is known that when qi passes through the liver, it becomes pure yang. Within this pure yang qi lies the invisible and indistinct water (真一之水, refer to yellow river chart), named the "Yang Dragon".

As the lungs belong to yin, cutting off the excess yang of the heart, it is known that when fluid reaches the lungs, it becomes pure yin. Within this pure yin fluid, it carries the positive yang qi, concealed and unseen, named the "Yin Tiger".

Qi ascends, and fluid descends—originally, they should not intersect. However, within the qi, there is the true unity of water (真一之水), seeing the fluid and uniting with it. Within the fluid, there is the positive yang qi, seeing the qi and gathering together. (1 Merge in 5 refer to yellow river chart)

If, during the time of transmission, one follows the proper methods, preventing the loss of kidney qi and collecting the true unity of water within the qi, and ensuring that the fluid of the heart is not scattered and acquiring the positive yang qi within the fluid, when the parent and child meet, mutually caring for each other, then one will attain the size of a grain of millet within a day. Without deviation in efficacy for a hundred days, after two hundred days, the sacred embryo will solidify, and after three hundred days, the immortal fetus will be complete. The form will be like a pellet, the color resembling vermillion oranges, known as the "Elixir." It will forever settle in the lower field (5+5+5, yellow court, or 1+5 = 6 lower Dāntián, also refer to the yellow river chart), preserving its form in this world. It will endure for countless ages, becoming an immortal on land.

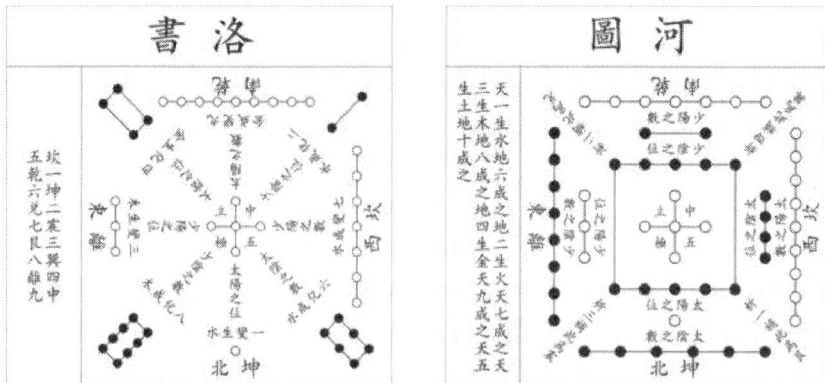

Lü Zu said: The kidneys produce water, and within the qi, there is the true unity of water, named the Yin Tiger. The Tiger encounters the fluid and unites with it. The heart's fire produces fluid, and within the fluid, there is the positive yang qi, named the Yang Dragon. The Dragon encounters the qi and unites with it. Thus, similar things gather, and in the realm of substances, they naturally separate. This is the inherent principle.

When qi is generated, fluid descends, and within the qi, there is the true unity of water, all of which follows the fluid and descends, transmitting to the five organs! When fluid is generated, qi ascends, and within the fluid, there is the positive yang qi, all of which follows the qi and ascends, emerging from the 12 staircases! True water follows the descent of fluid, and the Tiger cannot engage with the Dragon; true yang follows the ascent of qi, and the Dragon cannot engage with the Tiger. When the Dragon and Tiger do not engage, how can the yellow sprout be obtained? If the yellow sprout is absent, how can the great medicine be obtained?

Zhong Zu said: Once the qi of the kidneys is generated, it is like the sun rising over the sea; neither mist nor dew can obscure its brilliance. As the fluid descends, it is like a sparse curtain; is it sufficient to overcome the strength of the qi? When the qi is vigorous, the true unity of water naturally becomes abundant.

Once the fluid of the heart is generated, it is like a harsh winter's cold that can slaughter creatures; mere breaths cannot withstand its chill. As the qi ascends, it is like a green curtain; is it enough to overcome the fluid? When the fluid is abundant, the positive yang qi may be strong or weak, and it cannot be predetermined.

Lü Zu said: The generation of qi and the generation of fluid each have their own timing. When it is the time for the emergence of qi, with the flourishing of qi, the true unity of water naturally becomes abundant. When it is the time for the emergence of fluid, with the abundance of fluid, the positive yang qi also flourishes. The waxing and waning are not yet stabilized—why is this so?

Zhong Zu said: The qi of the kidneys is easily dispersed, and what is difficult to obtain is the true Tiger. The fluid of the heart is challenging to accumulate, and what is easily lost is the true Dragon. In the ten thousand scrolls of the Elixir Classic, discussions do not go beyond yin and yang; the essence and purity are nothing other than Dragon and Tiger. Among those who uphold the Dao, one or two may truly understand. Some may be well-read and possess extensive knowledge, and though they comprehend the principles of Dragon and Tiger, they may not recognize the timing of their union or understand the methods of cultivation. This is why many accomplished individuals in ancient and modern times, despite their advanced age and dedicated practice, only achieve partial success and longevity through generations, without attaining transcendence. It is likely because they were unable to engage in union with the Dragon and Tiger and extract the yellow sprout to form the Elixir.

PS: remember how I summarized this chapter in a few sentences?

心氣化液 = Essence of the Heart qi transforms into liquid
腎水化氣 = Essence of Kidney liquid transforms to qi

Liquid drops from the Heart (middle dantian) merge in the Yellow Court with the steaming water in the Pot (lower dantian.
After merging, it forms the yellow/golden medicine and the residual will return in reverse back to the Middle and Lower Dantian.
Yang to Yin and Yin to Yang.

Graphics by: Marianne Nakamura

修真傳道論－－論龍虎第八

呂祖曰：龍本肝之象，虎乃肺之神。

是此心火之中生液，液為真水，水之中，杳杳冥冥，而隱真龍，龍不在肝，而出自離宮者，何也？

是此腎水之中生氣，氣為真火，火之中，恍恍惚惚，而藏真虎，虎不在肺，而生於坎位者，何也？

鍾祖曰：龍，陽物也，升飛在天，吟而雲起，得澤而濟萬物，在象為青龍，在方為甲乙，在物為木，在時為春，在道為仁，在卦為震，在人身中五臟之內為肝；

虎，陰物也，奔走於地，嘯而風生，得山而威制百蟲，在象為白虎，在方為庚辛，在物為金，在時為秋，在道為義，在卦為兌，在人身五臟之內為肺。

且肝，陽也，而在陰位之中，所以腎氣傳肝氣，氣行子母，以水生木，腎氣足而肝氣生，肝氣既生，以絕腎之餘陰，而純陽之氣上升。

肺，陰也，而在陽位之中，所以心液傳肺液，液行夫婦，以火剋金，心液到而肺液生，肺液既生，以絕心之餘陽，而純陰之液下降。

肝屬陽，以絕腎之餘陰，是以知氣過肝時，即為純陽，純陽氣中包藏真一之水，恍惚無形，名曰「陽龍」。

肺屬陰，以絕心之餘陽，是知液到肺時，即為純陰，純陰液中，負載正陽之氣，杳冥不見，名曰「陰虎」。

氣升液降，本不能相交，奈氣中真一之水，見液相合，液中正陽之氣，見氣自聚。

若于傳行之時，以法制之，使腎氣不走失，氣中收取真一之水，心液不耗散，液中採取正陽之氣，子母相逢，兩相顧戀，日得黍米之大，百日無差藥力全，二百日聖胞堅，三百日胎仙完，形若彈丸，色同朱橘，名曰「丹藥」，永鎮下田，留形住世，浩劫長生，此陸地神仙。

呂祖曰：腎水生氣，氣中有真一之水，名曰陰虎，虎見液相合；

心火生液，液中有正陽之氣，名曰陽龍，龍見氣相合。

方以類聚，物以群分，理當然也。

氣生時，液亦降，氣中真一之水，莫不隨液而下傳於五臟乎！液生時，氣亦升，液中正陽之氣，莫不隨氣而上出於重樓乎！真水隨液下行，虎不能交龍；

真陽隨氣上升，龍不能交虎。

龍虎不交，安得黃芽？黃芽既無，安得大藥？

鍾祖曰：腎氣既生，如太陽之出海，霧露不能蔽其光；液下如疏簾，安足以勝其氣？氣壯則真一之水自盛矣。

心液既生，如嚴天之殺物，呼呵不能敵其寒；氣升如翠幘，安足以勝其液？液盛則正陽之氣，或強或弱，未可必也。

呂祖曰：氣生液生各有時：

時生氣也，氣盛則真一之水自盛；

時生液也，液盛則正陽之氣亦盛。

盛衰未保，何也？

鍾祖曰：腎氣易為耗散，難得者真虎；

心液難為積聚，易失者真龍。

丹經萬卷，議論不出陰陽；

陰陽兩事，精粹無非龍虎。

奉道之士，萬中識者一二。或多聞廣記，雖知龍虎之理，不識交合之時，不知採取之法。所以今古達士，皓首修持，止於小成，累代延年，不聞超脫，蓋以不能交媾於龍虎，採黃芽而成丹藥。

【第二十四章】Chapter 24

Most Common Translation

企者不立，	Those who tiptoe can not stand,
跨者不行，	Those who stride can not progress,
自見者不明，	Those who see only themselves are not enlightened,
自是者不彰，	Those who assert oneself does not shine,
自伐者無功，	Those who criticize themselves achieve nothing,
自矜者不長。	Those who boast of themselves do not thrive.
	Those who are self-conceited do not prosper.
其在道也，	All in the way of Dao,
曰餘食贅行。	Having too much food and doing unnecessary things.
物或惡之，	Some entities (objects/things or beings) might dislike it,
故有道者不處。	Hence, those who possess the Dao do not dwell there.

My literal translation

Trying to stand tall by lifting the heels ends up in instability; taking big strides to move quickly results in not covering much distance. Boasting about one's own insights leads to a lack of clarity; being self-righteous leads to a lack of recognition. Self-praise doesn't bring about achievements; arrogance doesn't make one a leader among others.

From the perspective of the Dao, these impatient and showy behaviors can only be described as excess baggage. Because they are repulsive, those who follow the Dao never engage in such actions.

Hence, every baby step count.

【第二十五章】Chapter 25

Most Common Translation

有物混成，	Something emerges from chaos, formless yet present,
先天地生。	Before Heaven and Earth were born.
寂兮寥兮，	In the calm emptiness, (like a morning star),
獨立不改，	Solitary (self-reliant), and Unchanging,
周行而不殆，	Orbiting tirelessly in a perpetual cycle,
可以為天下母。	Can serve as the mother of all under heaven.
吾不知其名，	I do not know its name.
字之曰道，	If I have to assign a word to it, that word is Dao.
強為之名曰大。	Forcibly giving it a name, we label it as "Great" - the transcendent.
大曰逝，逝曰遠，	Great means time (flows through all time), time means far (distance, space),
遠曰反。故道大，	Far means returning (cycle, orbiting), hence, Dao is great,
天大，地大，王亦大。	The heaven is great, the earth is great, the king (ruler of the earth, means human) is great.
域中有四大，	Within the domain, there are four great. (which is: the Dao, heaven, earth, and human)
而王居其一焉。	And the king resides in one of them.
人法地，地法天，	Man follows the natural Law of the Earth, Earth follows the natural law of heaven,
天法道，道法自然。	Heaven follows the natural law of Dao. Dao follows its-self, indeed.

My literal translation

There is a substance that forms chaotically, preceding the creation of heaven and earth. Silent, calm, and empty! Independent and unchanging, like the morning star, it perpetually cycles without fatigue.

It can be considered as the origin of all things in the universe. (someone says it is the Big Bang theory)

I don't know how to name it, for now, I will call it 'Dao,' reluctantly naming it 'Great.'

'Great' is characterized by the infinite passage of time, boundless space, and perpetual renewal in motion.

Thus, not only does the Dao possess the characteristic of greatness, but so does the sky, the earth, and humanity.

In the cosmos, there are four categories with the attribute of greatness, and humans are one of them.

Human laws follow the laws of the earth, the laws of the earth follow the laws of heaven, the laws of heaven follow the Dao, and the Dao follows all by itself, and that is it.

Extract from Laozi He Shang Gong Zhang Ju - Xiàng yuan (the original phenomenon)

In the beginning, there was a blending of substances, and the primal force gave birth to heaven and earth. It is said that the Dao is formless, creating all things out of chaos, existing before the existence of heaven and earth. Profound and quiet, standing alone without change – 'profound' meaning there is no sound, 'quiet' meaning there is emptiness without form. Standing alone, it has no equal partner. Without change, it abides in constant transformation.

It circulates without deviation, and the Dao pervades and moves through heaven and earth, entering everything without exception. In brightness, it does not scorch; in shadow, it does not decay. It penetrates everything without exception, without being negligent. It can be considered the mother of all under heaven.

The Dao nurtures and fosters the essence and energy of all things, like a mother nurturing her child. I do not know its name; I simply call it Dao. I do not see the form and appearance of Dao, and I do not know how to name it. Since I observe that all things come into existence from Dao, I call it Dao. To force a name upon it, I call it Great.

Not knowing its name, I forcefully call it Great because it is high and has no upper limit, vast and without exterior, embracing everything without exception. Thus, I call it Great. Great is said to be elusive. In its greatness, it is not fixed like the constant above of the sky or the constant below of the earth. Instead, it constantly moves away, having no fixed abode. Elusive is said to be distant. Speaking of its distance, it extends endlessly, permeating the breath (QI FLOWS) of heaven and earth, reaching everywhere. Distant is said to be returning. Saying it is distant does not mean it surpasses all limits; it ultimately returns within the realm of human existence. (it refers to the qi flow within our body)

Therefore, the Dao is great, heaven is great, earth is great, and the sovereign (King) is also great. The greatness of Dao lies in its encompassing of heaven and earth, embracing everything without exception. The greatness of heaven lies in its covering, extending over everything. The greatness of earth lies in its support, carrying everything. The greatness of the sovereign lies in their authority, governing everything. Within the domain, there are four greatnesses: Dao, heaven, earth, and the sovereign. All things that are named or designated fall short of their ultimate nature.

When speaking of the Dao, there is a source from which it arises. Only when there is a source can it be called Dao. Therefore, the Dao mentioned the greatness within the realm of names, not like the greatness without names. However, the unnameable greatness cannot be named, so it is called the domain. Heaven, earth, and the sovereign are all within the realm of the unnamable, thus it is said that within the domain there are four greatnesses. The sovereign resides in one of them. Within the boundaries of the Eight Extremes, there are four greatnesses, with the sovereign residing in one.

People should emulate the earth, being tranquil, harmonious, and gentle. By cultivating, they yield the five grains; by digging, they find sweet springs. They work without complaining and achieve without boasting. The earth follows the way of heaven; heaven is serene, selfless, and nurturing, giving rise to all things without seeking anything in return. Heaven follows the Dao; the Dao is clear, silent, operating in the background (the original wording is: 陰行精氣, in qi practice, it means heaven operates through the yin energy) and all things naturally unfold. The Dao follows naturalness. The nature of the Dao is spontaneous, and it does not adhere to any specific principles.

老子河上公章句 -> 道經 -> 象元

有物混成，先天地生。謂道無形，混沌而成萬物，乃在天地之前。寂兮寥兮，獨立而不改，寂者，無音聲。寥者，空無形。獨立者，無匹雙。不改者，化有常。周行而不殆，道通行天地，無所不入，在陽不焦，託蔭不腐，無不貫穿，而不危怠也。可以為天下母。

道育養萬物精氣，如母之養子。吾不知其名，字之曰道，我不見道之形容，不知當何以名之，見萬物皆從道所生，故字之曰道。強為之名曰大。不知其名，強曰大者，高而無上，羅而無外，無不包容，故曰大也。大曰逝，其為大，非若天常在上，非若地常在下，乃復逝去，無常處所也。逝曰遠，言遠者，窮乎無窮，布氣天地，無所不通也。遠曰反。言其遠不越絕，乃復反在人身也。

故道大，天大，地大，王亦大。道大者，包羅天地，無所不容也。天大者，無所不蓋也。地大者，無所不載也。王大者，無所不制也。域中有四大，四大，道、天、地、王也。凡有稱有名，則非其極也。

言道則有所由，有所由然後謂之為道，然則是道稱中之大也，不若無稱之大也，無稱不可而得為名，曰域也。天地王皆在乎無稱之內也，故曰域中有四大者也。而王居其一焉。八極之內有四大，王居其一也。人法地，人當法地安靜和柔也，種之得五穀，掘之得甘泉，勞而不怨也，有功而不置也。地法天，天澹泊不動，施而不求報，生長萬物，無所收取。天法道，道清靜不言，陰行精氣，萬物自成也。道法自然。道性自然，無所法也。

【第二十六章】Chapter 26

Most Common Translation

重為輕根，	Heavy is the root of light,
靜為躁君。	Calm is the ruler of restlessness.
是以聖人終日行不離輜重。	The sage travels through the day, never separating from crucial necessities. (note 1)
雖有榮觀，	Even though there may be splendid sights and beautiful scenes,
燕處超然，	Stay with a calm state of mind, and be transcendence. (note 2)
奈何萬乘之主，	How can the ruler of myriad chariots (original wording is 10,000 chariots),
而以身輕天下？	Prioritize personal interests, disregarding (lightening) the world one governs?
輕則失本，	Light and heedless loses its foundation,
躁則失君。	Restlessness results in the loss of the ruler's status.

Note 1

輜重, is an ancient military terminology, later extended to societal contexts: In ancient times, '輜重' referred to all military and daily supplies for an army, including provisions, clothing, weapons, and equipment.

Here, it extends to become the mental state that a sage must consistently maintain.

Additionally, given that one of the key contents of the 輜重 is primarily food and a well-nourished state is fundamental for life, some scholars propose it correlates with the concept of the 'dantian.' Hence, the sage must consistently protect and value this aspect throughout the day.

Note 2 (Very Important)

Please read both verse 2 and verse 3 together, and we can refer to:

Note 2 in the Lu Dongbin 100 words: It says: Responding to things without losing one's way. (不迷性自住)

And the quote of Qingjing Jing: Always observing and responding to external matters with their genuine nature without any bias, can acquire the true nature of the one-self. Often interchange and interact with calm mind and peacefulness. Hence, mind peacefulness (tranquil and serene) as always.

Furthermore, I'd like to recall a profoundly significant quote from the Diamond Sutra, a topic we have previously explored.

It is: When the mind has a dwelling, it is not true dwelling, we should let the mind arise without dwelling anywhere. 心有所住即非住，應無所住而生其心。(PS: it is extremely important when we are practicing either spiritual meditation or qi.)

After attaining enlightenment through the Diamond Sutra, the Sixth Patriarch Huineng (六祖惠能) summarized his realization in the "Platform Sutra of the Sixth Patriarch" with the following statement: "The essence of enlightenment is naturally pure and serene; by employing this mind, one can directly achieve Buddhahood.", (菩提自性，本來清靜，但用此心，直了成佛。), serving as both an opening statement and a concluding remark. In other words, the main theme of the whole Platform Sutra.

As a side note, I'd like to mention once again that in our tradition, there's a concluding phrase: Through the retreat of awareness of all of our six senses, unveiling the emergence of the original primordial spirit. (識神隱退，元神現).

I once jokingly told Wing Ho that the Diamond Sutra is summarized in 14 or 17 words. The Sixth Patriarch used 16. We only need 8 words. (Diamon sutra should charge more ☺)

Fruit for thought: When we were kids, it felt like forever to get to our destination on a bus or train. We'd keep asking, "Are we there yet?" But as adults, time doesn't seem to drag on like that. WHY? Can we be a child again?

Note 3 - He Shang Gong has a different interpretation about Verse 4 and 5 (雖有榮觀，燕處超然) of this chapter, although the meaning is similar. It is worth bringing out.

His concept is that "榮觀" refers to the palace, "燕處" is the residence of the emperor's consorts (spouses, ladies, lovers.), and "超然" means to keep a distance and not reside there.

Indeed, the literal meaning suggests that despite the existence of palaces for the emperor's consorts, a virtuous emperor should maintain a certain distance from them. In other words, it implies the importance of controlling one's sexual desires. While there may be room for improvement, particularly for males, through practical efforts in this regard.

雖有榮觀，燕處超然。榮觀，謂宮闕。燕處，后妃所居也。超然，遠避而不處也。

PS: In ancient times, a lack of punctuation allowed for diverse interpretations based on different sentence arrangements, contributing to a heightened level of complexity in its potential meanings. This complexity adds to its multi-dimensional nature.

My literal translation

Stability is the foundation of a lofty spirit, while tranquility reigns over restlessness.

Therefore, a sage carries his true self every day when setting out on a journey.

Despite the allure of wealth and grandeur, he remains calmly detached.

However, some rulers of powerful nations only seek to satisfy their own desires, neglecting the well-being of the state.

Frivolity leads to the loss of fundamentals, and arrogance leads to the loss of the throne.

【第二十七章】Chapter 27

Most Common Translation

善行無轍跡，	Good deeds leave no trace,
善言無瑕謫，	Good words have no flaws to be criticized,
善數不用籌策，	A proficient psychic needs no crystal ball, or, Good calculations require no elaborate strategies,
善閉無關楗而不可開，	A well-closed door has no bolt, yet cannot be opened,
善結無繩約而不可解。	A well-tied knot has no rope, yet cannot be untied.
是以聖人常善救人，	That is why a wise saint is always good at helping others,
故無棄人；	Hence, does not abandon anyone;
常善救物，	Those who are skilled at preserving things,
故無棄物，	Thus, does not discard anything.
是謂襲明。	It is called concealing his wisdom and cleverness within (embracing enlightenment).
	Or transmitting (inheriting) the light.
故善人者，	Therefore, a virtuous person,
不善人之師；	Is a teacher to those without virtue;
不善人者，	A person without virtue,
善人之資。	Is a resource for the virtuous.
不貴其師，	Those who do not honor or value the teacher,
不愛其資，	Do not cherish the resource (or task) given,
雖智大迷，	Though intelligent, but are greatly lost,
是謂要妙。	This is called the subtle essence.

My Literal Translation

The actions of a Daoist leave no trace; the words of a virtuous Daoist leave no handle. The calculations of a virtuous Daoist require no tools or chips. The shielding of a virtuous Daoist needs no bolts and cannot be opened. The constraints of a virtuous Daoist require no ropes and cannot be released.

Therefore, the sage, by adhering to the virtuous Dao, saves humanity without anyone being abandoned. By following the virtuous Dao, all things are saved, and nothing is left behind.

This is what is meant by inheriting and transmitting the light.

Hence, the virtuous Daoist is the teacher of those who do not follow the Dao, and those who do not follow the Dao are the resources of the virtuous Daoist. Failing to respect such a teacher and not cherishing such resources, even with wisdom, one remains in confusion. This is a crucial mystery.

Extract from Laozi He Shang Gong Zhang Ju - Skillfully Employ

Good actions leave no trace; those who practice virtuous deeds seek it within themselves, without descending the hall or leaving the door. Therefore, there are no traces. Virtuous words have no flaws; speaking virtuously means choosing words carefully, resulting in flawless speech surpassing all under heaven. Proficient calculations require no scheming; those who calculate matters with the Dao adhere to one principle without deviation. Their calculations are not excessive, hence no need for scheming, and the outcome is already known.

Being adept at closing without bolts, yet unable to be opened; closing desires and guarding the spirit with the Dao is more effective than having doors with bolts. Being skilled at tying without ropes, yet unable to be untied; skillfully tying matters with the Dao can bind hearts, unlike ropes that can be untied. Therefore, the sage is always skilled at saving people. By teaching loyalty and filial piety, the sage seeks to save lives, hence does not abandon people, allowing each to attain their rightful place.

Consistently skilled at saving all things, the sage teaches people to follow the four seasons to save all injured things, without abandoning anything. The sage does not belittle a name but values jade as one. This is called inheriting brightness. The sage is skilled at saving both people and things; this is called inheriting the great Dao of brightness.

Therefore, the virtuous person is the teacher of the non-virtuous; those who practice virtue are considered teachers by the sage. The non-virtuous person is the resource of the virtuous; the resource is utilized. For those who walk in unvirtuous ways, the sage still guides and instructs them to act virtuously, enabling them to be of use. Not esteeming their teacher, they lack assistance alone. Not cherishing their resources, they have nothing to employ. Though they may possess great intelligence, they are still deeply confused, even if they consider themselves wise. Speaking of such individuals, they are profoundly deluded. This is called essential subtlety. To comprehend this meaning is called understanding the subtle and essential Dao.

老子河上公章句 -> 道經 -> 巧用

善行無轍迹，善行道者求之於身，不下堂，不出門，故無轍迹。善言無瑕謫，善言謂擇言而出之，則無瑕疵謫過於天下。善數不用籌策，善以道計事者，則守一不移，所計不多，則不用籌策而可知也。善閉無關楗而不可開善以道閉情欲、守精神者，不如門戶有關楗可得開。善結無繩約而不可解。善以道結事者，乃可結其心，不如繩索可得解也。是以聖人常善救人，聖人所以常教人忠孝者，欲以救人性命。故無棄人；使貴賤各得其所也。常善救物，聖人所以常教民順四時者，欲以救萬物之殘傷。故無棄物。聖人不賤名而貴玉視之如一。是謂襲明。聖人善救人物，是謂襲明大道。故善人者，不善人之師；人之行善者，聖人即以為人師。不善人者，善人之資。資，用也。人行不善者，聖人猶教導使為善，得以給用也。不貴其師，獨無輔也。不愛其資無所使也。雖智大迷，雖自以為智。言此人乃大迷惑。是謂要妙。能通此意，是謂知微妙要道也。

【第二十八章】 Chapter 28

Most Common Translation

知其雄，	Know the masculine,
守其雌，	Guard to the feminine,
為天下谿。	And become the world's stream.
為天下谿，	Become the world's stream,
	(Original wording is Stream under the sky or heaven)
常德不離，	Constant Virtue will not depart,
復歸於嬰兒。	And one will return to infancy.
知其白，	Know the white (bright),
守其黑，	Guard to the black (dark),
為天下式。	And become the world's model (Law).
為天下式，	Become the world's model (Law),
常德不忒，	Constant Virtue will not falter,
復歸於無極。	And one will return to Wújí, (limitlessness" or "non-duality).
知其榮，	Know the honor,
守其辱，	Hold to the disgrace,
為天下谷。	And become the world's valley.
為天下谷，	Become the world's valley,
常德乃足，	Constant virtue will be sufficient,
復歸於樸。	And one will return to simplicity. (note 1a)
樸散則為器，	simplicity, when scattered, becomes a vessel,(note 1b)
聖人用之則為官長。	Used by the sage, it becomes a chief. (note 1c)
故大制不割。	Therefore, the great law (the Dao) never cuts up. (note 1d)

Note 1 - The Chinese character 樸 (pǔ) indeed has various meanings, and its interpretation can depend on the context.

1a. 樸 (pǔ) - Simplicity
1b. 樸 (pǔ) - Big Timber or Tree Bark
1c. 樸 (pǔ) - Weapon; a type of ancient weapon, a narrow and long knife with a short handle, used with both hands.
1d. 樸 (pǔ) - Summarizes the three attributes: simplicity, big timber or tree bark, and weapon.

In addition, 朴 (pǔ), which is an alternate form of 樸, is interchangeable and means simplicity, aligning with the meaning mentioned in note 1a.

Therefore, simplicity aligns with the Dao. In philosophy, when fragmented, it manifests as the vessel (refer to Yi Jing: The metaphysical realm is termed the Dao, while the physical/material realm is termed the vessel - 形而上者謂之道，形而下者謂之器).

Contrarily, from an applied perspective, the fundamental essence is simplicity. In practical usage, it resembles a versatile material (like the big timber), capable of adapting to various shapes and sizes depending on the type of vessel required for a specific situation.

In the same vein, when simplicity is wielded adeptly, your command becomes a potent instrument, akin to a well-crafted weapon (like a knife), establishing you as the leader of your country or group.

Common Literal Translation

Knowing the vigorous vitality of the masculine, peacefully adhering to the yielding nature of the feminine, gathers the streams of the world.

Gathering the streams of the world, the virtue of nature coexists, returning again to the pristine state of an unblemished infant.

Understanding the bright prospects, steadfastly abiding in the process of darkness, verifies the truths of the world.

Verifying the truths of the world, the sincerity of natural virtue remains unswayed, returning to the state of boundless limitlessness.

Understanding the preciousness of honor, faithfully enduring the humility of disgrace, achieves the world's inclusivity.

Achieving the world's inclusivity, the fullness of natural virtue abounds, returning to the realm of the original source.

Bestowing upon the original source can serve as a symbol of trust; when utilized by sages, it naturally becomes a leadership tool.

In this way, supreme wisdom and the simplicity of the Dao are inseparable.

My 5 cents

This passage also delves into the principles of internal cultivation, particularly focusing on Qi cultivation. To enhance comprehension, it would be beneficial to reference the Yellow River Chart and the Inscription of Luo (Hetu luoshu 河圖洛書), as the original text employs specific terms from Hetu Luoshu. Alternatively, a supplementary chapter could be considered a year or later, allowing everyone to delve deeper into this topic. Nonetheless, here are some fundamental ideas for your quick reference:

Strive for the Yang without sacrificing the Yin qualities; through integration, a sensation akin to a flowing stream within the body may be experienced. A common occurrence when attaining the state of "Qi converges into the bones" (氣斂入骨) is a natural phenomenon (please refer to our previous discussion). Subsequently, one may attain a state of mental tranquility and internal softness, resembling infancy (chapter 10). This phase allows for the perception of the internal body and external environment as a unified whole. Understand the bright (white) from the dark (black), guarding the Ming Dian (明點) within our body (inner vision). To verify, review our previous notes and consult the diagram illustrating the [interconnectedness of the eight extraordinary meridians (vessels)], or the stream that flows through the 12 meridian lines. Where at Hetu, it represents the white and black dots (officially named, though currently unrecalled).

In practical application, dark dots at energy intersections or meridian points within the body may signify illness or insufficient energy levels. Hence, you are either lightening them all up or not using the shadow dots (lower-level achievements). (Note: The concept is all light out, similar to a Christmas tree, with a thousand lotus petals opening at the crown).- then you are officially achieving the asura level while your physical body is maintained in this physical world.

Achieving harmony among these elements results in a synergistic effect, creating the world valley (originally wording described as becoming the valley under the sky/heaven, and you know where it is, right?). In this context, "valley" pertains not to a spiritual valley as in chapter 6 but signifies a life valley—an area where all life energy is nurtured and cultivated.

For the purely spiritual aspect, I will reserve further discussion until later, as it hasn't been covered in our sessions yet. Perhaps, in due time and under appropriate circumstances, we can explore this dimension further. Hope it does not need to wait for a Yuga of any kind 😊

Laozi think about you and make notes:

To know the masculine, guard the feminine, and thereby serve the world – why is this? (this think about you note changed the character from stream (溪) to (奚), and (奚) means why?, and also the sentence structure.

為天下溪 = Become the world's stream, if read as one sentence

為天下, 奚 = The purpose is to serve the word, why?

Desiring the masculine to be like the feminine. Why? It is also about being close to the essentials. Understanding the essentials brings peace to the spirit, attaining the essence of the world.

Constant virtue does not depart, returning to infancy. By focusing on purity and simplicity, one aligns with the state of an infant. Knowing the essence and acting effortlessly, moral principles remain unwavering. It is a return to the state of infancy.

To know the bright, guard the dark, and thereby set an example for the world. The essence of brightness is the same as the origin (the primordial qi), while darkness is associated with the moon (tai yin). In humans, the kidneys house the essence. Guarding the dark is like not using it, and the world follows this natural order.

Constant virtue does not lend itself, returning to the state of limitless. Knowing how to guard the dark, moral principles remain, not borrowing from others. If one borrows, there will be repayment. It is better to have it within oneself. Following the methods of the Xuan Nu Jing, Gong Zi, and Rong Cheng, all desire to borrow; who will be the one to lend? Hence, it is decreed that one should not borrow. Only by self-guarding and cutting off thoughts can one achieve the state of boundless limitlessness.

"To know the honorable, guard the disgraceful, and thereby become the world's valley. Where there is an honor, there must be a disgrace. The Daoist fears disgrace, so does not covet honor, but rather directs aspirations towards the Dao."

May the wish for longevity be like the desire of valley waters to flow eastward and return to the sea. (In China, the western side are mountains, East is the seas. Water flows from high to low, it is nature). To be the valley for the world, constant virtue is sufficient, returning to simplicity. Aspire to be like valley waters longing to return to the sea, where virtue remains constant. Simplicity, in its essence, is the foundation of the Dao. Walking the Dao leads to the return to simplicity, aligning with the Dao. When simplicity is scattered, it becomes tools; the wise use it for leadership. Using it for tools departs from the Dao, and it should not allow simplicity to be scattered. The wise, by not letting it scatter, govern people and bring about great peace. Therefore, a grand plan has no divisions. Those who pursue worldly affairs, high positions, abundant wealth, fine clothing, delicious food, and precious treasures cannot achieve longevity. Longevity is a great blessing; for Dao practitioners who seek greatness, they endure without allowing worldly matters to divide their hearts.

知其雄，守其雌，為天下奚。"欲令雄如雌。奚，何也，亦近要也。知要安精神，即得天下之要。"常德不離，復歸於嬰兒。"專精無為，道德常不離之，更反為嬰兒。"知其白，守其黑，為天下式。"精白與元[22]同色，黑太陰中也。於人在腎，精藏之，安如不用為守黑，天下常法式也。"常德不貸，復歸於無極。"知守黑者，道德常在，不從人貸，必當償之，不如自有也。行《玄女經》、龔子、容成之法，悉欲貸，何人主當貸若者乎？故令不得也。唯有自守，絕心閉念者，大無極也。"知其榮，守其辱，為天下谷。"有榮必有辱。道人畏辱，故不貪榮，但歸志於道。

唯願長生，如天下谷水之欲東流歸於海也。"為天下谷，常德乃足，復歸於樸。"志道當如谷水之志欲歸海，道德常足。樸，道本氣也。人行道歸樸，與道合。"樸散為器，聖人用為官長。"為器以離道矣，不當令樸散也。聖人能不散之，故官長治人，能致太平。"是以大制無割。"道人同知俗事、高官、重祿、好衣、美食、珍寶之味耳，皆不能致長生。長生為大福，為道人欲制大，故自忍不以俗事割心情也。

Extract from Laozi He Shang Gong Zhang Ju)

-Back to Simplicity (Unadorned and straightforward quality)

Understand the masculine, embrace the feminine, and become the world's valley. Embody the qualities of strength and honor while practicing humility and softness. Even when aware of one's own prominence, it is essential to cultivate humility, letting go of excessive assertiveness and embracing a gentle approach. By doing so, the world will naturally align, much like water flowing into a deep valley. Serving as the world's valley ensures the preservation of constant virtue. Embracing humility and yielding like a deep valley ensures that virtue remains within oneself, never departing.

Revert to a state of innocence, akin to an infant, with a tranquil mind and a lack of excessive knowledge. Understand the bright aspects and cling to the obscure, becoming a model for the world. Use brightness to symbolize clarity and obscurity to symbolize subtlety. Even when recognizing one's own brilliance, it is crucial to adhere to a sense of subtlety, resembling darkness where nothing is visible. This way, one can serve as a model for the world, ensuring the perpetuity of virtue. Being a world model guarantees the consistency of virtue, and individuals embodying this role will find virtue always present within themselves, free from deviation.

Return to a state of limitlessness. If virtue is unwaveringly upheld, a long and healthy life is achievable, aligning with the boundless ultimate.

Recognize one's honor, uphold one's disgrace, and be the world's valley. Honor symbolizes nobility, while disgrace symbolizes impurity. If one can understand one's own nobility, it is essential to embrace it with a sense of humility and impurity. In doing so, the world will naturally gravitate towards them, like water flowing into a deep valley. Being the world's valley ensures that constant virtue is abundant and sufficient.

If individuals can embody the role of the world's valley, virtue will consistently abide within themselves. Return to a state of simplicity. One should return to a state of simplicity and authenticity, refraining from unnecessary embellishments. When simplicity is scattered, it becomes a vessel, and a vessel is meant for utility. All things in their simplicity become useful vessels. Similarly, when the Dao is scattered, it manifests as spirit and illumination, flows as the sun and moon, and divides into the five elements. The sage utilizes this for governing and becomes the leader of officials. When the sage ascends, they become the foundational leader of all officials. Hence, the grand design is not severed.

When the sage utilizes it, they employ the grand Dao to govern the world without causing harm or severance. In self-discipline, the sage uses the grand Dao to govern desires, not harming the essence and spirit.

老子河上公章句

《反朴》

知其雄，守其雌，為天下谿。雄以喻尊，雌以喻卑。人雖自知其尊顯，當復守之以卑微，去雄之強梁，就雌之柔和，如是則天下歸之，如水流入深谿也。為天下谿，常德不離，人能謙下如深谿，則德常在，不復離於己。復歸於嬰兒。當復歸志於嬰兒，惷然而無所知也。知其白守其黑，為天下式。白以喻昭昭，黑以喻默默。人雖自知昭昭，明白當復守之以默默，如闇昧無所見，如是則可為天下法式，則德常在。為天下式，常德不忒，人能為天下法式，則德常在於己，不復差忒。復歸於無極。德不差忒，則常生久壽，歸身於無窮極也。

知其榮，守其辱，為天下谷。榮以喻尊貴，辱以喻污濁。人能知己之有榮貴，當復守之以污濁，如是則天下歸之，如水流入深谷也。為天下谷，常德乃足足，止也。人能為天下谷，則德乃常止於己。復歸於樸。復當歸身於質樸，不復為文飾。樸散則為器，器，用也。萬物之樸散則為器用也。若道散則為神明，流為日月，分為五行也。聖人用之則為官長。聖人升用則為百官之元長也。故大制不割。聖人用之則以大道制御天下，無所傷割，治身則以大道制御情欲，不害精神也。

【第二十九章】Chapter 29

Most Common Translation

將欲取天下而為之，	To desire to take the world and act upon it,
吾見其不得已。	I see that it cannot be done forcibly.
天下神器，	The world is like a divine instrument,
不可為也。	It cannot be manipulated.
為者敗之，	Those who attempt to manipulate it are defeated,
執者失之。	Those who grasp it lose it.
故物或行或隨，	Therefore, things may advance or follow,
或歔或吹，	Exhale or inhale,
或強或羸，	Be strong or weak,
或挫或隳。(或載或隳)	Be thwarted or ruined.
是以聖人去甚，	Hence, the sage refrains from excess,
去奢，去泰。	Rejects extravagance, rejects arrogance.

My literal translation

Wanting to arbitrarily manipulate the world, I see that one will never achieve the goal. The world is a sacred existence and cannot be manipulated at will. Arbitrary manipulation will corrupt it, and holding onto it too tightly will lead to its loss. Therefore, various existences can be left to move independently, or allowed to follow; they can be allowed to be calm and gentle, lightly whispering, or allowed to be swift and rapid, blowing fiercely. They can be allowed to be strong and prosperous, or allowed to decline and decay; they can be allowed to be stable or allowed to be destroyed. Hence, the sage refrains from excessive interference rejects self-indulgence, and avoids extremes in conduct.

In business/economic terms, the market will naturally recalibrate based on the inherent dynamics of demand and supply, primarily through price adjustments. Hence no need to interfere with it.

In farming, is it?

【第三十章】 Chapter 30

Most Common Translation

以道佐人主者，	Guiding/helping a ruler with the Dao,
不以兵強天下，	Not relying on military strength to control the world,
其事好還。	Affairs will naturally return to goodness.
師之所處，	Where the army is stationed,
荊棘生焉。	Thorns and thistles will grow.
大軍之后，	After the great war,
必有凶年。	There will surely be ominous years.
善有果而已，	Goodness brings its rewards;
不敢以取強。	There is no need to strive for strength.
果而勿矜，	Achieve and refrain from boasting,
果而勿伐，	Achieve and refrain from attack,
果而勿驕，	Achieve and refrain from arrogance
果而不得已，	Achieve and only when there is no alternative,
果而勿強。	Achieve and refrain from coercion.
物壯則老，	When things flourish, they decline,
是謂不道，	This is called the way of non-Dao,
不道早已。	The way of non-Dao will inevitably lead to one's downfall.

My literal translation

Those who assist the Lord with the principles of the Dao do not urge the nation to assert dominance through force in the world.

Seeking dominance through force easily invites retribution: wherever the armed forces are stationed, desolation follows; after excessive military actions, persistent famine ensues.

Those who follow the Dao achieve results in moderation, refraining from seizing success forcefully and acting tyrannically. They do not rely on their achievements, nor do they boast or flaunt them.

They don't use their accomplishments as a basis, and they don't use them to show off or be arrogant. They only consider achievements as a necessary recourse when unavoidable, without using them to dominate the world.

Things that become strong eventually age; when plants and trees reach their peak strength, they wither and fall. Likewise, when people reach their peak strength, they experience decline and aging. Those who speak of strength cannot endure for long. This is known as going against the Dao. To wither and age is to sit without following the Dao. Departing from the Dao leads to an early demise. Those who do not follow the Dao die prematurely.

【第三十一章】 Chapter 31

Most Common Translation

夫佳兵者，	Good weapons (also military force and/or military skills, applies for the whole chapter),
不祥之器。	are implements of ill omen,
物或惡之，	May be hated by all creatures.
故有道者不處。	Therefore, followers of the Dao avoid them (not dwelling on it).
君子居則貴左，	A nobleman in dwelling values the left, (note 1)
用兵則貴右。	In warfare values the right. (note 1)
兵者，不祥之器，	Weapons are implements of ill omen,
非君子之器。	Not the tools of a nobleman.
不得已而用之，	Only as a last resort would he use them,
恬淡為上，	Quietly preferring calm and restraint.
勝而不美。	Victory is not beautiful,
而美之者，	And those who find it beautiful,
是樂殺人。	Delight in killing others.
夫樂殺人者，	Those who delight in killing
則不可以得志於天下矣。	Cannot fulfill their ambitions in the world.
吉事尚左，	In auspicious events, the left (side, note 1) is honored,
凶事尚右。	In inauspicious events, the right (side, note 1) is honored.
偏將軍居左，	The lieutenant general occupies the left,
上將軍居右，	The general occupies the right,
言以喪禮處之。	Address it with words spoken in mourning or funeral rites.
殺人之眾，	Individuals involved in killing,
以哀悲泣之，	Mourned with sorrow and pity tears.
戰勝，以喪禮處之。	In victory, mourning rites are performed.

Note 1 - Values the left = life, good deeds. Values the right = death, bad deeds.

Reference: Chapter 21, note 4: The Heavenly Court (天曹左契) (Note 4, from the Daoist religion, 天曹 the God official, 左契, good deeds are recorded on the left side, cherish life, while bad deeds are recorded on the right, death. Or good people are lining up on the left side after death)

And traditionally, in daily meetings with the king (emperor or ruler) to discuss state affairs, civil officials stood on the left side of the emperor, while military officials stood on the right. Besides the mentioned religious beliefs, another explanation is that the ruler must sit facing south, with the left side representing the east (wood element, associated with vitality, geographical features like lakes, seas, and forests, symbolizing life), and the right side representing the west (metal element, associated with high mountains, minerals, often associated with frequent warfare, hence a conquering aspect.

Furthermore, in situations where only military officials are present at a meeting, the higher-ranked officials position themselves on the right side, and the most senior official stands at the forefront. This arrangement helps in cases where certain kings may be less attentive or more preoccupied, as it facilitates the recognition of the key figures addressing them. It's worth noting that some kings, as historical records indicate, were notably absent from national daily meetings, with the longest recorded absence reportedly spanning over 20 years.

This tradition also influenced Buddhism in China, where the placement of Buddha's images or statues involves facing south, following a specific left and right arrangement.

PS: This concept later evolved in the folk tradition, and interestingly, when our eyelids twitch, it is believed that twitching on the left side is considered auspicious, while on the right side is considered ominous. By combining this with the time of day and the immediate circumstances, one can discern auspicious or inauspicious signs, predicting potential events that may unfold.

Further developments have led to various versions of interpretations in the present day. There are different explanations for the twitching of the left and right eyelids, and even the upper and lower eyelids have their distinct interpretations. These interpretations vary depending on factors such as one's own situation, interactions with friends, family, and other personal connections.

As an aside, in ancient Europe, when swordsmen and their girlfriends went out, especially if the swordsman had many adversaries, the girlfriends typically stood or walked on the left side, slightly behind. This positioning was chosen because, in the event of a sudden attack, it wouldn't hinder the swordsman's ability to draw their sword, and it also made it easier for them to protect their girlfriend. (Since most people wielded swords with their right hand. In warfare values the right 😊 !)

Another deeply moving story is that of Japan's sword saint, Miyamoto Musashi, and his girlfriend, Otsū. When Musashi embarked on his journey to travel and refine his skills, facing numerous combats along the way, it was impractical for him to bring his girlfriend. Moreover, he couldn't let his adversaries know about his connections. Otsū, deeply in love with Musashi, wanted to know everything that happened to him. She made the courageous decision to follow him from miles away, unbeknownst to Musashi, ensuring he remained unaware. After Musashi's duels with other samurai, she would gather information from the locals or personally witness the actual scenes. This was her way of expressing love and understanding for everything Musashi went through. (A different interpretation of "knowing the male, yet holding to the female" from the Dao De Jing, perhaps.) It is so touching, whenever I recall this story, even now.

https://www.youtube.com/watch?v=rYEexeuz2fc

One of the beliefs among Japanese warriors (samurai) is to stride through hell and dwell in the realm of the asura. (what does it mean?)

My literal translation

Weapons, instruments of ill omen, are generally despised by people. Therefore, those who follow the Dao do not rely on them. A noble person values the left side in residence, but in the use of military force and warfare, they value the right side—these principles are contradictory. Sharp weapons and such ominous things are not commonly used by noble individuals. They are only used as a last resort, with tranquility and simplicity as the ideal. Even if victory is achieved through them, one should not boast. Those who boast in this manner find joy in killing, and those who find joy in killing cannot attain success in the world. Auspicious events are valued on the left, while inauspicious and mourning events are valued on the right. The subordinate general positions on the left, and the commanding general positions on the right—this indicates that the order and rituals of the military are akin to the rituals of mourning. Therefore, those preparing for war and killing should approach it with a heart full of sorrow; even if victorious, they should handle it following mourning rituals.

PS: In the era of Laozi, China experienced one of the most tumultuous periods of warfare in its history. During that time, China was fragmented into numerous small nations, each vying for control over the entire territory or, at the very least, seeking to expand their boundaries.

Therefore, it is not surprising that Laozi extensively discusses his ideas about war in the Dao De Jing.

A well-known quote often attributed to Clausewitz, though my memory may be fallible, suggests that a large-scale war is a recourse only when all alternative methods of conflict resolution prove ineffective.

During my high school years, one of my cherished novels was "War and Peace". In a poignant scene, one of the main characters, Andrew (if my memory serves me right), faces his imminent demise, lying on the ground and gazing at the serene blue sky above. In that moment, a sudden clarity illuminates his mind, revealing the profound essence of war. Simply put, it is intricately connected to the migration and blending of diverse beliefs, cultures, and races of people, despite the painful undertones of the process. His central idea regarding the historical trajectory of war appears akin to a sidetrack on a lengthy train journey. It may seem divergent from world history in the immediate sense, yet, when observed over time and from a broader perspective, it manifests as a straight line, dutifully fulfilling its mission. (Remember the historical background: there is no internet or World wide web in those days.)

Furthermore, a close high school friend of mine, we shared lots of common hobbies, such as martial arts, philosophy, etc., who later studied War and Peace (not the novel) at London College, UK. shared his sentiments and insights about large-scale wars. According to him, the primary objectives of such conflicts are to purify societies of negative qualities and accumulated adverse energies over the years. Interestingly, in subsequent conversations with several high-ranking military generals, I discovered a common perspective. They emphasized that, particularly in the later stages or concluding periods of wars, the majority of soldiers engaged are often prisoners, individuals with lower education, or those with questionable moral character who derive satisfaction from violence. In contrast, scientists, highly educated individuals, and those of good character are generally reserved as a last resort and play crucial roles in rebuilding the nation after the war. Although it sounds no humane, it is a fact. Our real-life situation.

Coincidentally, Sukh recently brought up the topic of war which happened recently, and once again, I shared with her a quote from the Bhagavad Gita, although I'm aware it's not her favorite. In the story, Lord Krishna is invited to assist a king in the war. Despite the king being a good friend of Lord Krishna, Krishna goes to the battlefield. Simultaneously, he sends a relative to support the opposing side. Ultimately, the king loses the war, but through conversations with Lord Krishna, he gains profound spiritual insights. I explained to Sukh that God does not take sides and does not intervene to support any party in a conflict. I believe I've mentioned this perspective in our group chat before.

Extract from He Shang Gong - Yan Wu (偃武 Ceased the war)

The finest weapons are instruments of ill omen; 'fine' means ornate, 'omen' means auspicious. Weapons stir the spirit, disturb the harmony, and are tools of those who lack goodness. They should not be adorned. When people abhor them, harm will come when weapons are in motion. Therefore, there is nothing in the world more detestable than weapons. Hence, those who possess the Way do not rely on them. Those who possess the Way do not dwell in their use. When a noble person resides, they honor the left, favoring the gentle and weak. In the use of military force, they favor the right, valuing strength and firmness. This is a reversal of the principles of both martial strategy and the Way of the noble person, as the values upheld are distinct.

Warfare is an instrument of ill omen; 'war' is a last resort. It is a tool of those lacking virtue, not an instrument valued by noble individuals. It is employed out of necessity, such as in times of decline, adversity, or disaster, when one desires to protect oneself by resorting to it. Tranquility and simplicity are esteemed. There is no greed for land, and the focus is on benefiting people and their wealth. Victory is not glorified; even in triumph, it is not viewed as a means to benefit oneself.

And those who find beauty in it delight in killing. Those who rejoice in triumph through killing, revel in the joy of taking lives. However, those who delight in killing cannot attain their aspirations in the world. A ruler who takes pleasure in killing cannot establish their rule over the world. To be a sovereign ruler, one must cherish and value human life, refraining from arbitrary executions and punishments. Auspicious events favor the left, as the left signifies the origin of life.

In inauspicious events, favor the right, as the dark path involves killing. The subordinate general positions on the left, being humble and residing in the light, signifies their reluctance to specialize in killing. The commanding general positions on the right, being esteemed and residing in the darkness, signifies their dedication to the mastery of killing. Handle it with funeral rites.

The commanding general, residing on the right, aligns with funeral rites favoring the right, as the deceased is esteemed in the darkness. In the multitude of killings, mourn with sorrow and lamentation. If one's virtue is insufficient and cannot transform people through the Tao, causing harm to innocent civilians, it is a profound loss. In the event of victory, handle it with funeral rites.

In ancient times, after a victorious battle, the general would assume the position of the chief mourner, dressed in plain garments and weeping. A wise ruler values virtue and belittles the military, reluctant to employ it for the purpose of extermination. With a heavy heart, akin to mourning, they understand that the incessant use of military force in future generations is a cause for grief and sorrow.

老子河上公章句 - 《偃武》

夫佳兵者，不祥之器，佳，飾也。祥，善也。兵者，驚精神，濁和氣，不善人之器也，不當修飾之。物或惡之，兵動則有所害，故萬物無有不惡之者。故有道者不處。有道之人不處其國。君子居則貴左，貴柔弱也。用兵則貴右。貴剛強也，此言兵道與君子之道反，所貴者異也。

兵者，不祥之器，兵，革者。不善之器也。非君子之器，非君子所貴重之器也。不得已而用之。謂遭衰逆亂禍，欲加萬民，乃用之以自守。恬淡為上。不貪土地，利人財寶。勝而不美，雖得勝而不以為利己也。

而美之者，是樂殺人。美得勝者，是為喜樂殺人者也。夫樂殺人者，則不可以得志於天下矣。為人君而樂殺人者，此不可使得志於天下矣，為人主必專制人命，妄行刑誅。吉事尚左，左，生位也。

凶事尚右，陰道殺人。偏將軍居左，偏將軍卑而居陽者，以其不專殺也。上將軍居右。上將軍尊而居陰者，以其專主殺也。言以喪禮處之。上將軍居右，喪禮尚右，死人貴陰也。殺人之眾，以哀悲泣之；傷己德薄，不能以道化人，而害無辜之民。戰勝，以喪禮處之。

古者戰勝，將軍居喪主禮之位，素服而哭之，明君子貴德而賤兵，不得以而誅不祥，心不樂之，比於喪也，知後世用兵不已故悲痛之。

【第三十二章】Chapter 32

Most Common Translation

道常無名，	The Dao is nameless,
朴雖小，	Though simplicity (朴), it is small. (朴 See chapter 28)
天下莫能臣也。	Under heaven, none can subjugate it.
侯王若能守之，	If lords and kings can uphold it,
萬物將自賓。	All things will naturally submit.
天地相合以降甘露，	Heaven and Earth unite to bestow sweet dew,
民莫之令而自均。	And the people will harmonize without command.
始制有名，	Beginning with distinctions, names arise, (see Chapter 1)
名亦既有，	Once names exist,
夫亦將知止。	We should know when to stop.
知止可以不殆。	Knowing when to stop prevents danger (also means exhaustion, if we understand this chapter in Qi.)
譬道之在天下，	By analogy, the Dao is under the heaven (original word is under the skies, ref: TCHYD)
猶川谷之於江海。	Is like valleys' relation to rivers and seas.

My Literal Translation:

The Dao is forever elusive in manifesting its identity, although it is small in appearance, it holds a subtle and unassuming essence that can nonetheless command the allegiance of the entire world. If rulers and nobles can uphold and preserve it, all things will naturally submit and fall into harmony. The qi of heaven and earth converges to bestow a nurturing dew, with no need for human distribution as nature spontaneously evens out.

Once a semblance of order is established, names and distinctions emerge, and with the presence of names, one should be aware of the INTRANSGRESSIBLE limits. (In Qi, it means, The shackles of life, or the shackles of spiritual cultivation realms. 生命的桎梏，或是, 修行境界的桎梏).

Understanding these limits and timely restraint ensures peace and security. It is akin to the Dao guiding all people under heaven to return, much like rivers and streams finding their way to the vast sea.

【第三十三章】 Chapter 33

Most Common Translation

知人者智，	Knowing others is wisdom,
自知者明。	Knowing oneself is enlightenment.
勝人者有力，	Conquering others through strength,
自勝者強。	Conquering oneself is true power.
知足者富，	Being content and self-satisfaction is wealth,
強行者有志，	Being determined leads to success.
不失其所者久，	Not losing one's way leads to longevity,
死而不亡者壽。	To die without perishing is longevity, or Surviving death is a form of immortality.

My literal Translation

Understanding others is wisdom; self-awareness is enlightenment. Overcoming others requires strength, conquering oneself demands true power. Contentment is true wealth, perseverance in action is a sign of ambition. Remaining steadfast in one's chosen path ensures longevity.

Though the body may perish, a soul that persists, and a spirit that endures, unforgotten, is a form of eternal life/immortality. In other words, free from reincarnation.

My 5 cents

What prompts our profound concern about death?

In the labyrinth of life, the future is obscured, and the past remains an enigma. Therefore, uncovering the secrets of our past (because we forgot) and gaining insights into the future becomes crucial (because we can not see through)—a key that leaves an indelible mark. This ability is an inner vision, a capacity to peer through the layers of bygone days, the current moment, and the days yet to come. Various traditions, such as Buddhism, delineate numerous stages of enlightenment, each with its distinctive name. The ability to perceive the events of the past three lives and anticipate the next three lives is a common milestone, yet there are still further stages on the path to ultimate enlightenment. Hence, delving into specific questions becomes futile, as the answers we hold are mere fragments of the vast mosaic until we attain the zenith of understanding.

As I mentioned to Wing Ho many years ago, the inclination to utilize a tool for deciphering the past, present, and future stems from residual abilities inherited from realms beyond. While such a capability may prove beneficial in certain aspects, it does not represent the ultimate objective for us. The preceding chapter in the Dao De Jing has already encapsulated this notion, should you wish to reaffirm it.

【第三十四章】Chapter 34

Most Common Translation

大道泛兮，	The expansive energy of the Great Way (Dao),
其可左右。	is sufficient to influence all things.
萬物恃之而生而不辭，	All things rely on it for life and the Dao do not boast or reject it.
功成不名有，	Dao achieves success without claiming credit,
衣養萬物而不為主，	Nourishing and clothing all things without dominating them.
常無欲，	Always without desire,
可名於小；	And can thus be named insignificant.
萬物歸焉而不為主，	All things return to it without being dominated,
可名為大。	And it can thus be named great.
以其終不自為大，	Because it does not seek greatness for itself,
故能成其大。	Thus, achieves greatness.

My literal translation

The expansive energy of the great Way is sufficient to influence all things. It treats all living beings with reliance, avoiding self-praise and boasting, naturally achieving success without making a conspicuous display. It provides shade and protection for all things without assuming a dominant position, almost to the point of insignificance. When all things return to it, it does not assert dominance, allowing it to be named as significant. Therefore, the sage consistently avoids considering oneself as great, and this, in turn, accomplishes their true greatness.

【第三十五章】Chapter 35

Most Common Translation

執大象，	Execute the big image (note 1) adhere to" or "uphold" the big picture, (image) (Dao)
天下往；	And the world will follow. Everything under the sky should go through. (note 2)
往而不害，	Guide without harm, Go through without any experiencing psychological instability or uneasiness,
安平太。	And peace will prevail.
樂與餌，	Delight (original word: Music and food) nourishment,
過客止。	Travelers should avoid. (note 3)
道之出口，	The exit of Dao, (or the exit to the Dao),
淡乎其無味，	Subtle and tasteless,
視之不足見，	Staring intensely is insufficient to perceive, (note 4)
聽之不足聞，	Hearing it falls short of truly listening,
用之不足既。	Using it, is not enough to deplete,

Note 1 - The character "象" encompasses various meanings and extensions. Within this chapter, its central interpretation lies in "大象", representing the Big Dao. Additionally, "象" conveys the concept of an image or symbol, aligning with the three fundamental principles in the interpretation of the Yi Jing (1. symbol or phenomenon, 2. philosophy, and 3. divination and/or numerology). You might recognize it as a theme revealed in your inner vision, often interpreted by skilled fortune tellers, The primary challenge encountered by many adept fortune tellers lies in navigating the intricacies of time, flux, and space.

In a spiritual context, it is commonly used to signify scenes within one's inner vision, or seed syllables (種子字) （Sanskrit：बीजाक्षर bījākṣara）, as elucidated in the side note on inner vision. Furthermore, you might perceive it as if the image is encapsulated within a crystal ball, akin to the tool employed by a psychic or wizard, and it is common as an inner vision.

But in spiritual activities, the inner vision crystal ball is in our minds (head), not something external or a tool.

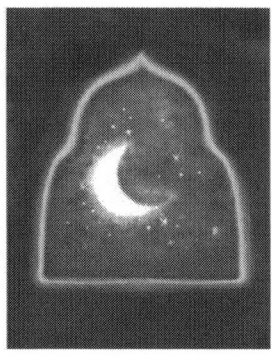  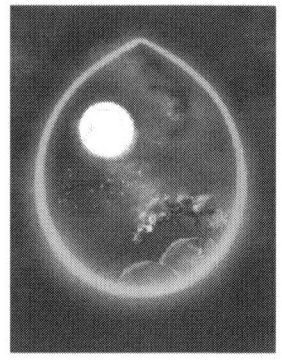

PS: A joke

The original phrase is "執大象", where "象" can also mean an elephant. Therefore, it can be interpreted as "holding the big elephant". I attempted to use Google translation, and indeed, it translated the phrase as "holding the big/giant elephant". This expression draws inspiration from a Buddhist story involving a king who summoned several naturally born blind individuals to discover the nature of an elephant by placing the creature in front of them. I think this tale is also popular in the Western word too.

Note 2 - The word "往" (Wǎng), holds dual meanings in this context. (In the Dao De Jing, common usage involves dual and opposite literal meanings, and another frequently employed syntactical structure is inverted or reversed syntax.).

"往" (Wǎng), denotes "go, depart", and it also conveys the sense of "past, formerly", implying an association with events that have occurred. Furthermore, in ancient usage, it is interchangeable with "望" (wàng), indicating the act of looking towards or following.

Note 3 - Spiritually speaking, during practice, it's advisable not to become overly attached or addicted to any specific "forms" or "images", unless you can control it or you have a purpose or some specific issues happening recently, which is often challenging for most people to resist, because it is so entertaining, and feeds our ego. (wows, I managed to achieve this stage..etc..)

Diamond Sutra: there is no semblance of self (form), no semblance of others (form), no semblance of sentient beings (form), and no semblance of life or old agers (form). (Note: The most common manifestation is observed in sages.)

PS: While we've delved into this verse previously, let's revisit and explore it more comprehensively:

This verse can be comprehended from various perspectives: 1. Psychological, 2. Philosophical, and 3. Mythological.

From a psychological standpoint, it captures the characteristics and self-attributes emerging from the ego, shaped through interactions with oneself and others. 'Self-form' arises in the dynamics between individuals, 'others' exist as a consequence of the 'self-form,' 'sentient beings' emerge from interactions with a multitude of individuals, and 'life' or 'old age' signifies the temporal extension of the self-centric perspective.

In a philosophical context, it symbolizes the continuum of time—past, present, and future—exerting its influence on the sentimental nature of our minds.

From a mythological angle, as previously indicated.

In essence, this verse unfolds not only as a psychological exploration but also as a philosophical contemplation and a mythological narrative or a matrix of mix.

Note 4 - Refer to Chapter 14

Some Common literal translations

1. Embracing the natural way of the Great Dao represents the destination that people all over the world aspire to reach. Going there, one will encounter no harm but instead, relish in a life of tranquility, peace, and contentment. The enchanting music and delectable feasts often captivate passing travelers, making them linger in indulgence. However, when the Great Dao is expressed in the form of language, it becomes bland and tasteless. It appears like a drop in the vast ocean and sounds insignificant, yet its utility brings boundless benefits.

2. Whoever adheres to the Great Way will have the world following them. When people adhere to the Great Way, they will not harm each other, and the world will be stable and peaceful. However, the allure of sensory temptations such as indulging in fine food and entertainment easily leads some astray from the Great Way! These teachings may seem bland and unworthy of attention to some, but understanding and applying them can lead to endless wonders!

My 5 Cents

This chapter also outlines the process of managing inner vision and progressing to the next realm using metaphorical expressions. There are several prerequisites for this journey: a resilient and steady mind, a pure soul, and the ability to focus on an image without the usual fluctuations experienced by many practitioners.

There are two paths to achieve this. The first involves the cultivation of Qi, typically divided into three steps: cultivating life essence to transform Qi, cultivating Qi to transform spirit, and cultivating spirit to return to emptiness (練精化氣，練氣化神，練神回虛). The fourth and being last is "Returning to Emptiness and entering the Dao". (還虛入道).

The second path involves direct cultivation of the mind and heart (refer to note 5, here, we are referring to the 2nd heart), often at the cost of life energy in most cases, especially if we want fast achievement. It is crucial to note that impurities in one's karma can interact negatively, (law of attraction), leading to mental issues or instability if the mind and heart are not pure.

Nevertheless, both are not an easy path. Maybe we can discuss this later.

Note 5 - The Huayan Sutra (Buddhāvataṃsaka Sūtra (Chinese: 華嚴經; pinyin: Huáyán jīng, Flower Garland Sutra) states: "The mind is like a skilled painter, capable of depicting all worldly phenomena.

We must understand that our world is shaped by the mind; everything is created by the mind alone. But what is the mind?

We have three types of Hearts 心 (minds) in Chinese, as always quoted by the Shurangama (楞嚴) Sutra:

Fleshly Heart (肉團心): This is the physical heart formed by the essence of our parents' blood.

Discriminating, contemplation, or worrying Heart (Mind) (緣慮心): This mind uses the senses (sight, hearing, smell, taste, touch, and thought) to constantly discriminate, choose, and contemplate various situations and realms. It attaches to and distinguishes between different circumstances. Due to the discrimination and attachments of this mind, we often forget about the deeper, more tranquil, purer, and freer Spiritual Mind!

Spiritual Heart (Mind) (靈知心): This mind remains undisturbed amid a myriad of changes, enduring through countless situations without turmoil. It is not swayed by the fluctuations of the world. Just like space, despite the constant birth, disappearance, and changes of all things in the world, the emptiness itself remains undisturbed and unshaken.

The Spiritual Mind has endured through past, present, and future, showing no differences across these three temporal phases. It is equal, utterly equal – this is our Buddha nature!

Laozi think about you and make notes:

Hold the great image, and the world will follow. The sovereign who upholds righteous principles, emulates the grand way, and governs in accordance with the principles of the universe, will draw the world towards him. The paths will be clear, and people will come from far and wide, much like the wind. The Dao operates by transforming, rising from a high point and descending. It is specifically referred to as being embodied by the sovereign, hence the singular importance attributed to the ruler.

There should be no dual rulership, and thus emperors and kings must consistently follow the Dao. Only then can the principles be extended to officials and the common people. This is not limited to Daoist practitioners (who follow the guidance of Dao); even rulers who do not explicitly follow Daoist practices can abandon and neglect these principles.

The highest sage ruler is one who thoroughly embodies the Dao, teaching and transforming through practical examples. When the world is governed according to these principles, there will be peace and auspicious signs, all attributed to the efforts of the virtuous ruler. The middle sage ruler may have some imperfections, but with sincerity and openness to correction, and by appointing virtuous and capable individuals, he governs with the Dao.

Even with the existence of the state, challenges may arise. Diligence is required, and the assistance of competent advisors is crucial. If, however, the ruler neglects the Dao, the state will decline, and the responsibility lies not with the ruler but with those who have departed from the Dao. This departure is considered a deviation, akin to water flowing against its natural course (the original wording is not flowing from the west, the natural geography of China land). Even with capable ministers, it is difficult to achieve governance under such circumstances, especially when dealing with a multitude of diverse policies and political intricacies. Rulers who deviate from the Dao, neglect true wisdom, and believe that they can sustain the world without adhering to these principles are misguided.

The path of the sovereign following the Dao should not be easily abandoned. The Dao is revered and divine, and ultimately, it does not yield to human desires. Therefore, the ruler should diligently uphold these principles. (The original wording is 故放精耶,

which means losing of life essence, or hence, put your effort into this. It is also a dual expression sentence)

Variations arise incessantly, intending to admonish and instruct. The Dao remains hidden and elusive, but in the midst of chaos, order is inevitably restored. The intent of the Dao must be proclaimed. Therefore, emperors and high officials must diligently and attentively discern it. 'Beneficial but not harmful.' When rulers follow the Dao, the Dao comes and goes. Rulers take joy in the Dao, understanding that the divine cannot be deceived. They fear not only the laws of man but also the judgment of celestial beings, refraining from wrongful deeds. Loyalty and filial piety from ministers emanate from their sincere and natural hearts. The laws of the ruler cause no harm, and punishments are justly administered, resulting in easy governance and the ruler's contentment. 'Tranquility and great joy.' Such governance brings immense joy. 'Adornments surpass those of passing guests.' Various calamities and unusual phenomena in the world are like the movement of the sun and moon, surpassing the limits set by the heavens. The consequences of piercing transgressions are brought about by exceeding the bounds of propriety. When celestial bodies follow their designated paths and guests do not deviate from their roles, the spread of epidemic energies comes to a halt. (also, a metaphorical expression) 'The Dao expresses itself, bland and tasteless.' The words of the Dao are simple and without artifice, seemingly tasteless to common people. In this tastelessness, there exists a profound and significant flavor, hence the sages find joy in the taste of tastelessness. 'Not enough to be seen, not enough to be heard, not enough to be used.' The Dao delights in simplicity and sincerity, lacking in excess words. Observing the Dao's teachings and listening to its admonitions may seem insufficient to be seen or heard, yet they are challenging to put into practice. The ability to implement and apply the Dao's principles ensures that the blessings and fortunes derived from them are inexhaustible.

"執大象天下往。" 王者執正法，像大道，天下歸往，曠塞重驛，向風而至。道之為化，自高而降，指謂王者，故貴一人。制無二君，是以帝王常當行道，然後乃及吏民。非獨道士可行，王者棄捐也。上聖之君，師道至行以教化。天下如治，太平符瑞，皆感人功所積，致之者道君也。中賢之君，志信不純，政復扶接，能任賢良，臣弼之以道。雖存國，會不蕩蕩，勞精躬勤，良輔朝去，暮國傾危，制不在上，故在彼去臣。所以者，化逆也，猶水不🅾不西。雖有良臣，常難致治。況群耶雜政，制君諱道，非賤真文，以為人世可久隨之。王者道可久棄捐，道尊且神，終不聽人，故放精耶。

變異汾汾，將以誠誨。道隱卻觀，亂極必理，道意必宣，是以帝王大臣，不可不用心殷勤審察之焉。"佳而不害。" 王者行道，道來歸往。王者亦皆樂道，知神明不可欺負。不畏法律也，乃畏天神，不敢為非惡。臣忠子孝，出自然至心。王法無所復害，形罰格藏，故易治，王者樂也。"安平大樂。" 如此之治，甚大樂也。"與珥過客止。" 諸與天災變怪，日月運珥，倍臣縱橫，刺貫之咎，過罪所致；五星順軌，客逆不曜，疾疫之氣，都悉止矣。"道出言，淡無味。"道之所言，反俗絕巧，于俗人中，甚無味也。無味之中，有大生味，故聖人味無味之味。"視不足見，聽不足聞，用不可既。"道樂質樸，辭無余，視道言，聽道誡，或不足見聞耳而難行。能行能用，慶福不可既盡也。

Extract from He Shang Gong - humaneness and morality

Hold the great image, and the world will follow. 'Hold' implies safeguarding. 'Great image' signifies the Dao. The sage preserves the grand Dao, and thus the myriad people in the world turn their hearts and follow it. When one governs oneself according to the Dao, celestial insights descend, circulating within oneself. Going forth without causing harm brings peace, tranquility, and greatness. If the multitude turns and follows without harm, the nation experiences peace and attains great harmony. Governing oneself without harming celestial insights ensures personal well-being and longevity.

Delight in feeding and adornments, attracting passing guests. 'Feeding' represents beauty. 'Passing guests' refers to transient moments. If people can find joy in the beauty of the Dao, they remain content. Contentment means departing from excess and dwelling in simplicity, like a passing guest. The Dao's expression is bland, akin to tastelessness. The Dao flows in and out through the mouth (remember Grandmaster He practiced breathing technique), not as distinct flavors like the five tastes of sour, salty, bitter, sweet, and umami. Its appearance is not visible, as the Dao lacks a form, unlike the five colors of blue, yellow, red, white, and black. Its sounds are not audible, as the Dao is not like the five musical notes of do, re, mi, sol, and la. (Recall DDJ Chapter 12)

Using it brings inexhaustibility. 'Not enough to be seen,' implies that the Dao is not something one can obtain visually. 'Not enough to be heard,' suggests that the Dao cannot be heard like the five musical notes. 'Not enough to be used,' signifies that the Dao, when applied to govern a nation or oneself, is limitless. Using the Dao to govern a nation ensures peace and prosperity while applying it to oneself extends life without any notion of exhaustion.

老子河上公章句 -《仁德》

執大象，天下往。執，守也。象，道也。聖人守大道，則天下萬民移心歸往之也。治身則天降神明，往來於己也。往而不害，安、平、太，萬民歸往而不傷害，則國家安寧而致太平矣。治身不害神明，則身安而大壽也。樂與餌，過客止，餌，美也。過客，一也。人能樂美於道，則一留止也。一者，去盈而處虛，忽忽如過客。道之出口，淡乎其無味，道出入於口，淡淡非如五味有酸鹹苦甘辛也。視之不足見，足，得也。道無形，非若五色有青黃赤白黑可得見也。聽之不足聞，道非若五音有宮商角徵羽可得聽聞也。用之不足既。既，盡也。謂用道治國，則國安民昌。治身則壽命延長，無有既盡之時也。

【第三十六章】Chapter 36

Most Common Translation

將欲歙之，	When you desire to contract it,
	When you want to inhale (note 1)
必固張之；	you must firmly expand it;
	You must exhale first,
將欲弱之，	When you desire to weaken it,
必固強之；	you must firmly strengthen it;
將欲廢之，	When you desire to abolish it,
必固興之；	you must firmly promote it;
將欲奪之，	When you desire to take it away,
必固與之，	you must firmly give it.
是謂微明。	This is called subtle enlightenment. (note 2)
柔弱勝剛強。	Softness and weakness overcome hardness and strength.
魚不可脫於淵，	A fish can not leave the abyss (water),
國之利器不可以示人。	the advanced weapon of a nation should not be revealed to others.

Note 1

"歙" means to inhale or to "converge".

In ancient times, it shared similar characteristics with 翕 and 洽.

翕 represents harmony, convergence, and smoothness, while 翕 is interpreted by Master He as 噏. Both characters convey the idea of inhaling, while (噏) also resembling the sound of XI.

Additionally, 洽 means to blend with, be in harmony, to penetrate, and to negotiate.

Note 2

微明 is a very complicated term, from word to word, it is minimal of faint brightness, or dim light. The light before dawn, where the sky is still in grape blue.

What does "微明" mean? Conceal this principle to cultivate inner tranquility, deep reflection, and retire with leisure, akin to a fish not escaping the abyss.

Zhuangzi (莊子) metaphorically likens the above-mentioned strategies to the sharpness of a nation's advantageous tool (blade). Comprehend this subtle clarity, yet refrain from revealing it to others.

Master, He interpreted 微明 is: Its way is subtle; its impact is clear and obvious. (其道微，其效明,)

Common Literal Translation:

To restrain it, you must temporarily expand it; to weaken it, you must temporarily strengthen it; to abolish it, you must temporarily promote it; to take hold of it, you must temporarily give it. This is called the subtly enlightened state, where the mechanism lies in the victory of gentleness over strength. Just as a fish cannot survive without the deep waters (hidden), a nation's sharp tools should also remain concealed, not to be shown to everyone.

【第三十七章】 Chapter 37

Most Common Translation

道常無為而無不為，	The Dao is uncontrived, yet there is nothing it does not do. (note 1)
侯王若能守之，	If lords and kings can keep (guard) it,
萬物將自化。	all things will transform themselves.
化而欲作，	Transformed and wishing to act,
吾將鎮之以無名之朴。	I will restrain them with the namelessness simplicity: 朴 (pǔ) (note 2).
無名之朴，	Through, the nameless simplicity [朴 (pǔ)],
夫亦將無欲。	Desires will gradually fade away.
不欲以靜，	Without desire, tranquility prevails,
天下將自定。	And the world will settle by itself.

Note 1 - This is a very popular verse/quote of DDJ

Note 2 - Chapter 28: note 1

My Literal Translation

The Dao is perpetually characterized by its nature of non-interference, making it all-encompassing. If rulers can uphold the principles of Dao, everything will naturally transform.

In the process of this transformation, should personal desires arise, I will use the fundamental and uncarved tool [朴 (pǔ)] of Dao to bring about calm.

If, after this calming influence, a certain obstinate and persistent pursuit arises, I will cut off that pursuit and restore it to a chaotic state. By returning it to chaos (DDJ 16 and 21), it loses its stubborn nature. Without such stubborn inclinations and in a state of tranquility, the world will naturally settle, free from the risk of tumultuous disturbances or collapse.

My 5 Cents

This chapter seems to discuss the principles of governing a nation, suggesting that managing a nation is akin to managing oneself in meditation; how to handle your naughty mind and internal desires that come from within.

Viewing it from this perspective, the parallels become clear and easily understandable.

【第三十八章】Chapter 38

Most Common Translation

上德不德，是以有德；	High virtue is not virtuous, therefore it truly possesses virtue.
下德不失德，是以無德。	Low virtue never loses virtue, therefore it lacks virtue.
上德無為而無以為，	High virtue does nothing, yet nothing is left undone.
下德為之而有以為。	Low virtue does something, and it leaves much to be done.
上仁為之而無以為，	High benevolence does something, yet nothing is left undone.
上義為之而有以為，	High righteousness does something, and it has something to be done.
上禮為之而莫之應，	If one extends a courtesy without receiving a response,
則攘臂而扔之。	Then, roll up one's sleeves and forcibly intervene (throw out, throw on the table). (note 1)
故失道而后德，	Therefore, when the Dao is lost, there is virtue.
失德而后仁，	When virtue is lost, there is benevolence.
失仁而后義，	When benevolence is lost, there is righteousness.
失義而后禮。	When righteousness is lost, there is courtesy.
夫禮者，忠信之薄而亂之首。	Courtesy is a superficial expression of loyalty and trust, the beginning of social unrest (turmoil).
前識者，道之華而愚之始。	Foreknowledge is the extravagant embellishment of the Way, the beginning of foolishness.
是以大丈夫處其厚，	That's why a wise person stays in the substantial,
不居其薄；	Does not linger in the superficial or shallow.
處其實，	Dwells in the kernel/seeds, (Dwells on the actual)
不居其華。	Not in the husk. (not on illusion)
故去彼取此。	Therefore, get rid of that, and take this.

Note 1- The word "扔"(Rēng) in Chinese has two meanings. The more common one is to throw out or throw away, cast aside. The other meaning is to forcefully place something on a table or to forcibly intervene, but this usage is rare. It's only found in this specific chapter of the Dao De Jing and is not commonly used.

Why is that, let us have some basic historical background of DDJ.

Laozi and Confucius lived in approximately the same era, known as the late Zhou period. Laozi, born between 571 BCE and 471 BCE, was born in the state of Chu in the Eastern Zhou Dynasty. Confucius, with the given name Kongzi (551 BCE – 479 BCE), was born in the state of Lu.

Several centuries before the births of Laozi and Confucius, the Great Zhou Dynasty was established in a vast territory. Given the lack of modern communication devices like ours today, they had to rely on messengers, often using people with horses, and even carrier pigeons to transmit information. Consequently, the transmission of messages was time-consuming.

In such a vast realm, efficient governance faced challenges, particularly due to delays in communication. The rulers, also known as the Heavenly Son (a title signifying a chosen son from the heavens, essentially deified, and elevated to a higher status, giving rise to various complications), often found it difficult to issue timely commands.

To manage such a large nation more effectively, the rulers established various systems, including the system of territories. Besides the ruler's domain, the rest of the nation was divided into several smaller states. Each of these states, governed by acknowledged princes or kings (諸侯 Zhūhóu), had autonomous authority over matters such as legislation, execution, politics, culture, economy, and military affairs.

Unless confronted with extremely challenging issues, local princes (kings) had complete authority over all matters, big or small. The kingship was hereditary, meaning power was passed down through generations within a family or lineage, often through political or commercial lines of succession. (Line of hereditary succession). This gradually led to the consolidation of local powers.

Even if a certain prince encountered irreversible problems, such as rebellion, the emperor would command another prince or several princes to mobilize forces for joint suppression. Policies were determined independently by the various princes.

Several centuries later, the Zhou royal family declined, and the Zhou emperor practically became a symbolic figure, with uprisings occurring in various regions. Local princes vied for dominance, seizing the titles of kings and competing for resources and territorial expansion. This period of upheaval, marked by the collapse of rituals and music, persisted for over two hundred years. Laozi and Confucius were born in this tumultuous era.

However, their perspectives differed significantly. Confucius advocated for the restoration of ancient Zhou rituals and music, emphasizing moral standards such as benevolence and righteousness. In contrast, Laozi's philosophy centered around the concept of Wu Wei (non-action) and tranquility, presenting a stark contrast to Confucius's emphasis on active moral principles.

Confucius tirelessly traveled to different regions, promoting his ideas of rituals, music, benevolence, and righteousness to local princes. Unfortunately, his teachings were largely rejected during his time, and Confucius often left disappointed, sweeping his sleeves. PS: In ancient times, people wore oversized long sleeves as part of their tradition. However, his diligence eventually paid off as he became a grand master's in education and his teaching was widely spread. Through the establishment of the Three Bonds and Five Constants (the Three Bonds being between Heaven, Earth, and Humanity; and the Five Constants being the relationships between ruler and subject, father and son, husband and wife), Confucius aligned rulers with the principles of Heaven, further legitimizing the hereditary system.

As Confucius had numerous students and gained a significant following, his teachings were later embraced by rulers in subsequent eras. This widespread acceptance allowed Confucianism to thrive for over two thousand years, influencing rulers and societies.

Therefore, this passage in Note 1 and Chapter 18 of the Dao De Jing is believed to be written based on this historical fact. However, scholars of Confucianism generally disapprove of this view. As a result, there has emerged the current popular interpretation of this section.

You guys know me. It is too serious. Let us have a joke:

Chinese Medicine Master: Thank you very much for your unlimited support towards my pursuit, especially for selling our home to support my teaching in the Chinese medicine inheritance class.

Wife, somewhat reluctantly: I wasn't really willing. My dad (also your Chinese medical teacher) also agrees. I just had no choice.

Chinese Medicine Master: Think about it. In the future, when our students become successful, everyone will thank you for your selfless act today.

Wife: Don't paint a rosy picture for me. Confucius had enough students, with three thousand disciples. He's famous enough, everyone in China knows him. But do you know who his wife was?

Note: In history, there is indeed no recorded information about who is Confucius's wife. However, details about Confucius's descendants are documented. (Extracted from a Chinese TV episode)

Common Literal Translation

Those with superior virtue do not flaunt their virtuous reputation, and therefore, they have virtue. Those with inferior virtue boast about their virtuous reputation to show that they have not lost virtue, and therefore, they lack virtue. Those with superior virtue do not strive for recognition, hence they do not adhere rigidly to a specific virtue or appearance. On the other hand, those with inferior virtue always maintain a virtuous appearance and engage in many actions.

Actions arising from a heart of benevolence and love do not depend on virtue or outward appearances. Actions driven by a sense of moral responsibility display virtue and outward appearances for validation. Actions guided by rituals and norms, if not reciprocated appropriately, lead to coercion and forceful compliance. Therefore, without adherence to the Dao, considerations of virtue are futile. The descent of virtue highlights people's benevolent and loving hearts, the absence of which stimulates a sense of moral responsibility in society. The decline of moral responsibility prompts the revision of various rituals and norms.

Rituals and norms, with loyalty and trust as their main essence, are products of the diminishing appeal of moral influence. Consequently, society begins to descend into chaos. Various prevailing social beliefs are merely the expansion and embellishment of the previous path and using them to embark on a new path is a foolish beginning. Therefore, a great person who sheds external appearances should continuously strive towards increasing depth, without being confined by the constraints of superficial customs. The focus should be on the core essence of why things are the way they are, without being entangled in temporary expansions. Therefore, one must make [this and that], [is and what], such a kind of choices.

My 5 cents

Inadvertently, we have entered the realm of the De Jing (the second part of DDJ), a text that presents a considerable challenge in translation. It is also a continuation of the Dao Jing's Chapter 18, and therefore, I refrained from adding many annotations during the translation of Chapter 18. Note: Scholars generally divide the Dao De Jing into two parts - the Dao Jing and the De Jing, referring to the Way (Dao) and Virtue (De), respectively.

Firstly, what is "德" (De)?

In the common understanding of people nowadys, "德" (De) refers to one's conduct, character, and the exemplary nature of elevated behavior. In Chinese, "德" (De) is often associated with "道" (Dao) or linked to "行" (xing), as seen in the term "德行" (De Xing), which encompasses a person's virtuous conduct, demeanor, and so on. It is said that virtue originates from the heart and manifests through one's actions. As stated in the "周礼·地官" (Zhou Li · Di Guan), "In the heart lies virtue, and in its application lies conduct". (在心为德，施之为行).

The character "德" (De) is composed of three components: "心" (heart/mind), "彳" (step/walk), and "直" (straight). The "心" represents emotions and mental states, "彳" is associated with movement or behavior, and "直" (original form "值") conveys the idea of meeting or encountering. In Buddhist terminology, this represents the response to circumstances. It signifies the immediate and spontaneous reaction of the mind and behavior in the face of current situations.

Due to established conventions, let's look at Confucius's interpretation of "德" (De):

Norms which followed by all of humanity.

From the Analects (《論語·述而》): "When the Way (德) is not followed, the learning (學) is not discussed".

Conduct and demeanor.

From the Analects (《論語·顏淵》): "The virtue (德) and demeanor of a gentleman, the virtue (德) of a good man, are like the wind; the grass (the inferior virtue) must bend when the wind blows".

Kindness, grace, and favors.

From the Analects (《論語·憲問》): "Confucius said: 'How should one repay kindness? Repay hatred with uprightness and repay kindness with kindness.'"

From Mencius (《孟子·公孫丑上》): "Moreover, with the virtue (德) of King Wen, even after a hundred years, it still had not fully permeated the world".

Apart from the above-mentioned aspects, "德" (De) can also refer to one's intention, will, or belief. For example, the expression "一心一德" can be translated as "single-minded devotion" or "wholehearted commitment", emphasizing the unity of heart and virtue.

There's another interpretation suggesting that "德" (De) and "得" (De, getting, achieve, I use De1 hereafter in this paragraph to show the difference, cause the pronunciation are the same) share ancient meanings, and their characters are interchangeable. Hence, the Dao De Jing could be alternatively interpreted as Dao De Jing or Dao De1 Jing. Based on recent archaeological discoveries in the Mawangdui tombs in China, where a version of the Dao De Jing (now known as the "Jia Ben Bo Shu") was unearthed, the chapters on Dao and De were reversed, forming "德道經" (De Dao Jing). Similarly, this could be understood as "得道經" (De Dao Jing).

Here, I have emphasized multiple times that Laozi often employs inverted sentence structures in his writing. In many passages, we can read using an inverted method, (PS: it is also a key to unlock DDJ), such as in Chapter 18 and this chapter. Simply put, if understood straightforwardly, it suggests that when the Dao is lost, virtue emerges; when virtue is lost, benevolence appears, and so on. When employing the inverted reading method, it guides us on how to return to the Great Dao. That is, entering benevolence from righteousness, entering virtue from benevolence, and entering the Dao from virtue. Chen Bo's Tai Chi/Ji diagram (Diagram 1 originally called the "Diagram of the WuJI (Infinite)") also uses this technique to express the harmony and opposition of heaven and earth. Harmony leads to becoming human, while opposition leads to becoming a transcendent being.

Diagram 1:

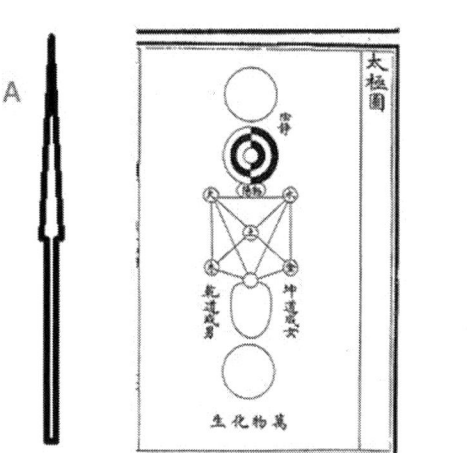

- Path A represents the journey backward from being human to the state of ONEness. Conversely,

Path B entails following the natural flow to become a successful or fruitful human.

(PS: I am not sure if we have discussed this diagram before, together with other tai chi diagrams, if not, please let me know)

Another joke: GOD = DOG, Evian Water = Naive Water.

I think inversion reading is gaining popularity in the Western world now. Many years ago, I read a philosophy-related novel called "Sophie's World" (Sofies verden, first version 1991) by Jostein Gaarder, where he consistently incorporated this idea throughout the book.

Therefore, from my perspective, whether it is the Dao De Jing or the De Dao Jing, they are essentially the same. As mentioned in another separate cover about historical context, the Dao De Jing was scattered on the ground during its transportation. The disarrayed bamboo slips were later meticulously arranged and reconstructed by scholars. It is for this reason that we may unintentionally observe certain chapters appearing in a non-linear sequence.

From my perspective, "德" (De), which sounds similar to "duck" in Cantonese (too bore again, adding a playful note), possesses several attributes:

- As the vessel of the Dao, "德" (De) is the manifestation of the Dao in this world.
- "德" (De) serves as the intermediary/agent/media between all things and the Dao, facilitating transformation.
- Similar to the branching of rivers, "德" (De) nourishes all things, akin to the veins in our bodies, continuing and intricately branching into every part of our body (note 2).
- Based on this transformative quality, it is the inherent nature of all things.
- It is also because of this "德" (De) that the cycles of all things continue endlessly, with vitality transforming, and the processes of birth and death occurring in an orderly manner.

Note 2 - I have emphasized repeatedly that: when doing Qi flow exercises, it's important to keep it smooth, soft, and gentle, not rigid or harsh. Our blood vessels reach every part of our body, and our Qi needs time to flow through them and nourish everything. In addition, our smallest blood vessels (capillaries) and nerves need time to grow and become bigger and thicker to handle the extra Qi. If we rush this process, common health issues related to Qi might show up. Check my notes for more info on common Qi problems.

Extract from He Shang Gong - A discourse on virtue

High/Supreme Virtue vs lacks Virtue (Inferior virtue):

Supreme virtue refers to the ruler of ancient times, without a renowned title, possessing unparalleled virtue. Therefore, it is called supreme virtue. Those lacking virtue are described as not instructing the people with virtue, adhering to natural ways, and nurturing human nature and lives. Their virtue is not apparent; hence it is termed lacking in virtue. (上德不德，上德，謂太古無名號之君，德大無上，故言上德也。不德者，言其不以德教民，因循自然，養人性命，其德不見，故言不德也。)

Therefore, having virtue means that their virtue aligns with heaven and earth, and harmonious energy prevails, ensuring the completeness of the people's virtue. (是以有德。言其德合於天地，和氣流行，民德以全也。)

Inferior virtue does not lose its virtue. Inferior virtue refers to the ruler with a recognized title, whose virtue does not surpass that of superior virtue; hence, it is called inferior virtue. Not losing virtue means that their virtue is visible, and their accomplishments are commendable. (下德不失德，下德，謂號謚之君，德不及上德，故言下德也。不失德者，其德可見，其功可稱也。)

Therefore, lacking virtue refers to those with a recognized title, but lacking virtue in their character or actions (是以無德。以有名號及其身故。)

Supreme virtue of non-action refers to the tranquility of the Dao, where there is no deliberate or forced action. (上德無為謂法道安靜，無所施為也。)

And without using, it means not employing names or titles for recognition. (refer to DDJ chapter 1) (而無以為，言無以名號為也。)

Inferior virtue involves speaking to teach and instruct, as well as implementing government affairs. (下德為之言為教令，施政事也。)

Yet having something to rely on, it means using names and titles for self-recognition. (而有以為。言以為己取名號也。)

Supreme benevolence refers to a ruler who practices benevolence, and their benevolence is unsurpassed, hence it is called supreme benevolence. The one who does this is bestowing kindness upon others. (上仁為之上仁謂行仁之君，其仁無上，故言上仁。為之者，為人恩也。)

Yet without relying on it, achievements and tasks are accomplished without holding on to them. (而無以為，功成事立，無以執為。)

Supreme righteousness is to act with righteousness to discern and separate. (also refer to DDJ chapter 28) (上義為之為義以斷割也。)

Yet having something to rely on, taking action for self-interest, using violence (original wording is killing) to establish authority, and exploiting the lower class for self-benefit. (而有以為。動作以為己，殺人以成威，賊下以自奉也。)

Supreme ritual refers to a ruler who practices the highest forms of ritual, and their ritual is unparalleled, hence it is called supreme ritual. The one who does this is establishing rituals and order, and arranging dignified ceremonies. (上禮為之謂上禮之君，其禮無上，故言上禮。為之者，言為禮制度，序威儀也。)

Yet without anyone responding, it means that the extravagance of rituals is flourishing while their substance is declining. Superficial adornments and deceptions are abundant, and when put into practice, they deviate from the Dao, making them unresponsive. (而莫之應，言禮華盛實衰，飾偽煩多，動則離道，不可應也。)

Then, he rolls up his sleeves and throws it away. This means that excessive and unresponsive rituals lead to conflicts and disputes between superior and inferior, hence the metaphorical action of rolling up sleeves and throwing them away. (則攘臂而扔之。言禮煩多不可應，上下忿爭，故攘臂相仍引。)

Therefore, losing the Dao precedes the decline of virtue, indicating that when the Dao weakens, virtue deteriorates. (故失道而後德，言道衰而德化生也。)

The waning of virtue precedes the emerging presence of benevolence, indicating that as virtue weakens, the manifestation of benevolent love then emerges. (失德而後仁，言德衰而仁愛見也。)

Losing benevolence precedes the rise of righteousness, signifying that as benevolence weakens, the distinctions of righteousness become evident. (失仁而後義，言仁衰而分義明也。)

Losing righteousness precedes ritual. When righteousness declines, the proper conduct of ceremonial exchanges involving jade and silk (Jade artifacts and silk textiles; a general term for wealth, or nation-to-nation exchanging gift) needs to be in operation. (失義而後禮。言義衰則失禮聘，行玉帛也。)

Rituals, being the manifestation of loyalty and trust, when ritual was neglected, disrupting the foundation and the order (causality), leading to a daily decline in the strength of loyalty and trust. (夫禮者，忠信之薄言禮廢本治末，忠信日以衰薄。)

And it becomes the source of chaos. Rituals value form (verbal) over substance, hence righteousness and integrity gradually diminish, while perversions and disorder increase day by day. (而亂之首。禮者賤質而貴文，故正直日以少，邪亂日以生。)

The one who claims knowledge without understanding the essence of the Dao is referred to as having prior awareness. At the time when a person loses the Dao, they attain the superficial appearance of the Dao. (前識者，道之華不知而言知為前識，此人失道之時，得道之華。)

And this marks the beginning of ignorance. Referring to those with prior awareness as the initiators of ignorance and obscurity. (而愚之始。言前識之人，愚闇之倡始也。)

Therefore, a great man dwells in his depth, whereas a great man refers to a ruler who has attained the Dao. Dwelling in one's depth means residing in simplicity and sincerity. (是以大丈夫處其厚，大丈夫謂得道之君也。處其厚者，謂處身於敦樸。)

Not residing in shallowness, not dwelling where the Dao is neglected, and avoiding causing disturbance and chaos in the world. (不居其薄，不處身違道，為世煩亂也。)

Dwelling on the actual means abiding by loyalty and trust. (處其實，處忠信也。)

Not dwelling on illusion, avoiding the pursuit of superficial appearances. (不居其華。不尚華言也。)

Therefore, abandon the former and embrace the latter. Discard the superficial and pursue the substantial. (故去彼取此。去彼華薄，取此厚實。)

Postscript

India, Mahatma Gandhi: The best way to find yourself, is to lose yourself in the service of others. PS: I found this image from Mother Teresa.

American, Maya Angelou: You can only become truly accomplished at something you love. Do not make money your goal. Instead, pursue the things you love doing, and then do them so well that people can't take their eyes off you.

Apple, Steve Jobs: The only way to do great work, is to love what you do.

■■■

PS: I always say that being able to turn your hobbies or things you enjoy into your job is a real blessing, while doing a job you do not hate, is also a blessing already.

【第三十九章】Chapter 39

Most Common Translation

昔之得一者，	In ancient times, those who attained oneness:
天得一以清，	Heaven attained oneness and became clear,
地得一以寧，	Earth attained oneness and became tranquil,
神得一以靈，	Spirit attained oneness and became divine, (or sorceress, or approach to God level)
谷得一以盈，	Valley attained oneness and became full (sufficient),
萬物得一以生，	All things attained oneness and came to life,
侯王得一以為天下貞。	Lords and kings attained oneness and established the stability or nobility of the world. (virtuous, chaste, pure; loyal)
其致之。	This is the ultimate way.
天無以清將恐裂，	If Heaven lacks clarity, it may be on the verge of breaking.
地無以寧將恐發（note 1），	If Earth lacks tranquility, it may be on the verge of erupting.
神無以靈將恐歇，	If Spirit lacks divinity, it may be on the verge of resting.
谷無以盈將恐竭，	If the Valley lacks fullness, it may be on the verge of drying up/used up.
萬物無以生將恐滅，	If all things lack life, they may be on the verge of extinction.
侯王無以貴高將恐蹶。	If lords and kings lack nobility and elevation, they may be on the verge of stumbling.
故貴以賤為本，	Valuable originates from considering the lowly as the essential essence,
高以下為基。	High is built upon based on the low as the foundation.
是以侯王自謂孤寡不穀（谷）。(note 2)	Therefore, lords and kings often refer to themselves as "lonely", "orphaned", and "without plenty" (in terms of resources or abundance).
此非以賤為本邪？非乎？	Is this not valuing the lowly as the foundation? Is it not so?
故致數輿無輿。	Hence, achieving without boasting or displaying it.
不欲琭琭如玉，	Without desiring to shine conspicuously like jade,
珞珞如石。(note 3)	Dull and rough like stone.
	Treat "yingluo" (瓔珞), neck pendants as normal stones.

Note 1 - In ancient times, "發" and "廢" sometimes were interchangeable, even though their meanings are quite opposite when considered separately. "發" signifies glory, getting rich, or starting off, while "廢" means abrogate, terminate, or discard.

Some scholars suggest that the original word should be "廢", pronounced as "發", sharing the meaning of abrogate, terminate, or discard.

Note 2 - Some versions use "穀", while others use "谷".

"穀" refers to crops, while "谷" means valley. Regardless of the specific Chinese character used, the fundamental meaning remains the same.

Note 3

珞珞, Apart from signifying the jewelry as mentioned, it can also represent a sound. Interpreted as a sound, the verse suggests treating the sparkling jade as ordinary stones. When stored in a cloth pouch, the collision produces a sound similar to that of stones.

Master He Shang Gong has another point of view or interpretation: "(琭琭)" symbolizes scarcity, while "(珞珞)" symbolizes abundance. Jade is considered valuable because it is scarce, and stone is deemed common because it is plentiful. The expression suggests not wanting to be esteemed like jade or scorned like a stone but rather staying neutral amid these distinctions.

Remarks:

Yingluo (瓔珞), Ancient neck pendants, it is not only common neck pendants, but they are also the "most" highest valuable both in value and prestige status jewelry. In India, it is called Keyūra. In Buddhism, it is specified as those who are worn by the female deva. Daoism shares similar meanings and values. In the old days of China, only those royal ladies with the emperor could wear it.

In the Buddhist tradition, distinguishing between a Buddha and a Bodhisattva in a depiction such as a photo or painting often involves observing the presence of adornments. Buddhas, embodying enlightenment and supreme awakening, are typically portrayed without any jewelry, reflecting a state of pure transcendence. On the other hand, Bodhisattvas, compassionate beings aspiring for enlightenment, may be depicted wearing ornaments such as the Keyura (Yingluo), symbolizing their compassionate journey towards Buddhahood. Therefore, the presence or absence of jewelry, particularly the Keyura, can be a discerning factor in recognizing whether the depicted figure is a Buddha or a Bodhisattva in Buddhist art.

Common Literal Translation

In the past, there was the attainment of harmonious unity: the sky, due to its harmonious unity, was clear and bright; the earth, due to its harmonious unity, was tranquil and stable; the spirit (you may also understand it as our primordial spirit), due to its harmonious unity (embracing both the vital and spiritual aspects), was lively and animated; the void (the valley), due to its harmonious unity, was everywhere filled; all things, due to their harmonious unity, grew and thrived; and rulers and kings, due to their harmonious unity with the people, maintained their positions of authority—these virtues and abilities (such as clarity, tranquility, and vitality) naturally manifested because they achieved harmonious unity.

If the sky lacked harmonious unity, it would fear eventual fragmentation; if the earth lacked harmonious unity, it would fear significant upheavals; if the spirit lacked harmonious unity, it would fear withering and decline; if the void lacked harmonious unity, it would fear depletion and emptiness; if all things lacked harmonious unity, they would fear extinction; if rulers and kings lacked harmonious unity with the people, they would fear eventual overthrow. Therefore, within a harmonious and unified entity, the noble should consider humility as the foundation, and the high should consider the low as the basis.

Hence, rulers and kings often speak of themselves as lonely, weak, and without support—isn't this because they fully recognize the necessity of considering humility as the foundation? Therefore, seeking numerous virtues and abilities results in the absence of true virtues and abilities. One should not always strive to be splendid and noble like precious jade, nor persist in being coarse and lowly like a stone.

My 5 Cents

As mentioned, this chapter proves challenging to translate yet remains exceptionally popular. Achieving Oneness, which stands in close proximity to the Dao, involves a multifaceted approach. Delving into its essence, we find that various lineages offer distinct interpretations, especially concerning the practices of Qi cultivation or spiritual purification. To illustrate, let's consider the following example.

DDJ Character	Qi Practice	Spiritual
Sky / Heaven	Middle Dāntián	Wisdom Eye / Upper Dāntián
Earth / land	Low Dāntián	Low Dāntián
Spirit	Upper Dāntián	Upper Dāntián
Valley / void	Wisdom Eye	Void
All Things	Whole Body Inner and Outer	Whole Body Inner and Outer
Lords/kings/Dukes	Zhōngmài / 中脈 / Central Meridian	Zhōngmài / 中脈 / Central Meridian

In certain lineages, this chapter might be transformed into a mantra for disciples to chant. For your convenience, I have provided the Mandarin Pinyin below:

(Original Text in Chinese)　　　Mandarin Pinyin (pronunciation)

昔之得一者，　　　　　　　　Xī zhī dé yī zhě.
天得一以清，　　　　　　　　Tiān dé yī yǐ qīng,
地得一以寧，　　　　　　　　De dé yī yǐ níng,
神得一以靈，　　　　　　　　Shén dé yī yǐ líng,
谷得一以盈，　　　　　　　　Gǔ dé yī yǐ yíng,
萬物得一以生，　　　　　　　Wànwù dé yī yǐ shēng,
侯王得一以為天下貞。　　　　Hóu wáng dé yī yǐwéi tiānxià zhēn.

I know some lineage chanting in Cantonese, but I am uncertain about its effectiveness when using Mandarin. May be English may work either. It's important to note that, regardless of pronunciation, the act of chanting involves mentally referencing the relevant location or Dāntián. I'm not suggesting you practice this; it's simply provided as a reference for informational purposes.

This form of chanting (pure verbal chanting usually without mental reference to the related locations) aligns closely with the essence found in various religious practices worldwide, akin to those embracing the concept of Oneness, observed in Sikhism, Hinduism, and many others. It also shares similarities with popular sacred relaxation music used for meditation.

PS: I do not practice this chanting myself.

As an additional note, which could be referenced in the future, several chapters in the Dao De Jing are employed for chanting, extending beyond the confines of Chapter 39.

Note: And it is needless to say, you may understand this chapter inversely.

Extract from He Shang Gong – De Jing - The Root of Dao's Way:

In ancient times, "obtaining the One" means going towards it. The One is the non-action (Wúwéi), the child of the Dao. Heaven obtains the One to achieve clarity; it is said that because Heaven obtains the One, it can manifest clear and bright phenomena. Earth obtains the One to achieve tranquility; it is said that because Earth obtains the One, it can remain calm and undisturbed. Spirits obtain the One to achieve (Divine) spirituality; it is said that because spirits obtain the One, they can transform and be formless. Valleys obtain the One to achieve fullness; it is said that because valleys obtain the One, they can be full and never cease. All things obtain the One to achieve life; it is said that all things require the Dao to be generated.

Dukes/Lords and kings obtain the One to establish integrity in the world. "Integrity" (nobility) here means admonishing the six matters below. If Heaven lacks clarity, it may fear disintegration. This means that Heaven must have the interplay of Yin and Yang, alternating between day and night; it cannot always desire clarity without end, or it may risk falling apart and not functioning as Heaven. If Earth lacks tranquility, it may fear upheaval. This implies that Earth must have the qualities of high and low, firm and yielding (soft), the regulation of seasons, and the five elements (eternal energy); it cannot always desire tranquility without end, or it may risk erupting and not functioning as Earth. If spirits lack spirituality, they may fear stagnation. This suggests that spirits must have rulers and officials, imprisonment and death, rest, and abandonment; they cannot always desire spiritual transformation without end, or they may risk becoming empty and stagnant, not functioning as spirits. If valleys lack fullness, they may fear depletion. This means that valleys must have expansion and contraction, emptiness, and fullness; they cannot always desire fullness without end, or they may risk drying up and not functioning as valleys. If all things lack life, they may fear extinction. This indicates that all things must undergo birth and death according to the times; they cannot always desire eternal life without end, or they may risk extinction and not function as things.

If dukes and kings lack humility, they may fear downfall. This means that dukes and kings must humble themselves and serve the people, seeking talents diligently; they cannot always desire superiority over others without end, or they may risk stumbling and losing their positions. Therefore, to value the high as the foundation, it is necessary to consider the low as the basis. If one desires to be honored and esteemed, one should consider humility and lowliness as the foundation, just like Emperor Yu cultivating the fields and Emperor Shun tending to the rivers, or Duke of Zhou living in a humble white house. To build high, one must start with a low foundation, just like constructing walls and structures, starting from the low to achieve the high; if the foundation is not firm, it will inevitably collapse later.

Hence, dukes and kings refer to themselves as "lonely, few, and without support". "Lonely and few" implies being alone and lacking support, similar to a chariot without the support of many spokes to a hub. Is this not considering humility as the basis? It means that dukes and kings, despite their exalted status, can refer to themselves as lonely and few, recognizing the importance of humility. Isn't this understanding the principle? No! It is an expression of regret. Therefore, when pursuing several carriages, there are no carriages. "Pursuing" here means attaching spokes, wheels, hubs, balances, and shafts to a chariot. Without calling it a chariot, it becomes one, illustrating that dukes and kings do not use lofty titles for themselves, allowing them to achieve their nobility.

Not wanting to be dazzling like jade, nor dull like stone. "Dazzling like jade" symbolizes scarcity, while "dull like stone" symbolizes abundance. Jade is rare, and therefore precious, while stones are plentiful and hence considered cheap. It means not wanting to be esteemed like jade or considered lowly like stone but remaining in between.

老子河上公章句 -> 德經 -> 法本

昔之得一者：昔，往也。一，無為，道之子也。天得一以清，言天得一故能垂象清明。地得一以寧，言地得一故能安靜不動搖。神得一以靈，言神得一故能變化無形。谷得一以盈，言谷得一故能盈滿而不絕也萬物得一以生，言萬物皆須道以生成也。侯王得一以為天下貞。言侯王得一故能為天下平正其致之。致，誠也。謂下六事也。天無以清將恐裂，言天當有陰陽弛張，晝夜更用，不可但欲清明無已時，將恐分裂不為天。地無以寧將恐發，言地當有高下剛柔，節氣五行，不可但欲安靜無已時，將恐發泄不為地。神無以靈將恐歇，言神當有王相囚死休廢，不可但欲靈變無已時，將恐虛歇不為神。谷無以盈將恐竭，言谷當有盈縮虛實，不可但欲盈滿無已時，將恐枯竭不為谷。萬物無以生將恐滅，言萬物當隨時生死，不可但欲長生無已時，將恐滅亡不為物。侯王無以貴高將恐蹶。言侯王當屈己以下人，汲汲求賢，不可但欲貴高於人無已時，將恐顛蹶失其位。故貴以賤為本，言必欲尊貴，當以薄賤為本，若禹稷躬稼，舜陶河濱，周公下白屋也。高以下為基言必欲尊貴，當以下為本基，猶築牆造功，因卑成高，不下堅固，後必傾危。是以侯王自謂孤、寡、不穀。孤寡喻孤獨，不穀喻不能如車轂為眾輻所湊。此非以賤為本邪？言侯王至尊貴，能以孤寡自稱，此非以賤為本乎，以曉人？非乎！嗟嘆之辭。故致數輿無輿，致，就也。言人就車數之為輻、為輪、為轂、為衡、為轝，無有名為車者，故成為車，以喻侯王不以尊號自名，故能成其貴。不欲琭琭如玉，珞珞如石。琭琭喻少，落落喻多，玉少故見貴，石多故見賤。言不欲如玉為人所貴，如石為人所賤，當處其中也。

【第四十章】 Chapter 40

Most Common translation

反者,道之動;	The contrary is the movement/mechanism of the Dao.
弱者,道之用。	The weak/softness is how the Dao work.
	The weak embody the usefulness of the Dao.
天下萬物生於有,	All things under heaven are born from being,
有生於無。	Being is born from non-being.

Most Common Literal Translation

The extremity of things will inevitably reverse which is the law of movement in the Dao. Profoundly soft and weak, it is the source of the Dao's influence. All things under heaven are born from their own maternal source, and this maternal source emerges from the primordial emptiness of heaven and earth.

My 5 Cents

In the state of meditation or energetic flow, the seamless interchange between the positive and the negative represents a hallmark of the Dao. Transitioning effortlessly into and out of stillness is a step closer to the Dao. The Dao's application is marked by its supple and dynamic alignment with the natural flow of events. The significance of the diverse entities in the world lies in their naming, and these names find their origin in the nameless essence of the Dao. (DDJ Chapter 1)

【第四十一章】Chapter 41

Most Common Translation

上士聞道，	The scholar-official who hears of the Dao, (note 1)
勤而行之；	applies diligent practice;
中士聞道，	The average scholar-official who hears of the Dao,
若存若亡；	Seemingly grasps it, seemingly lets it slip away;
下士聞道，	The below average Scholar-official who hears of the Dao,
大笑之，	Laughs heartily,
不笑不足以為道。	As not laughing is insufficient to be considered as the Dao.
故建言有之：	Hence, quoting the words of ancient sages as evidence:
明道若昧，	Clarity (Brightness) in the path (Dao), appears as confusion (dark, or dim)
進道若退，	Advancing on the path seems like stepping back,
夷道若纇。	The seemingly flat pathway, when traversed, unfolds like a knot on silk, revealing a remarkably rough and uneven terrain.
上德若谷，	High virtue is like a valley (note 2),
大白若辱，	Great purity seems tarnished,
廣德若不足，	(Those who process) Broad virtue seems insufficient,
建德若偷，	(Those who possess) vigorous virtues may appear as laziness and lethargy,
質真若渝。	The natural quality of truth seems constantly changing.
大方無隅，	The great square has no corners,
大器晚成，	Great talents mature late, (note 3)
大音希聲，	The great sound sounds like (xi) or a sacred melody. (note 4)
大象無形。	The great image has no shape. (note 5)
道隱無名，	The Dao is hidden and nameless,
夫唯道善貸且成。	Indeed, the Dao is benevolent, bestowing, and can be accomplished.

Note 1 – Regarding (士 Shi), In Laozi's era, the majority of people were illiterate, and commoners lacked the ability or opportunity to learn to read. Those who could read and write were generally nobility and enjoyed special privileges. Because of their literacy, they became Emperor's officials, further securing their privileged status. As time passed, they formed a solid power base. Those holding official positions were collectively referred to as "士大夫 Shìdàfū". – Scholar official or scholar bureaucrat.

Later, as their new generations also learned to read, they were simply called "士子 Shì zi", referring to the early students/pupils.

Similar to Buddhism, Buddhism gradually entered China around the Jin Dynasty (266-420). In the beginning, it was accessible primarily to the nobility and literati. Therefore, some Western scholars refer to the Buddhism of that time as "elite Buddhism".

Similarly, although Daoist teachings originated in China, during times when the general population was largely illiterate, especially in Laozi's era, Daoist transmission was more covert. The tradition often involved a master guiding a few disciples in remote mountains. If a Daoist adept wished to propagate teachings externally, it typically had to begin through the literati and nobility. This pattern continued with later Daoist sects, such as the Upper Clarity (Shangqing sect 上清派).

In this context, the use of the term "scholar-official" in this chapter becomes clear. Although the term "students" (士子 Shì zi) could be accurate, it may overlook the subtle nuances embedded in these verses.

P.S.: In the quest for the Dao within the renowned medical scriptures, the Huangdi Neijing (黃帝內經), who seeks enlightenment from the immortal? It is none other than the Yellow Emperor.

A legendary saying from Patriarch Lü Chunyang (Lü Dongbin (呂洞賓): "Wealth and nobility are inherently like a dream; there has never been a deity who did not study and read.

"Who is talking about me? Naughty boy"

Note 2 - Laozi frequently employs the term "valley", which holds diverse meanings, varying with each chapter. It can signify the spirit inside the valley, the characteristics and six attributes of a mountain-enclosed valley, the (image) associated with a valley, such as a vortex, the vital essence embodied in a valley, and more, including the echoed sound resonating from the valley.

Note 3 - 大器晚成. Translating the term "大器" literally gives us "big container" or "big equipment". But in today's language, because of this popular chapter, we commonly use it to refer to someone exceptionally talented, often with natural abilities. This isn't just about small skills; it's about possessing extraordinary talents that can lead to significant success in their chosen pursuit.

The word "晚" translates to "late" or "night". When combined with "大器晚成", it conveys the idea that great talents mature over time. To express this more romantically, it can be said that magnificent accomplishments unfold gradually, resembling a masterpiece that blooms gracefully with time, much like a fine wine that matures to perfection.

A scholar 陳柱, suggests that the original term is (免), which means to excuse from or evade. Therefore, according to this interpretation, (大器晚成) could be translated as great talent doesn't necessarily require success or achieving something specific. This corresponds to the statement "大音無聲、大象無形" (Great sound has NO sound, great form has NO form- formless). This aligns with the teachings of the Heart Sutra, stating, "Ultimately, Nirvana is attained, with no wisdom and no attainment, because there is nothing to be attained; the Bodhisattva relies on Prajnaparamita and thus attains perfect understanding." In essence, those with great inherent wisdom realize enlightenment and Nirvana without acquiring anything tangible, as it is inherent in their nature.

In Daoism, a similar concept exists to describe highly talented practitioners known as 樸玉 (Simple/ unadorned/plain Jade). These individuals engage in consistent daily practice without apparent signs of improvement. Yet, they persist wholeheartedly without regret. While their achievements may not be readily visible, they eventually attain remarkable success which cannot be visioned or measured.

A side note: Mo Yan, a contemporary literary writer, offers another interpretation of 大器晚成 (Great Talent Matures Late) in his Late Bloomer:

The portrayal of a late bloomer（晚熟的人）：

"When others are clever and quick-witted,
We appear foolish and dull.
As others exhaust their cunning strategies and decline into decline,
We, at that very moment, happen to have our souls transcend."

莫言（Mo Yan）（近代文學作家）對大器晚成的另一演繹：
在他的（晚熟的人）寫下：
當別人聰明伶俐時
我們又傻又呆
當別人心機用盡，漸入頹境時
我們恰巧靈魂出竅。

Note 4 - Refer to Chapter 14

Note 5 - Refer to Chapter 35, note 1, holding an elephant. 😊

Most Common Literal Translation

Excellent individuals, upon hearing the methods of enlightenment, diligently study and immediately take action.

Ordinary individuals, upon hearing the methods of enlightenment, may have a mix of belief and doubt, understanding and non-understanding.

Vulgar and narrow-minded individuals, upon hearing the methods of enlightenment, may scoff and burst into laughter.

If one is not ridiculed by such individuals, it is not enough to prove the preciousness of the Great Way.

Thus, in the record of "The Counselor":

The bright path seems dim, the forward path seems backward, the smooth path seems rugged, the highest virtue seems like a valley, the purest seems to have flaws, the most extensive virtue appears insufficient, the process of cultivating virtue seems lazy, and the simple and sincere seems not firm.

Great goals are achieved by overcoming obstacles, precious vessels are shaped through meticulous carving, beautiful music arises from the combination of individual notes, greatness forms from intangible influences, and the Great Way is concealed within the unnamed.

Only those who follow the rules of the Great Way can begin well, end well, and ultimately succeed.

More detailed common translations and interpretations

The superior person possesses extraordinary knowledge and profound insights, with a broad and expansive spirit. Upon hearing of this Dao, they are bound to diligently follow and practice it, never daring to be negligent. It is likened to climbing a mountain where reaching the summit is essential, or crossing a body of water where exploring the depths is imperative. Upon hearing of it, one's understanding extends to the realm of the unheard, and in practicing it, one's actions lead to places where there seems to be no path.

The Dao transcends common understanding and is not something that can be grasped by the lower and limited intellect. Only those with elevated roots and sharp intellect can comprehend it. For individuals with elevated roots, their aspirations align with the Dao, and upon hearing of it, they embody it and actively put it into practice. Therefore, it is said that the superior person, upon hearing of the Dao, diligently follows and practices it. In general, this refers to individuals who, through repeated lifetimes of practice, have achieved a certain level of accomplishment. Just continue their path in this life.

The middle-ranking individual refers to those with a generally rooted and faithful disposition towards the Dao, possessing a moderate level of innate understanding. While they harbor an aspiring heart towards the Dao, their attitude remains ambivalent, wavering between belief and doubt. They may be aware of it without truly comprehending or perceive it without complete clarity. Their stance is characterized by a mixture of faith and skepticism. Alternatively, due to habitual tendencies, they may intermittently engage in practices, alternating between periods of diligence and moments of lethargy. Progress may be accompanied by regression, hence the expression "existence or non-existence, as the case may be."

The inferior person refers to those lacking Dao-nature, namely those who do not believe in the Dao. This category includes individuals with worldly wisdom and sharp intellect. They possess a strong subjective consciousness, cling stubbornly to their own views, and cannot objectively analyze issues. They may use mockery to showcase their perceived intelligence or dismiss others' words as baseless and absurd. Such individuals, without a sense of humor, fall short of embodying the Dao.

As mentioned in Zhuangzi's "Free and Easy Wandering", cicadas and small birds are unaware of the aspirations of the great Peng, and those with limited knowledge cannot compare to those with greater knowledge. Similarly, as stated in the chapter on Autumn Floods, a well-frog cannot speak of the sea because it is confined to its limited perspective, a summer insect cannot speak of ice because it is bound by the constraints of its time, and those who deviate from the Dao cannot speak of the Dao because they are confined by their dogmatic beliefs. It is not that they are not taught; rather, they are genuinely incapable of being taught. This helps to avoid accumulating numerous karmic hindrances.

The person who understands the Dao is devoid of cleverness. Their thoughts are clear and tranquil, not displaying their intelligence outwardly. When interacting with others, they forget about right and wrong arguments. In the midst of worldly affairs, they remain unaffected by favor or disgrace. They appear ordinary and simple, seemingly foolish. If there is any appearance of not understanding, it is because they are truly enlightened. Their great wisdom appears as foolishness, reflecting a demeanor and actions that, when observed externally, may seem quite simple and dull.

Wisdom encompasses all, it is clarity, radiant yet not dazzling, and obscured. Obscured refers to the cultivation of ethical practices where one's radiance is not dazzling, nurturing clarity through obscurity, abandoning form and discarding intellect, yet truly understanding and enlightened. Therefore, it is said to be as if obscured.

To cultivate the formless Dao, one must focus the mind and realize the Dao by seeing one's true nature. Refining the spirit to return to emptiness, entering the Dao through the void, is the path to enlightenment. (悟道 乃是要見性. 練神還虛，還虛入道)

In spiritual practice, one must eliminate worldly wisdom, cleverness, and correct distorted views. It involves discarding delusions, discriminations, and attachments to enhance spiritual awareness. By removing worldly wisdom and cleverness, it is said that advancing on the path is akin to retreating. Those who progress on the path have a tranquil inner state, remain unaffected by external circumstances, and follow the Dao. They respond to the world with an open heart, achieving great completeness while appearing deficient to ordinary observers. Therefore, it is said that advancing on the path seems like retreating.

"夷" refers to smooth and level, while "纇" signifies roughness or unevenness. The great Dao, appearing seemingly rough and uneven, is, in fact, fundamentally smooth and easy. Laozi expresses that the Dao is inherently straightforward, but those who follow it tend to forget their roots, deviating further from the Dao, and creating obstacles that hinder their progress.

The simplest Dao requires adherence to its principles. Awakening to the Dao and recognizing one's true nature is actually quite straightforward. With wisdom, the right knowledge, and the ability to let go of delusions, discriminations, and attachments, one can return to the Dao. Ethical individuals, whose hearts align with the Dao, walk the great Dao with meticulous care in all their actions. Though it may seem rough, they move as if treading on thin ice (如履薄冰), as always emphasized in the Tai Chi practice – foot work.

The person of highest virtue has a mind like an expansive emptiness, with a capacity akin to that of the vastness of heaven and earth. Their virtue is broad and immense, resembling an empty valley that accommodates and accepts everything without resistance, and fostering them. Therefore, it is said that the highest virtue is like a valley.

"白" represents purity, inner radiance, and cleanliness. "辱" implies staining or defilement, and it also has the connotation of being disgraceful or undesirable. There is also a contrasting meaning with "black", hence the phrase "大白若辱" – "great purity resembling disgrace".

A person of great purity, resembling disgrace, focuses on inner cultivation while disregarding external appearances, allowing the essence to remain unblemished. Such an individual resides in a state of radiant self-possession, shining like a bright moon in the clear sky without a single cloud obstructing its brilliance. Despite this inner radiance, they do not discriminate between high and low, do not judge things in terms of right or wrong, and do not forcefully seek high positions when in humble circumstances. They can dwell in lower positions with ease and contentment. Therefore, it is said that great purity resembles disgrace.

An example of this concept is found in the image of Zhang Sanfeng, a renowned Daoist and Tai Chi master, legendary said he is the founder of Tai Chi Quan. He was known for his messy appearance, earning him the nickname "邋遢道人" (Luo Tuo Dao Ren), which translates to "Dirty and Smelly Daoist." Zhang Sanfeng was so absorbed in his pursuit of Dao and martial arts that he paid little attention to his attire and outward appearance. His unkempt appearance symbolizes the idea that true purity may seem disgraceful or messy to the outside world.

Imagine an individual whose nickname masks his abilities and accomplishments, portraying him as someone untidy or unkempt. How messy should he be?

Joke: In the Japanese comic/manga series "Dragon Ball", there exists a warrior character who not only boasts a formidable fighting prowess but also possesses a repugnant appearance. This warrior emanates a foul odor, exhibits dirtiness, and is characterized by an unappealing look, complete with a runny nose and muddy saliva streaming from his mouth. Remarkably, when he steps onto the stadium to compete for his medal, opponents find it impossible to defeat him or even approach him closely.

The person of extensive virtue has a heart that encompasses the vastness of heaven and earth, and their capacity is as boundless as the expansive sea. They would rather consider any inadequacy in their virtue as a personal shortcoming, even if their achievements advance daily, without boasting of progress. They refrain from self-praise and do not indulge in arrogance. They seem to lack a sense of self-satisfaction, hence it is said that extensive virtue appears insufficient.

"真" represents purity and simplicity, while "渝" signifies change and transformation. Understanding that everything in the world is inherently a manifestation of the Dao, the Dao itself remains unchanging, neither born nor extinguished. In the shadow of the Dao, all things follow the inherent principles of their own Dao, undergoing the rhythmic changes of yin and yang. Therefore, it is said that the true nature is like change, or in other words, "質真若渝". (will discuss more depth into it in next chapter)

The human heart fluctuates with the passing moments, inclining towards personal gain and adapting to prevailing trends. The heart of a sage, however, remains steadfast and pure like jade, impervious to being swayed. It can navigate the vicissitudes of the world, undergoing endless transformations, without being constrained by any fixed norms.

大方無隅" literally means "great square without corners". Here, "隅" refers to the corners or angles in a square. The phrase suggests that a sage has cultivated themselves over time, smoothing out the corners of their character, and achieving a state of roundedness or harmony. In ancient times, there was a belief in a square Earth with a circular Heaven. "大方無隅" can also be interpreted mathematically, where 72 multiplied by 5 equals 360, reflecting completeness or wholeness associated with a circle (note 6). This metaphorically conveys the idea that through continuous spiritual practice, a sage refines their own character, becoming smooth, rounded, and harmonious.

In the 1960s, practitioners of Wu Style Tai Chi, aiming to simplify teachings for the general public, mostly rich or sick individuals, who lack physical movement, **introduced the square form. This was designed to impart fundamental principles, with the hope that** as individuals became adept at the square form, they would naturally progress to refining their movements, smoothing out the corners, and embodying roundness and harmony. However, contrary to this intention, the square form evolved into a distinct system of its own, nearly overshadowing the traditional round form. (PS: we are practicing one of the earliest round forms, close to the small round form of the Yang style)

"大器晚成" has become a well-known phrase, but according to an alternative interpretation, aside from the character "免", the original expression might be " Great talent but no accomplishment" (大器無成). In this context, a person of great potential seems to have achieved nothing. This aligns with the idea expressed in the phrase Great sound is silent, great form is formless "大音无声、大象无形".

If we follow the original wording of this verse, the interpretation of "大器晚成", can be explained as follows: "器" refers to something capable of containing or holding. "大器" metaphorically represents great talent. "晚成" implies that achieving greatness is not an easy or immediate task. To complete a significant undertaking in the world, one must go through an extended and arduous process; it cannot be accomplished hastily.

The sage conceals and nurtures profound virtues, accumulating and nurturing them deeply within, awaiting the opportune moment to act. They observe the situation, act when the time is right, and seize the opportunity to manifest their principles. The cultivation of virtue becomes a tool for transforming the world for the benefit of all. Hence, the great talent matures slowly. One must first understand the clear path, progress on the path, and learn from myriad teachings to reach the common root of the ancient Dao. Only then can one walk the path, establish virtue, and attain the highest virtue of the superior person, which requires a connection spanning generation and generation to follow. It is not achieved with a single touch but is termed as a late accomplishment. Even if they don't fly, their flight would challenge the heavens; even if they don't make a sound, their sound would astonish people.

"大音希声" can be translated into English as "The grand sound is rare to hear." In common terms, the most significant sound is often paradoxically difficult to perceive.

The immense sound exceeds the capacity for hearing, surpassing the range that the ears can recognize in terms of frequency and amplitude. Therefore, it is heard but not listened to.

From a profound perspective, "大音" can be understood as the sound of no sound, and "希声" as the sound of no sound as well. The grand sound is without sound, permeating the Dharma realm. It cannot be spoken by the mouth, nor heard by the ears. It is like the celestial music described by Zhuangzi, where the celestial music is soundless but resonates according to things. "The great clump of air, its name is wind. It is simply non-active, yet when active, myriads of openings roar." It sounds like a silent quiet, but within this silence, there resonates a thunderous impact that shakes the human heart.

The profound mysteries of the Great Dao transcend language and written words. The transmission of true essence methods is through the imprint of the mind, manifested through the expression of Zen consciousness. Therefore, the Great Dao, cannot be fully articulated by the mouth, referred to as the grand sound (大音), nor comprehended by the ears, described as the rare sound (希声).

The sage imparts teachings through actions rather than words, embodying the principle of non-verbal instruction. In this way, the grand sound is soundless, and the rare sound is subtly preserved, illustrating the ineffable nature of the Great Dao.

The colossal form transcends the scope of visual perception, hence it is tangible yet formless. "大象無形" can be translated as "The great form is formless". In the context of tangible entities, anything with a physical form is inherently limited in size. Only things without a defined structure can be limitless, much like the boundless expanse of empty space. Therefore, it is expressed as "The great form is formless".

The Dao has no form, no appearance; it cannot be apprehended by the mind, nor can it be recognized. It is named as the source of all things and functions within the realm of heaven and earth. Therefore, it is said: The Dao that can be spoken of is not the eternal Dao; the name that can be named is not the eternal name. (Dao De Jing, Chapter 1)

The Tai Shang Qing Jing Jing (太上清靜經) states: The Great Dao is formless, giving birth to heaven and earth. The Great Dao is emotionless, setting in motion the sun and moon. The Great Dao is nameless, nurturing the myriad beings. The Great Dao is without sound or scent, without trace or form. It is supremely mysterious and subtle, transcending to the utmost in profundity and ethereality. It is divine and empty, concealed within heaven and earth. Heaven and earth are unaware of it. It is hidden within all things. All things are unaware of it. When sought for its form, it has no form. When pointed to by a name, the name cannot be grasped.

"善貸且成": "Benevolently lending and enabling completion". "貸" implies bestowing kindness, giving, or extending help, while "成" means to grow or complete. The phrase conveys the idea that the Dao enables all things to begin and conclude in goodness. All things, from inception to completion, are inseparable from the Dao. If one does not embark on the path of the Great Dao for cultivation, there is no path for cultivation. If one does not follow the Great Dao for nourishment, there is nowhere for nourishment. Therefore, the Great Dao, as the circular mechanism of creation, is benevolent and supportive in all aspects, facilitating and completing all endeavors.

A person skilled in letting go and relinquishing will gradually succeed in the Dao. "貸" can also mean to give or offer, while "捨" denotes letting go, releasing, abandoning, or reducing. In the practice of the Dao, what is offered or let go of are various delusive thoughts. Abandoning and letting go reduces external cravings, aversions, and attachments, diminishing them until they are nonexistent. Through this process of reduction, one can return to the Great Dao.

Note 6 - The sky undergoes 36 changes, while the earth experiences 72 changes. When the 72 changes of the earth merge with the five eternal energies—metal, water, wood (life), fire, and earth—the resulting matrix (72x5 = 360) forms a complete circle. This circle operates endlessly, running without cessation. (三十六天罡, 七十二地煞 originally applies to stars)

*** A sage poses a question to his followers: "What happens if you have ten containers but only seven lids?"

Followers: Try to find the other 3 lids and every one second and agrees

Sage: "Why not give away the most useless three containers?" ***

Note: Besides the trend of minimalist living, there is a recent lifestyle concept called "Subtraction Life", emphasizing elimination, letting go, and detachment. In recent years, there has also emerged another attitude known as "lying flat".

Therefore, the summary of this chapter suggests that starting from "The superior person hears of the Dao and diligently puts it into practice", progressing through "The clear Dao appears obscured, advancing on the Dao is like meeting with obstacles, and the common Dao is like entangled silk... The great sound is rare, the great form is formless", one can grasp the essence of the Dao in daily life and activities. Only through experiencing and understanding these principles in practical situations can one comprehend the formless and unknowable nature of the "Dao", as stated in the Diamond Sutra: "If one sees all forms as non-forms, then one sees the Tathagata (Buddha, the true nature, ultimate Divine or the Dao)".

My 5 cents

Chapter 41 of the Dao De Jing holds significant popularity, often cited and shared across various contexts and situations. Its widespread use in diverse forms of quotation underscores its profound impact. This chapter is considered particularly valuable, prompting a detailed exploration of its themes and insights.

The above literal descriptions generally explain the content of this chapter from the perspectives of mindset, behavior, or philosophy.

From the perspective of inner cultivation, there is a saying, although I may not fully agree with it. Providing examples for everyone's reference is also harmless. "上" (Upper, Prestige Scholar-Official), "中" (Middle, Average Scholar-official), and "下" (Lower, below average Scholar-official) refer to the upper, middle, and lower Dāntián, respectively. When the lower Dāntián is cultivated to a certain state, the facial expression will unconsciously take on a smiling appearance. This is often depicted in the compassionate smiles of Buddha statues. They explain that without reaching this state, one is not qualified to be considered on the path or in a state of meditation.

As for the explanations related to the upper and middle Dāntián, they are considered less meaningful and will not be elaborated upon.

As usual, Laozi employs a significant amount of contrasting terms in this passage, such as clarity and obscurity, advancement and retreat, smoothing and treading, brightness and disgrace, expansiveness and insufficiency, and so on. **The important concept of this and that; is and what.** This is a common stylistic technique used by Laozi. Additionally, in this chapter, we can also utilize an inverted reading method to grasp the essence of what Laozi wants to present.

It is important to understand that the Great Dao, despite its selflessness, is willing to share with all things. However, the Dao remains hidden. When we are in a state of meditation, we can grasp a certain form of the Great Image through internal vision and hear the subtle sound within through inner hearing. By gently and slowly merging with this energy (which will be discussed in the next chapter, 42), it is crucial to recognize that great things come to fruition gradually. One must absolutely refrain from intentionally manipulating with the mind, in order to grind away the edges and corners and disrupt its gentle and harmonious nature.

Maintaining an unwavering inner tranquility, one can grasp the ever-changing inner messages (termed "messages" in Daoist language), discover the true essence of the Dao (or substance), understand one's own deficiencies, and utilize the energy of sound and image, or qi, to fill the gaps within oneself. This process untangles the shackles of life and spirituality.

Is the path of the Dao smooth? It can be both flat and filled with obstacles, seemingly smooth and soft, yet within this smoothness, there are hidden entanglements. Because it is necessary to unravel these entanglements on the path of the Dao, appearing to move backward is, in fact, a form of progress.

Once untangled, one can progress to another stage. It is essential to understand the principle of "knowing white, holding onto black", patiently awaiting the true illumination from the silence and darkness, expanding one's consciousness (the sea of awareness, or spiritual consciousness).

When ordinary beginners receive the inner messages of the Dao, they often become ecstatic and wish to share with others, hence laughing heartily.

More seasoned practitioners, having too many msg 😊, may become accustomed to or understand the boundless transformations of these messages, and may neither hold onto them nor let them go, as they recognize the transient nature of such experiences.

The superior individuals, having traversed the stages from the lower to the middle, can face any situation without being swayed by external influences, diligently adhering to the path of practicing without being disturbed.

Extract from He Shang Gong – De Jing - Similarities and Differences

The superior man hears the Dao and diligently follows it. The superior man hears the Dao and, with self-discipline and unceasing effort, follows it. The middle individual hears the Dao, sometimes retaining it and sometimes losing it. The middle individual hears the Dao, preserving his own life to endure, governing the state for peace. He embraces it joyfully, but then is tempted by wealth, beauty, and honor. Confused by desires, he again loses it.

The inferior man hears the Dao and laughs heartily. The inferior man, driven by greed, cruelty, and excessive desires, perceives the Dao as soft and weak, deeming it fearful. Seeing the Dao as simple and unadorned, he regards it as plain and ugly, hence his hearty laughter. Laughter is essential to the inferior man. If the Dao does not make him laugh, it is not worthy of being called the Dao. If it is not something the inferior man ridicules, it cannot be considered the Dao.

Therefore, it is said in a proverb: "To establish is to set up". Establishing words to convey the Dao should be like the following sentences: "Clear is the Dao, yet seemingly obscure". Those who understand the Dao are as if in darkness, seemingly blind and unaware. "Advancing on the Dao is like retreating". Those who strive for the Dao seem to be falling behind. "The plain Dao seems tangled". The great person of the Dao does not distinguish themselves, appearing like many others. "High virtue is like a valley". Those with high virtue resemble deep valleys, not ashamed of impurity and turbidity. "Great whiteness appears stained". Those who possess great purity may seem tainted but do not flaunt themselves. "Broad virtue seems insufficient". Those with broad and abundant virtue may appear foolish and inadequate. "Established virtue seems stolen". Those who establish and promote virtue may seem easily taken advantage of, allowing emptiness.

"Sincere simplicity appears changeable". Those who are simple and sincere may seem to lack clarity and understanding. "Great square has no corners". The person of great virtue and integrity has no crooked or deceptive corners. "Great vessel takes time to finish". The person of great capacity is like a precious vessel or gem, not easily completed. "Great sound is barely heard". The grand sound, like thunder, awaits its time to move, illustrating the need for patience in speaking. "Great form has no shape". The person of great principles and laws is unadorned and formless, yet substantial. "The Dao conceals and has no name". The Dao remains hidden, allowing no specific identification. Truly, the Dao is virtuous and lends itself to fulfillment.

As for fulfillment, it comes naturally. "Fulfillment is to arrive". Speaking of the Dao, it is like lending essence and energy to people, bringing about their completion and accomplishment.

老子河上公章句 -> 德經 -> 同異

上士聞道，勤而行之。上士聞道，自勤苦竭力而行之。中士聞道，若存若亡。中士聞道，治身以長存，治國以太平，欣然而存之，退見財色榮譽，惑於情欲，而復亡之也。下士聞道，大笑之。下士貪狠多欲，見道柔弱，謂之恐懼，見道質樸，謂之鄙陋，故大笑之。不笑不足以為道。不為下士所笑，不足以名為道。故建言有之：建，設也。設言以有道，當如下句。明道若昧，明道之人，若闇昧無所見。進道若退，進取道者，若退不及。夷道若纇。夷，平也。大道之人不自別殊，若多比類也。上德若谷，上德之人若深谷，不恥垢濁也。大白若辱，大潔白之人若汙辱，不自彰顯。廣德若不足，德行廣大之人，若愚頑不足也。建德若偷，建設道德之人，若可偷引使空虛也。質真若渝，質樸之人，若五色有渝淺不明也。大方無隅，大方正之人，無委屈廉隅。大器晚成，大器之人，若九鼎瑚璉，不可卒成也。大音希聲，大音猶雷霆待時而動，喻當愛氣希言也。大象無形，大法象之人，質樸無形容。道隱無名。道潛隱，使人無能指名也。夫惟道，善貸且成。成，就也。言道善稟貸人精氣，且成就之也。

【第四十二章】 Chapter 42

Most Common Translation

道生一，	The Dao gives birth to one,
	Dao projects its image as Oneness (Unity),
一生二，	Unity begets duality (Two),
二生三，	Two begets trinity (Three),
三生萬物。	And from the trinity springs forth the myriad of things and entities.
萬物負陰而抱陽，	All things carry yin yet embrace yang, (note 1)
沖氣以為和。	Harmony is attained through the merging of energies. (note 2)
人之所惡，	What people dislike,
唯孤、寡、不谷，	Are only orphan (loneliness), widowed, and lack of resources. (note 3)
而王公以為稱。	Yet, this is how kings describe themselves.
故物或損之而益，	Therefore, a loss may lead to gain, (note 4)
或益之而損。	Or gain may lead to loss.
人之所教，	What others teach,
我亦教之：	I also teach:
強梁者不得其死，	Those rigid and strong do not meet a good end. (note 5)
吾將以為教父.	I will take this as my mentor.

Note 1 - Take flowers for example: they originate from seeds buried in the ground. Before they sprout, they remain hidden in the soil's darkness (Yin), drawing nourishment from the earth. When touched by sunlight (Yang), they begin to grow, reaching toward the sun's energy while still benefiting from their roots. This cycle continues until their life comes to an end, at which point they return to the soil.

Also refer to chapter 28: know the white (bright), and Guard to the black (dark), and become the world's model (formula). Utilizing the Hé tú (River Map) diagram to illustrate this verse would make understanding easier, though it would also introduce additional topics for discussion.

Note 2 - 沖氣 (Chōng qì), has two interpretations. Firstly, it refers to the true qi generated by the harmonization and interaction of yin and yang energies.

The second is, during the practice of qigong, the congenital true qi (pre-heavenly true qi) arises before OR after the harmonization of yin and yang energies.

- The congenital true qi that arises before involves this innate energy clearing or harmonizing out the Yin-Yang duality.
- And the congenital true qi that arises after the harmonizing of the Yin-Yang energies.

This process illustrates a hierarchical distinction between superior and inferior achievements.

PS: 沖氣 Chōng qì, 沖: Originating from water, it carries meaning includes surging upwards, deep, empty, humble, and central.

Note 3 - The title "寡人" (guǎ rén) was used by monarchs before Qin Shi Huang, commonly during the Spring and Autumn period and the Warring States period. Subsequently, emperors typically referred to themselves as "朕" (zhèn). "寡人" and "孤" then became common self-references among feudal lords. "寡人" implies a person of limited virtue, often interpreted as a display of humility. It may also suggest the feeling of being isolated at the summit of power, experiencing the chill of loneliness, hence the self-reference. "孤" and "不穀" carry similar connotations of modesty. (Please also refer to Chapter 39, note 2)

Joke: The ancient Emperors in China called themselves 寡人, Despite the official explanation of humility, it's worth noting that the most common interpretation of "寡人" (guǎ rén) is someone who has lost their spouse. This implies that even though emperors had numerous wives in their palaces, they still considered themselves carrying an MBA degree (title) "married but available". 😊

Note 4 - This is pointing to verse 6 of this chapter – Harmony is attained through the merging of energies. It involves the blending of qi to achieve the harmony of both Yin and Yang, similar as the S shape within the commonly known Tai Chi/Ji Diagram.

Note 5 - This phase is from the inscription on the Zhou bronze vessel (周金人銘), The inscription on the Zhou bronze vessel is one of the most famous admonitory inscriptions before the Zhou dynasty. Based on the form of the Jin Ren Ming (Inscription of the Golden Man), it is likely one of the earliest forms of maxims.

Another explanation of this verse is: The spirit of those who strive to cultivate talents and pillars of society is immortal. (The translation is not based on the inscription on the Zhou bronze vessel; it is translated purely based on its wording.)

Some common literal translations and interpretations for reference:

Simplified Literal Translation:

The Dao manifests in the universe as unity, which then differentiates into duality. Further differentiation into Trinity, and forms various groups, and these groups, due to the independent interactions of individuals, give rise to specific existences. Each specific existence retains its tangible blessings through its inherent virtues, yet they harmonize with the Dao. What people detest the most are the weak, helpless, and arrogant, yet kings and nobles use these terms to refer to themselves. Therefore, for various specific existences, sometimes gain is achieved through loss, and sometimes loss is incurred through gain. I take heed of others' teachings: those who forcefully dominate never meet a good end, and I will take this as a lesson.

Wang Bi's "Commentary on the Dao De Jing"

Wang Bi (王弼) 226 AD, - 249 AD (age 23 years)

All things and forms return to unity. How is unity achieved? It is achieved through nothingness. From nothingness arises unity, and unity can be called nothingness. Once called unity, can there be no words? With words comes unity, how can there not be duality? With unity and duality, the trinity emerges. From the existence within nothingness, all numbers come to their limit, but beyond this is not the flow of the Dao. Hence, although myriad things are diverse, they merge into unity through blended breaths. Despite the different minds of the people and the diverse customs of foreign lands, those who attain unity are rulers and lords. With unity as the master, how can it be discarded? The more you strive, the further you are from it. Reduce and approach it, reduce it to its utmost limit, and you will reach its ultimate. Even when called unity, it still extends to three. If unity itself is not truly one, how can the Dao be approached? To reduce and benefit from it, is this not mere rhetoric?

It is not that I forcibly compel others to follow, but rather I adhere to nature, uphold its ultimate principle. Following it leads to auspiciousness, while opposing it leads to misfortune. Therefore, when people instruct one another, going against it leads to self-inflicted misfortune, just as when I advise others not to oppose it.

The mighty and powerful inevitably do not meet a good end. When people instruct others to be mighty and powerful, it must be just as I instruct people not to be mighty and powerful. Is it by holding up the example of the mighty and powerful not meeting a good end that one teaches? If it is said that following my teachings leads to auspiciousness, then those who oppose these teachings, fittingly, can serve as examples to instruct others.

王弼《道德經注》

道生一，一生二，二生三，三生萬物。萬物負陰而抱陽，沖氣以為和。人之所惡，唯孤寡不谷、而王公以為稱。故物或損之而益，或益之而損。

萬物萬形，其歸一也。何由致一？由於無也。由無乃一，一可謂無。已謂之一，豈得無言乎？有言有一，非二如何？有一有二，遂生乎三。從無之有，數盡乎斯，過此以往，非道之流。故萬物之生，吾知其主，雖有萬形，沖氣一焉。百姓有心，異國殊風，而得一者，王侯主焉。以一為主，一何可舍？愈多愈遠，損則近之，損之至盡，乃得其極。既謂之一，猶乃至三，況本不一，而道可近乎？損之而益，豈虛言也。

人之所教，我亦教之，我之非強使人從之也，而用夫自然，舉其至理，順之必吉，違之必凶。故人相教，違之必自取其凶也，亦如我之教人勿違之也。

強梁者不得其死。吾將以為教父。強梁則必不得其死。人相教為強梁，則必如我之教人不當為強梁也。舉其強梁不得其死以教耶？若雲順吾教之鈴吉也，故得其違教之徒，適可以為教父也。

Su Zhe's "Interpretation of Laozi":

(Su Zhe (苏辙) （1039 March — 1112 Oct）- Scholar

"The Dao is neither one nor two, and it coincides with things, yet the Dao is one while things are not one. Therefore, it is named as one, but the Dao is not singular. One combined with one makes two, and two combined with one makes three. This process continues, and thus the myriad things are born. Although there are countless differences among them, none fail to carry yin and embrace yang. Those who blend their breaths to achieve harmony conform to the natural order of things, as things are born from three and three from one. Such is the natural law.

People in the world do not understand the origins of all things. They all esteem the multitude and belittle the singular and small. However, those of high status, such as kings and nobles, often refer to themselves as lonely, lacking, and unfulfilled. The wise ones of antiquity already understood this.

In the world, people consider softness and weakness as detrimental, and strength and rigidity as beneficial, but they do not understand the truth. Therefore, I will teach all educators of the world with this lesson: Have they not seen how those who are strong and rigid do not meet a good end? The extreme of strength and rigidity is folly. When people realize that those who are strong and rigid cannot escape death, they will understand the folly of it. Only then can we discuss the Dao. Therefore, I will use this as my guiding principle.

苏辙《老子解》

道生一，一生二，二生三，三生萬物。萬物負陰而抱陽，沖氣以為和。夫道非一非二，及其與物為偶，道一而物不一，故以一名道，然而道則非一也。一與一為二，二與一為三，自是以往，而萬物生。雖有萬不同，而莫不負陰抱陽，沖氣以為和者，蓋物生於三，而三生於一，理之自然也。

人之所惡，惟孤寡不穀，而王公以為稱。世之人不知萬物之所自生，莫不賤寡小而貴眾大。然王公之尊，而自稱孤寡不穀，古之達者，蓋已知之矣。物或損之而益，或益之而損。人之所教，亦我義教之。強梁者，不得其死。吾將以為教父。

世以柔弱為損，強梁為益，不知其非也。故將使天下之教者，皆以此教之日：不見強梁者之不得其死乎？強梁，妄之極也。人知強梁之不免於死，則知妄之不可為；知妄之不可為，而後可與語道矣。故曰吾將以為教父。

My 5 Cents

The Dao is formless, neither born nor extinguished. It emerges from boundless chaos into the realm of form, embodying Wújí as Oneness. (See Wuji Diagram)

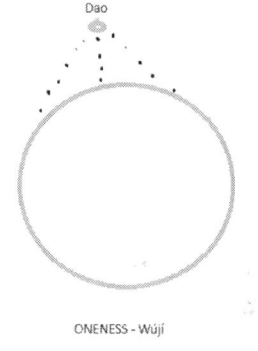

ONENESS - Wújí

Wújí (Oneness) is a mass of chaotic energy, where yin and yang are undifferentiated. The energy forms interact, giving rise to each other in a cycle of creation and destruction. Gradually, primordial true energy emerges, separating yin and yang. Once yin and yang are distinguished, they form TWO and THREE. Laozi pauses the phase as one, two, three, describing them slowly for convenience. In reality, from the emergence of primordial true energy, the distinction between yin and yang forms TWO and THREE. Primordial true energy constitutes the THREE. (See Diagram). All of them form Trinity.

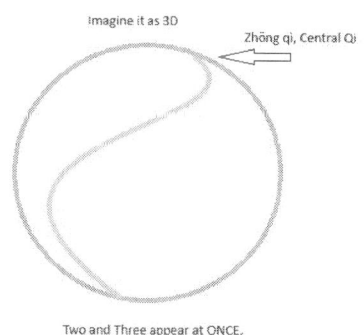

Two and Three appear at ONCE,
Once, Zhong Qi settles in between

Yet, at this stage, it remains in a state of Qi. The primordial true energy roams within the two energies (YIN and YANG), which, in accordance with their innate attributes, give birth to the elemental of 5 eternal energies. The interactions between the 5 eternal energies and primordial true energy gradually form all things in the world, allowing them to take visible forms. The process of transitioning from a Qi state to a material state can also be referenced in my annotations in TCHYD.

With the same token, when we engage in the cultivation of Qi practices and approach a state akin to Wújí, the Chaos (boundlessness), our innate true energy also surges forth. The interaction between this primordial true energy and the 5 eternal energies within our bodies gives rise to various effects or achievements. The attainment of the Golden elixir or cultivation of the spirit depends on the method of practice and the alchemical processes involved. I won't delve into details here. (Refer to the 5 kitchens scripture for more information).

Harmonizing Qi is about softness, smoothness, harmony, and non-contention. The central meridian is the king. The Yellow Court represents Earth and abundance/valley (in line with the content described in this chapter).

Some lineages read the beginning few verses of this chapter as:

Version 1

Dao gives birth to One One,	道生一一
Gives birth to Two Two,	生二二
Gives birth to Three Three,	生三三
Gives birth to a myriad of things.	生萬物

In this context, it aligns more closely with the principles of the I Ching and Bagua.

Version 2

Oneness, represented by Tàiyī (太一), when it divides into two, it signifies the emergence of time and space. The number three embodies our universe within this framework of time and space, symbolizing creation itself, where myriad beings reside. This perspective resonates closely with Western philosophical ideas.

Version 3

The doctrine of Overflow.

This viewpoint is similar to the Western philosopher Plotinus' (205-270 AD) Doctrine of Emanation. From the absolute energy of the divine, there is an overflow. With each layer of overflow, the divine characteristics diminish slightly. Looking at the creation story in the Bible, Genesis, from this perspective—God starting from darkness, water, then light, the earth, and all things—this can also be seen as the overflow of divine energy, with humans being the final creation. 😊

However, the concept of overflow gives rise to different interpretations of the Trinity. The first type of interpretation consists of intellectual capacity, soul, and the material world. The second type consists of the Oneness, intellect, and soul. The latter aligns well with the concept of Gnosticism as well.

And there are some more, which I think are irrelevant.

Epilogue: Regarding the Five Elements (The five eternal energies): Metal, Water, Wood, Fire, Earth, and the Four Great Elements: Earth, Water, Fire, and Wind. Where merging them, Earth (Earth), Water (Water), Fire (Fire), Wind (Metal). The vibration of Metal represents Wind (lung by other means).

The difference between the Four Great Elements and the Five Elements lies in Wood. (the fuel, we have discussed this before). Therefore, here Wood represents the innate vital energy (primordial true energy), also known as the source of life, or vitality.

Extract from He Sang Gong – De Jing – The transformation and manifestation of the Dao

The Dao gives birth to unity; it makes the One. The One gives birth to duality; it gives birth to Yin and Yang. Duality gives birth to trinity; Yin and Yang produce the harmonious, clear, and turbid three Qi, dividing into heaven, earth, and humanity. The trinity gives birth to all things. Heaven, earth, and humanity collectively give birth to all things; heaven bestows, earth nurtures, and humanity fosters them. All things carry Yin and embrace Yang; there is nothing that does not carry Yin and turn towards Yang, returning to the sun with a reverting heart. Blending their breaths to achieve harmony, all things contain primordial Qi, attaining softness and flexibility. It's like having a repository in the chest, marrow in the bones, and emptiness and Qi circulation in plants and trees, thus enabling longevity.

What people detest are only solitude, scarcity, and unfulfillment, yet kings and nobles consider them worthy. "Solitude, scarcity, and unfulfillment" are ominous names, yet kings and nobles use them as titles, symbolizing humility, emptiness, softness, and flexibility. Therefore, sometimes loss results in gain, pulling cannot acquire, pushing will naturally return. Or sometimes gain leads to loss. Those who seek to rise higher will fall, those who covet wealth will bring about calamity. People's teachings, referring to the teachings of the masses, advocate for the strong to overpower the weak, and for the hard to overcome the soft. I also teach. When I say I teach the masses, it is to encourage them to let go of strength and embrace weakness, to let go of softness and embrace hardness. Those who are forceful and overbearing do not meet a good end. "Forceful and overbearing" refers to those who do not believe in the subtle mysteries, who betray morality and do not follow the teachings, but instead rely on power and might. "Not meeting a good end" means being rejected by fate, struck by weapons, executed by royal law, unable to die a natural death. I will take this as my guiding principle. "Father" means one who guides. Laozi takes forceful and overbearing people as a lesson and a beginning of instruction.

老子河上公章句 -> 德經 -> 道化

道生一，道使所生者一也。一生二，一生陰與陽也。二生三，陰陽生和、清、濁三氣，分為天地人也。三生萬物。天地人共生萬物也，天施地化，人長養之也。萬物負陰而抱陽，萬物無不負陰而向陽，迴心而就日。沖氣以為和。萬物中皆有元氣，得以和柔，若胸中有藏，骨中有髓，草木中有空虛與氣通，故得久生也。人之所惡，惟孤、寡、不穀，而王公以為稱。孤寡不穀者，不祥之名，而王公以為稱者，處謙卑，法空虛和柔。故物或損之而益，引之不得，推之必還。或益之而損。夫增高者志崩，貪富者致患。人之所教，謂眾人所教，去弱為強，去柔為剛。我亦教之。言我教眾人，使去強為弱，去柔為剛。強梁者不得其死，強梁者，謂不信玄妙，背叛道德，不從經教，尚勢任力也。不得其死者，為天命所絕，兵刃所伐，王法所殺，不得以壽命死。吾將以為教父。父，使也。老子以強梁之人為教，誡之始也。

【第四十三章】Chapter 43

Most Common Translation

天下之至柔，	The supremely flexible (softness) conquers the supremely rigid.
馳騁天下之至堅，	Riding swiftly across the utmost hardness of the world,
無有入無間，	encountering no barriers.
	"Utilizing the space (nothingness) entering where there is no entering and no space to enter". (note 1)
吾是以知無為之有益。	Hence, I know the benefit of Wúwéi.
不言之教，	The teaching without words,
無為之益，	The benefit of Wúwéi,
天下希及之。	Few in the world can attain it.

Most Common Literal Translation

The person with the gentlest and kindest heart in the world can gallop through the strongest of wills.

Invisible energy freely moves in an unseen space-time.

From here, I perceive the benefits of the realm of Wúwéi.

This silent teaching ability, the benefits of the realm of Wúwéi, are difficult to widely spread throughout the world!

Note 1 - Just like water can pass through tightly packed sand or any crack without spilling. (PS: It is our nightmare to live under a wooden house with water leaks, where we do not know where it comes from ☹)

From He Sang Gong: The most yielding is water. The most firm is gold and stone. Water can penetrate the firm and enter the solid; there is nothing it cannot reach. There is no gap it cannot enter."

【第四十四章】Chapter 44

Most Common Translation

名與身孰親？	Which is closer (intimate), name or body?
身與貨孰多？	Which is more abundant, body or wealth?
得與亡孰病？	Which is worse (sickness), gain or loss?
是故甚愛必大費，	Therefore, excessive love (desires) leads to great expense. (note 1)
多藏必厚亡。	Hoarding leads to heavy loss.
知足不辱，	Being content prevents disgrace,
知止不殆，	Knowing when to stop avoids danger,
可以長久。	Thus, one can endure for a long time.

Note 1 - Let us see how Buddhism sees Love and Compassion, they share the same underlying meaning:

Love (in Pali and Sanskrit: तृष्णा (Taṇhā, tṛṣṇā, trishna)), also translated as desire, craving, affection, greed, or thirst, among others, literally means thirst. It is one of the Dvādaśanga pratītyasamutpāda; the twelve nidānas; (or simply the twelve causality) (note 2). Because of experiencing certain feelings (receiving), a need arises towards external conditions and the thought of not giving up, hoping to obtain (take). This is a fundamental impulse that all sentient beings experience.

Love can be generally classified into tainted love and untainted love. Tainted love is characterized by greed, while untainted love is characterized by faith.

Within our Desire Realm, love can also be broadly categorized as love with desire (note 3), love with attachment (note 4), and love without attachment (note 5). (Desire realm: The desire realm consists of six realms: Deva, asuras, humans, animals, hungry ghosts, and hell beings.)

As for compassion, I have already explained it in detail in this group. You can refer to the previous records.

Note 2 - The twelve nidanas; (or simply the twelve causality) (Sanskrit and Pali: निदान Nidāna) is one of the fundamental theories in Buddhism, which the Buddha attained through his own enlightenment. The twelve nidanas are as follows:

Fundamental ignorance (Pali: avidya)	無明
Formation (sankhara)	行
Consciousness (vinnana)	識
Name and form (namarupa)	名色
Sense faculties (salayatana)	六入
Contact (phassa)	觸
Feeling or sensation (vedana)	受
Craving, Love or thirst (tanha)	愛
Clinging or grasping (upadana)	取
Becoming, having or worldly existence (bhava)	有
Birth or becoming (jati)	生
Old age and death (jaramarana)	老死

They are all conditioned phenomena, subject to impermanence, and interconnected through the principle of "this arising, that arises; this ceasing, that ceases." The causal sequence of the Twelve causalities continues without interruption, leading beings to cyclic existence in the ocean of birth and death, without liberation.

Note 3 - Love with Desire (Desire Love)

Desire love (in Pali: kāma-taṇhā) is the love and attachment arising from sensual pleasure (kāma), which pertains to the enjoyment derived from the senses (five Skandha) and the happiness they bring. This belongs to the realm of desire.

Note 4 - Love with attachment refers to the common attachment established through dependence on worldly conditions.

Note 5 - Love without attachment refers to the attachment established through dependence on the cessation of worldly conditions.

My 5 Cents

The longing for love, whether seeking to give or receive it, naturally entails an expectation of mutual affection. When this expectation goes unfulfilled, it often results in disappointment. If this cycle persists, it can lead to profound distress. – Thirst of drinking water.

Likewise, the craving for worldly ambitions such as social status, wealth, success in diverse fields, or even accomplishments in art, sport, or spirituality, follows a comparable trajectory. It echoes the cycle of the 12-causality links, becoming a continuous loop that is challenging to break free from until genuine enlightenment is attained.

In the Disney movie "101 Dalmatians", the romantic couple initially has only one or two dogs (I don't remember exactly). They shower their beloved pet(s) with love, care, and attention, tending to every detail. This exemplifies the essence of love. A one-to-one kind of love.

By the end of the movie, they find themselves with 101 dogs. While it becomes challenging to provide individual attention to each dog as they did with just one or two, they still manage to ensure that all the dogs are treated well. Despite the constraints of time and resources, they extend their care to every single one of them. Does it also love?

The dogs are the same, the main character couples are the same, and the love behind them is the same. What has changed?

If you have over 1000 pearl hens, it will be akin to the scenario depicted in the video I just shared. But what about having 10,000? How does God treat us amidst such abundance? Could we not argue that this does not represent love?

Caring everything without caring........(refer to chapter 5 of DDJ)

【第四十五章】Chapter 45

Most Common Translation

大成若缺，	The utmost excellence appears flawed,
其用不弊。	Yet its utility knows no bounds.
大盈若沖，	The highest abundance seems vacant,
其用不窮。	Yet its utility knows no limits.
大直若屈，	The utmost directness seems indirect,
大巧若拙，	The utmost skill appears inept,
大辯若訥。	The utmost eloquence sounds hesitant.
靜勝躁，寒勝熱。(note 1)	Calmness triumphs over agitation, Coolness triumphs over heat.
清靜為天下正。	Pure tranquility is the essence of the world.

Note 1 - The common version of this verse in this chapter is: 躁勝寒, 靜勝熱, which means:

Agitation triumphs over coolness, while calmness triumphs over heat. Where, if translated literally, it means Movement can conquer coldness, and tranquility can conquer heat. He Sang Gong used the common version.

Extract From He Sang Gong – De Jing – Hong De

"Great accomplishment is like deficiency; it refers to the ruler who achieves great moral integrity. 'Like deficiency' means to extinguish fame and conceal reputation, as if to `eradicate deficiencies and be unprepared. If one's conduct is not impaired, if one's mind in using it is such, then there will be no exhaustion in due time.

"Great fullness is like emptiness; it refers to the ruler who achieves great fulfillment of virtue. 'Like emptiness' means to esteem without daring to be arrogant, to be wealthy without daring to be extravagant. His use is inexhaustible. If his mind in using it is such, then there will be no exhaustion in due time.

"Great rectitude is like bending; 'great rectitude' means to cultivate the Way and observe laws with upright integrity as one. 'Like bending' means not contending with ordinary people, as if one can bend and yield.

"Great skill is like clumsiness; 'great skill' means having many talents and skills. 'Like clumsiness' means not daring to show one's ability.

"Great eloquence is like taciturnity; 'great eloquence' means having unquestionable intelligence. 'Like taciturnity' means having a mouth without recklessness. 'Victory' means extreme. In spring and summer, the positive energy is fervent above, and all things thrive and grow; when reaching extremes, it turns cold, and when it's cold, things wither and die. Thus, people's speech should not be excessively fervent.

"Stillness triumphs over heat; in autumn and winter, all things are quiet below the earth, and when reaching extremes, it turns hot. Heat is the source of life. Clarity and stillness can rectify the world. If one can maintain clarity and stillness, then one will be the leader of the world. By keeping oneself upright, there will be no end to the time."

老子河上公章句 -> 德經 -> 洪德

大成若缺，謂道德大成之君也。若缺者，滅名藏譽，如毀缺不備也。其用不弊，其用心如是，則無敝盡時也。大盈若沖，謂道德大盈滿之君也。若沖者，貴不敢驕也，富不敢奢也。其用不窮。其用心如是，則無窮盡時也。大直若屈，大直，謂修道法度正直如一也。若屈者，不與俗人爭，若可屈折。大巧若拙，大巧謂多才術也。若拙者，亦不敢見其能。大辯若訥。大辯者，智無疑。若訥者，口無辟躁勝寒，勝，極也。春夏陽氣躁疾於上，萬物盛大，極則寒，寒則零落死亡也。言人不當剛躁也。靜勝熱，秋冬萬物靜於黃泉之下，極則熱，熱者生之源。清靜能為天下正。能清靜則為天下之長，持身正則無終已時也。

【第四十六章】 Chapter 46

Most Common Translation

天下有道，	When the world follows Dao,
卻走馬以糞；	Racing Horse works on a farm. (note 1)
天下無道，	When the world does not follow the Dao,
戎馬生於郊。	Battle Horse was born in the field.
禍莫大於不知足，	No calamity is greater than not knowing contentment,
咎莫大於欲得，	No fault is greater than wanting to possess.
故知足之足，	Therefore, the sufficiency of contentment is enough,
常足矣。	Always sufficient.

Note 1

The original wording of this verse is: racing horse haul manure. Which means using racing horse manure as farming, when there is no war.

Common Literal Translation:

If the operation of a country follows the Dao, it allows even warhorses to be returned to the fields for farming, if the operation of a country contrary to the Dao forces warhorses to produce only in the harsh environment of the battlefield. There is no greater calamity than not knowing self-satisfaction and no greater sin than persistent greed. Therefore, the wealth of understanding self-satisfaction is an enduring wealth.

【第四十七章】Chapter 47

Most Common Translation

不出戶，	Not going out,
知天下；	Know the world.
不窺牖，	Not peeping out the window, (note 1)
見天道。	Seeing the Way of Heaven.
其出彌遠，	The further one goes out,
其知彌少。	The less one knows.
是以聖人不行而知，	Therefore, the sage knows without traveling,
不見而名，	Names things without seeing them, (note 2)
不為而成。	Completes with Wúwéi. (note 3)

Note 1 - 窺牖：窺" translates to "peep" or "peek", referring to looking through a **small hole** or crevice. "牖" translates to "window", specifically referring to a window opening or aperture.

"窺" - Peep or Peek   "牖" - Window

Note 2 - Name, please refer to DDJ 1.

Some scholars suggest that instead of saying "names without seeing", it could be understood as "understanding without seeing". Because 名就明 sounds the same or similar in Chinese)

Note 3 - The common version of this verse is 不為而成, which literally means completed with doing nothing. While some version suggests that it should be 無為而成, which literally means completed with Wúwéi. I chose the latter one in translation and kept the common one in the Original Chinese.

Wang Bi's (226 – 249AD) "Commentary on the Dao De Jing":

Without leaving the house, one can understand the world; Without peering out the window, one can see the way of heaven.

Things have their roots and branches, and affairs have their masters. Although paths may differ, they all lead to the same destination. Although there are countless considerations, they all lead to the same conclusion. The Dao has its great constant, and principles have their great simplicity. By holding onto the ways of antiquity, one can control the present. Even though one dwells in the present, one can understand the origins of antiquity. Therefore, without leaving the house or peering out the window, one can still have knowledge.

The further one goes out, the less one knows. Seeking unity in multiplicity is futile. The Dao, when looked at, cannot be seen; when listened to, cannot be heard; when grasped, cannot be obtained. Yet if one knows it, there is no need to leave the house. If one does not know it, the more one ventures out, the more lost one becomes.

Therefore, the sage does not need to travel to understand, does not need to see to name. By understanding the essence of things, even without traveling, one can still have knowledge. By recognizing the origins of things, even without seeing, one can still grasp the principles of right and wrong and give them names.

Things come into being without being made. They follow their natural course. Therefore, even without doing anything, they are brought to completion.

王弼《道德經注》

不出戶，知天下；不窺牖，見天道。

事有宗而物有主，途雖殊而同歸也，慮雖百而其致一也。道有大常，理有大致，執古之道，可以御今。雖處於今，可以知古始，故不出戶窺牖而可知也。

其出彌遠，其知彌少。無在於一，而求之於眾也。道視之不可見，聽之不可聞，搏之不可得，如其知之，不須出戶。若其不知，出愈遠愈迷也。

是以聖人不行而知，不見而名，得物之致，故雖不行，而慮可知也。識物之宗，故雖不見，而是非之理可得而名也。

不為而成。明物之性，因之而已。故雖不為，而使之成矣。

Su Zhe's (1039-1112) "Interpretation of the Dao De Jing":

Without leaving the house, one can understand the world; Without peering out the window, one can see the way of heaven. The further one goes out, the less one knows.

The essence of nature pervades the universe, without distinction of far or near, ancient or modern. The reason why the sages of ancient times could know everything without leaving their houses or peering out their windows was simply because their nature was complete. People in the world are obscured by external things, their nature is scattered by what they see and hear, internally troubled by the complexities of body and mind, externally hindered by the barriers of mountains and rivers. Unable to see beyond what is immediately visible, unable to hear beyond what is immediately audible, the subtle barriers of doors and windows can blind and cut off perception. Not knowing that the sages return to their nature is sufficient, they desire to go out and seek it, hence the further they go, the less they know.

Therefore, the sage does not need to travel to understand, does not need to see to name, does not need to act to accomplish. The reach of one's nature is not limited to merely knowing and naming; it can naturally achieve without effort by following the natural course of things.

蘇轍《老子解》

不出戶，知天下；不窺牖，見天道。其出彌遠，其知彌少。

性之為體，充遍宇宙，無遠近古今之異。古之聖人，其所以不出戶牖而無所不知者，特其性全故耳。世之人為物所蔽，性分於耳目，內為身心之所紛亂，外為山河之所障塞，見不出視，聞不出聽，戶牖之微，能蔽而絕之，不知聖人復性而足，乃欲出而求之，是以彌遠而彌少也。

是以聖人不行而知，不見而名，不為而成。

性之所及，非特能知能名而已，蓋可以因物之自然，不勞而成之矣。

My 5 Cents

When you walk through a maze (labyrinth), no matter how hard you try, you can't see the whole picture. You need to look at it from above, like a bird (the bird's eye view), to see everything clearly, including the exit. From the angle above, you SEE, without a need to move. The higher you are above, the more you see. Think about how you see our Mother Earth from space. However, when you walk inside the maze, you move but can not see.

Similarly, in life, we often see things without really understanding them because of our feelings and perceptions. Over the years, through schooling and society, we've been taught how to perceive things. Our beliefs and values are ingrained in us.

We know what we should know without knowing the process or how it is processed, hence, we know the name. (what is the name, refer to DDJ 1)

We do not seek what we do not need to know.

We do not travel where we do not need to go.

That is Wúwéi

PS: If you guys want me to discuss the idea of NAME in more detail, let me know.

Extract from He Sang Gong – De Jing – Observing the Far

Without going out the door, one can know the world. The sage does not go out but knows the world; he sees the body to know the body, sees the family to know the family. This is how he perceives the world. Without peering out the window, one can understand the way of heaven. The way of heaven is the same as the way of man; heaven and man communicate, and their vital energies penetrate each other. When the ruler is pure, the qi of heaven is naturally correct; when the ruler has many desires, the qi of heaven becomes turbulent and murky. Fortune and misfortune, benefit and harm, all arise from oneself. The farther one goes, the less one knows. It means that by leaving one's home and observing other homes, or leaving one's own body and observing other bodies, one's observations become broader but one's insights become narrower. Therefore, the sage does not travel yet knows, does not rise to heaven nor plunge into the depths, but can know the world by knowing himself. Without seeing, he names; he prefers the Way above and virtue below. The sage starts with the small to know the great, observes the inner to understand the outer. He achieves without acting; if those above have nothing to do, those below will also be free from tasks. When the family has enough, all things will naturally come to fruition.

Remarks: those qi practitioners believe we, our body, are a smaller universe of all.

老子河上公章句 - 德經 - 鑒遠

不出戶知天下，聖人不出戶以知天下者，以己身知人身，以己家知人家，所以見天下也。不窺牖見天道，天道與人道同，天人相通，精氣相貫。人君清淨，天氣自正，人君多欲，天氣煩濁。吉凶利害，皆由於己。其出彌遠，其知彌少。謂去其家觀人家，去其身觀人身，所觀益遠，所見益少也。是以聖人不行而知，聖人不上天，不入淵，能知天下者，以心知之也。不見而名，上好道，下好德；上好武，下好力。聖人原小知大，察內知外。不為而成。上無所為，則下無事，家給人足，萬物自化就也。

【第四十八章】Chapter 48

Most Common Translation

為學日益，	Those who seek knowledge, learn, and take.
為道日損。	Those who seek the Dao, let go.
損之又損，	Let go and let go, (note 1)
以至於無為，	Until Wúwéi,
無為而無不為。	Wúwéi and nothing is left undone.
	Wúwéi and nothing can not be done.
取天下常以無事，	To rule the world effectively, one should often act without interference,
及其有事，	When there are matters to attend to, (note 2)
不足以取天下。	They alone are insufficient to govern the world. (note 3)

Note 1 - **Let it be:** https://www.youtube.com/watch?v=l6E0DIN_kgU

Let go and let it go 😊 : https://www.youtube.com/watch?v=L0MK7qz13bU

Note 2 - I have translated using the original wording, literally, it means: If there's something to worry about, he is not fit to oversee the world.

Note 3 - During Laozi's era, it was a time of warfare where small states within the nation battled each other for resources and power. These conflicts were often driven by personal ambitions rather than genuine concern for the well-being of their people.

Most common literal translation:

Engaging in scholarly pursuits leads to an increasing accumulation of various embellishments while following the Way results in a decreasing accumulation of embellishments. As the accumulation diminishes further and further, one eventually reaches a state of non-action where nothing is held onto or fixed. In this state of non-action, one can act effortlessly in accordance with nature. When governing the world, it is best to let things follow their natural course and remain unoccupied. If one pursues personal gain and forcefully drives things forward, it is insufficient for governing the world.

My 5 cents

In the pursuit of learning, wishes, and desires (including desires for knowledge) tend to increase day by day. In the pursuit of the Dao, desires tend to decrease day by day. As the decrease continues, desires are gradually diminished until there is no longer motivation for striving. Eventually, one returns to the state of non-action (Wúwéi). Through non-action, everything falls into its rightful place, each following its own course of development. Therefore, in Wúwéi (non-action), there is nothing that cannot be done. (PS: In economics, we have a term named: market equilibrium via pricing, that is the market will adjust itself, through price, demand, and supply, we do not need to interrupt at all.)

Extract from He Sang Gong – De Jing – Forget the knowledge.

To study increasingly means to engage in the study of politics, education, rites, and music. (This's what Confucius taught at his time), "Increasingly" refers to the embellishment of one's emotions and desires day by day. To follow the Way (Dao) leads to diminishing. "The Way" refers to the natural way. "Diminishing" means reducing the embellishment of emotions and desires day by day until they gradually disappear. This leads to inaction, where one remains tranquil and serene like an infant, without deliberately doing anything. In inaction, everything is accomplished effortlessly. When desires are cut off and virtue aligns with the Way, there is nothing that cannot be achieved and nothing that cannot be done. To govern the world, one should always aim for a state of non-action. Governing the world should be done without busyness or laborious effort. If there is constant busyness, governance becomes troublesome, people become unsettled, thus it is inadequate for governing the world. When there is a preference for busyness, politics, and education become burdensome, and people are not at peace. Therefore, it is insufficient for governing the world.

(PS: it is the same when cultivating Qi inside our body, remember our body is a small universe of a nation)

老子河上公章句 - 德經 - 忘知

為學日益，學謂政教禮樂之學也。日益者，情欲文飾日以益多。為道日損。道謂之自然之道也。日損者，情欲文飾日以消損。損之又損，損情欲也。又損之，所以漸去。以至於無為，當恬淡如嬰兒，無所造為也。無為而無不為。情欲斷絕，德於道合，則無所不施，無所不為也。取天下常以無事，取，治也。治天下當以無事，不當以勞煩也。及其有事，不足以取天下。及其好有事，則政教煩，民不安，故不足以治天下也。

【第四十九章】 Chapter 49

Most Common Translation

聖人無常心，	The sage has an impermanence mind (no set mind);
以百姓心為心。	He adopts the heart of the people as his heart.
善者，吾善之；	Those who are good, he treats them good;
不善者，吾亦善之，	Those who are not good, he also treats them good,
德善。	Virtue goodness.
信者，吾信之；	Those who are trustworthy, he trusts them.
不信者，吾亦信之，	Those who are not trustworthy, he trusts them too.
德信。	Virtuous trust.
聖人在天下歙歙，	The sage restrains and conceals themselves within the world, (note 1)
為天下渾其心。	Harmonizing people's thoughts to return to simplicity and purity.
百姓皆注其耳目，	The people all focus their ears and eyes on him,
	Or, people are all focused on their wise and cleverness,
聖人皆孩之。	And the sage treats them as children.
	Or, the sage leads the people back to a state of innocence and simplicity like that of infants.

Note 1 - 聖人在天下歙歙，為天下渾其心. 百姓皆注其耳目

These three sentences have another arrangement version:

聖人在天下，歙歙為天下渾其心. 百姓皆注其耳目. Which means: The sage is in the world, enduring silently for the sake of the world and thus making oneself confused. While the people are wise and self-aware.

Common literal translation

The sage often has no selfishness, taking the hearts of the people as their own. For the kind-hearted, I am kind to them; for the unkind, I am also kind to them, thus obtaining kindness and making everyone inclined towards goodness. For the trustworthy, I trust them; for the untrustworthy, I also trust them, thus obtaining honesty and making everyone adhere to trustworthiness. A virtuous sage, in their position, restrains their desires, causing the thoughts of the world to return to simplicity. The people all focus on their clear-sightedness; the virtuous person makes them all return to a state of purity like infants.

Extract from He Sang Gong – De Jing – letting virtue take its course.

The sage has no constant heart, the sage is constantly changing. He values flexibility as if he has no fixed mind of his own. He takes the people's hearts as his own. Whatever is convenient for the people, the sage follows. If the people are good, the sage follows their goodness. Even if some are not good among the people, the sage transforms them into goodness. Virtue is good. When the people's virtue is cultivated, the sage believes in the good. If the people are trustworthy, the sage believes in them. Even if some are not trustworthy among the people, the sage transforms them to be trustworthy. Trustworthiness is virtue. When the people's virtue is cultivated, the sage considers them trustworthy. The sage is anxious in the world, always fearful. Despite wealth and status, the sage dares not to be arrogant. He maintains a pure heart for the world. It's said the sage muddies their hearts for the people as if they were ignorant and blind. The people all focus their ears and eyes, using them for the sage's seeing and hearing. The sage treats them as children, loving and caring for them like infants, nurturing them without expecting anything in return.

老子河上公章句 -> 德經 -> 任德

聖人無常心，聖人重改更，貴因循，若自無心。以百姓心為心。百姓心之所便，聖人因而從之。善者吾善之，百姓為善，聖人因而善之。不善者吾亦善之，百姓雖有不善者，聖人化之使善也。德善。百姓德化，聖人為善信者吾信之，百姓為信，聖人因而信之。不信者吾亦信之，百姓為不信，聖人化之為信者也。德信。百姓德化，聖人以為信。聖人在天下怵怵，聖人在天下怵怵常恐怖，富貴不敢驕奢。為天下渾其心。言聖人為天下百姓混濁其心，若愚闇不通也。百姓皆注其耳目，注，用也。百姓皆用其耳目為聖人視聽也。聖人皆孩之。聖人愛念百姓如嬰孩赤子，長養之而不責望其報。

【第五十章】 Chapter 50

Most Common Translation

出生入死。	Born into life, enter death.
生之徒十有三，	Three out of ten follow the path of life. (note 1)
死之徒十有三。	Three out of ten follow the path of death.
人之生動之死地，	Those who live in between life and death,
亦十有三。	are also three in ten.
夫何故？	Why is this so?
以其生生之厚。	Because of their thick vitality. (Enjoyment is too thick, excessive) (note 2)
蓋聞善攝生者，	It is said that those skilled in preserving life, (note 3)
陸行不遇兕虎，	Travel on land without encountering rhinoceroses or tigers, (note 4)
入軍不被甲兵，	Enter battles without being harmed by weapons,
兕無所投其角，	Rhinoceroses have nowhere to thrust their horns,
虎無所措其爪，	Tigers have nowhere to sink their claws,
兵無所容其刃。	Weapons have nowhere to lodge their blades.
夫何故？	Why is this so?
以其無死地。	Death has no place for them.

Note 1 - This verse, with its original phrase "十有三" (ten has three), presents a complex and challenging interpretation. Scholars over the past 2000+ years have proposed two main opinions regarding its meaning.

1. 十有三, three out of ten, which can also extended to 30%.
2. 十有三, thirteen.

Version 1 - Three out of ten is the most common reading. In this regard, the first 5 verses mean:

Thirty percent of individuals follow the path of life, while another thirty percent follow the path of death. Additionally, there exists another thirty percent who navigate the precarious line between life and death.

Alternatively, another interpretation posits that:

Thirty percent are born for a long life,

Thirty percent are destined for a shorter lifespan.

Another thirty percent of people strive to prolong their lives through various efforts. (Conversely, another perspective suggests that thirty percent of people may inadvertently harm themselves, leading to a shorter lifespan)

Version 1 has been the preferred interpretation among scholars for over 2000 years.

Version 2 - 十有三, thirteen

What does this "Thirteen" mean?

Master He Sang Gong proposed that the "Nine major Qì qiào (氣竅)", or the nine apertures also known as Qi gateways, along with the four gates level, which made it thirteen, hold significance. However, he did not elaborate on the nature of these thirteen entities. Scholars have delved into historical texts and records and found that Han Fei Zi (Die at 233BC), a legalist philosopher who lived around the time of Laozi, mentioned this concept in one of his books, stating that "human has 360 joints, four limbs, and nine qiao 竅.

The nine apertures (qiao 竅) consist of two eyes, two ears, two nostrils, one mouth, and two additional apertures for urination and defecation, totaling nine in all.

Setting aside the debate over Han Fei Zi's appropriateness, let's explore the significance of the nine major Qì qiào (氣竅) within our bodies, which holds paramount importance for practitioners of qi. (In fact, I have discussed this with you guys when we practice BXQ).

The Nine major Qì qiào (氣竅) are:

1. Bai Hui, 2. Yin Tang (or simply Wisdom eye), 3. Yu Zhen (the Jade Pillow), 4. Da Zhui, 5. Shan Zhong, 6. Jiā jí (夾脊) or Shen Zhu (some lineages use this), 7. Shén què (神闕) or Belly Button, 8. Ming Men, and 9. Hui Yin.

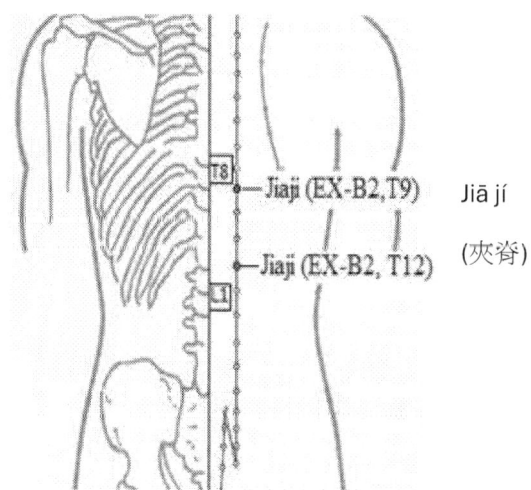
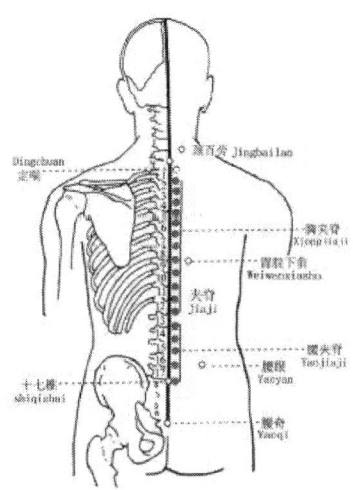

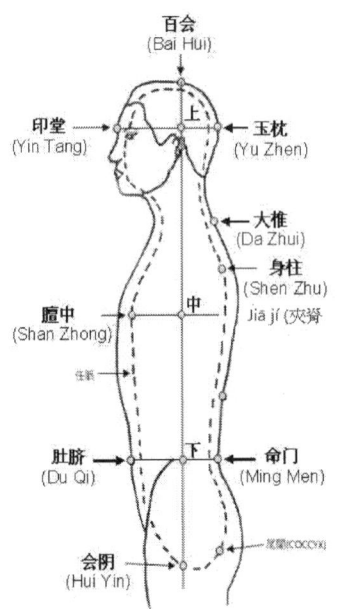

The diagram of Nine Qi qiào (氣竅)

PS: Another version proposes an alternate placement for the nine qiao. The most prevalent variation involves substituting the Da Zhui with the Wěi lǘ (尾閭).

Regarding the 4 gates:

In my opinion, using the four limbs as the four gates, as suggested by Han Fei Zi, lacks validation. Even if we consider the two Yong Quan on our feet and Lao Gong on our palms, it's unclear what this truly signifies.

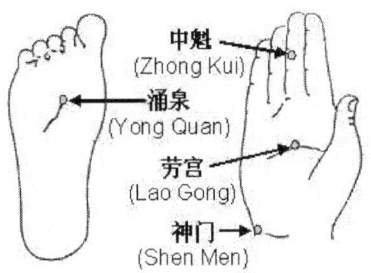

Others:

Daoists commonly refer to the three Dāntián as the main gates: the upper, middle, and lower. However, there's one gate left unmentioned. Combining the three Dāntián with the nine Qiao forms the most frequently used terminology today. However, it adds up to twelve only.

Some scholars also propose that the thirteen comprise thirteen emotional or mental states, such as happiness, anger, sadness, and so on.

There are various other opinions about the nature of these thirteen entities, but I've only touched upon the most pertinent and widespread ones here.

Note 1 (a) - **For the word 徒**

The most common translation of 徒 is a group of people. In DDJ 76, said, The life of a person is soft and weak; their death is firm and strong. The life of grass and trees is gentle and fragile; their death is withered and dry. Hence, those who are firm and strong belong to the realm of death, while those who are soft and weak belong to the realm of life.

Hence, those who are firm and strong are the group of people belong to the realm of death, while those who are soft and weak belong to the realm of life.

Zhuangzi, the Great Master (莊子，大宗師： 其一與天為徒，其不一與人為徒): Those who adhere to Oneness are disciples of heaven, while those who do not follow Oneness are disciples of humanity. In here, 徒 means disciples, the follower. In this context, interpreting this passage suggests that those who adhere to Oneness are disciples of life, while those who do not follow Oneness are disciples of death. The rest reside in the space between.

Note 2 - This verse refers to individuals who are caught in the struggle between life and death. It carries a dual meaning: those who excessively focus on their well-being, indulging in excessive vitamin intake and health-related obsessions, may inadvertently harm themselves or their finances. Conversely, those who pursue their desires and sensory pleasures with great enthusiasm may also find themselves heading towards demise.

Note 3 - It refers to the remaining ten percentage of peoples.

Note 4 - 兕: a female rhinoceros, or a container that holds wine. The ancient wording of 兕 refers to an unidentified wild ancient beast. Scholars later believe it is a female rhinoceros.

Side Note - Nan Huaijin, 南怀瑾（1918—2012）, A renowned modern Chinese master of traditional studies, he is also a well-known practitioner. Some of his lineages intersect with ours to a certain extent. According to his perspective, these three groups of thirty percent represent three different energies of life and death. If we apply this interpretation to this passage from this chapter of DDJ, it means that individual should diligently preserve their respective energies of life and death.

Common Literal Translation

Humans come into the world and are born, eventually entering the earth and dying. One-third of people belong to the category of longevity; one-third belong to the category of short-lived and dying; and one-third could have lived longer, but they themselves choose the path to death. Why is this so? Because they overindulge themselves. It is said that those who are good at nurturing their own lives, when walking on land, will not encounter fierce rhinos and tigers, nor will they be harmed by weapons in war. The rhinoceros cannot gore them, the tiger cannot extend its claws towards them, and weapons cannot pierce their bodies. Why is this so? Because they have not entered the realm of death.

Quiz: Why female Rhinos? (from the original wording?), not male?

What's the difference between a male and a female rhino?

Rhinoceros - Wikipedia

Males have much larger horns than the females. Hair can range from dense (the densest hair in young calves) to sparse. The color of these rhinos is reddish brown. The body is short and has stubby legs. (from Google)

My 5 Cents

From our lineage, it doesn't necessarily pertain to this particular chapter of the Dao De Jing, although they are closely related, if you want to ask.

There are various Qi qiào (氣簌) associated with different aspects of life. The three anterior points (Qi qiào in our front) are Yin in nature, possessing soft qualities that nurture life. Conversely, the four posterior (Qi qiào at our back) points are Yang, characterized by solid qualities that shape our physical bodies.

For the Bai Hui, it serves as a gateway where we can control our own death. Proficient Daoists have the ability to pass through this gateway at will, allowing them to die according to their wishes. In this context, although we are aware of the Bai Hui point, we focus our practice on the wisdom eye instead of actively working on the Bai Hui. Our soul or mind leaves our body through wisdom eye either, until we are at a very high proficient level.

Another Qi point related to death is Jiā jí (夾脊). In traditional Chinese medicine, there's a concept known as "病入膏肓" which translates to "sickness entering the gāohuāng (膏肓)". If this occurs, it signifies that the illness has reached a critical state with no possible cure. The gāohuāng (膏肓) is situated deep inside the Jiā jí (夾脊) region. Additionally, there's a belief that gāohuāng (膏肓) refers to the fatty area between the heart and the diaphragm, considered unreachable by conventional medicine in traditional Chinese medicine. In our lineage, we utilize the area surrounding the acupoint, which is also the Jiā jí (夾脊) area, to promote the overall health and well-being of our physical form. (For Tai Chi/Ji from, we practice releasing the Jiā jí (夾脊) area by Fans through the back)

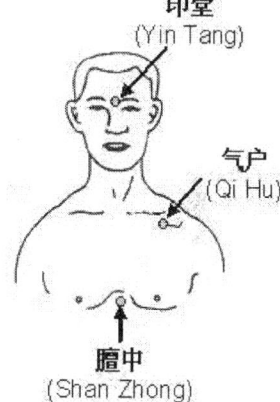

There is another Qi qiào (氣竅) located near the side of our shoulder known as Qi Hu. It serves as one of the prominent gateways through which our mature Qi infant ascends.

For the 4 main gates:

The most common saying is the upper, middle and lower Dāntián. It is commonly known as the three main gates. You should know all the attributes related to these three Dāntián, and I do not repeat in here. From the same token, the proper interpretation of the 4 gates or the achievements are:

1. Cultivate life essence to transform Qi, 練精化氣;
2. cultivate Qi to refine spirit, 練氣化神;
3. refine spirit to return to emptiness, 練神還虛; and
4. return to emptiness to enter the Dao. 還虛入道.

This also signifies the journey from the lowest Dāntián to the upper Dāntián and ultimately returning to the Dao through the Void. (PS: our neigong acts 4, 5, 6, and 7 are practicing these, just for your reference.)

Thus, when we understand the above said, we might get some idea of how Laozi talked about the three groups of life and death out of ten. And what He Sang Gong's thirteen stuff is about.

Wang Bi's (226-249 AD) "Commentary on the Dao De Jing"

Out of ten who engage in the pursuit of life, three are successful. Out of ten who engage in the pursuit of death, three are successful. And why is this so? It is because they cling to life so intently. Those who excel in preserving life avoid encountering rhinoceroses and tigers when traveling over land, and they do not arm themselves when entering a battlefield. Rhinoceroses find nowhere to thrust their horns, tigers find nowhere to sink their claws, and weapons find nowhere to lodge their blades. And why is this so? It is because they have nowhere to die.

Three out of ten, in the pursuit of life's path, when taken to its utmost, three out of ten may find success. Similarly, in the pursuit of death's path, when taken to its utmost, three out of ten may also find success. People's lives are deeply intertwined, with nowhere free from the grasp of life.

Those who excel in preserving life do not cling excessively to life itself, hence they have nowhere to die. The most harmful instrument is none other than weaponry, and the most dangerous creatures are none other than rhinoceroses and tigers. Yet, when weapons and military strategies find no place to exert their edge, and rhinoceroses and tigers find nowhere to unleash their claws and horns, it is indeed because they do not burden themselves with desires. What place is there for death's grasp?

The mole deems the abyss as shallow and thus digs its burrow within it; the hawk views the mountain as low and thus builds its nest upon it. Unable to be reached by snare or net, they can be said to dwell in a place without the threat of death. However, eventually enticed by sweet bait, they enter into a realm without life. Is this not due to an excessive attachment to life? Therefore, if creatures do not seek to depart from their essence or desire to alter their true nature, even if they enter a battlefield, they will remain unharmed, and even if they traverse land, they will remain inviolable. The innocence of the newborn is indeed precious and trustworthy.

王弼《道德經注》

出生入死，出生地，入死地。

生之徒十有三，死之徒十有三，人之生動之死地十有三。夫何故？以其生生之厚。蓋聞善攝生者，陸行不遇兕虎，入軍不被甲兵。兕無所投其角，虎無所措其爪，兵無所容其刃。夫何故？以其無死地。

十有三，猶雲十分有三分。取其生道，全生之極，十分有三耳。取死之道，全死之極，十分亦有三耳。而民生生之厚，更之無生之地焉。善攝生者，無以生為生，故無死地也。器之害者，莫甚乎兵。獸之害者，莫甚乎兕虎。而令兵戈無所容其鋒刃，虎兕無所措其爪角，斯誠不以欲累其身者也，何死地之有乎？夫蚖蟺以淵為淺，而鑿穴其中；鷹鶻以山為卑，而增巢其上。矰繳不能及，網罟不能到，可謂處於無死地矣。然而卒以甘餌，乃入於無生之地，豈非生生之厚乎？故物苟不以求離其本，不以欲渝其真，雖入軍而不害，陸行而不可犯也。赤子之可則而貴，信矣。

Su Zhe (1039-1112) 's "Interpretation of Laozi"

Born into life, entering death.

Nature knows no life or death, departing is life, and entering is death.

Of those who live, three in ten follow the path of life.

Of those who die, three in ten follow the path of death.

In the realm where people live and move, death's territory comprises three in ten.

Those who use objects to nurture themselves and enrich their essence are the followers of life.

Those who indulge in sensory pleasures and desires that harm themselves are the followers of death.

These two paths clearly distinguish between life and death.

Furthermore, I know that being active without rest, speaking without silence, thinking without forgetting, pursuing to the extreme—these lead one to the territory of death.

When speaking of the path of life and death with ten, each of the three aspects occupies three, is it not true that there are nine paths of life and death, leaving only one path of neither life nor death? The path of neither life nor death is what the Book of Changes calls 'tranquility without movement.' Laozi speaks of the nine paths but does not mention the one, allowing people to realize it on their own, to convey the subtlety of non-action and non-thought.

Why is this so? Because of the thickness of its vitality.

With life comes death, so those who follow life are also followers of death.

What people rely on in life is substantial, so the path of death always comprises nine out of ten.

It is said that those who are skilled at preserving life travel on land without encountering rhinoceros or tiger, and enter battles without being harmed by weapons. The rhinoceros has nowhere to thrust its horn, the tiger has nowhere to place its claws, and weapons have nowhere to lodge their blades. Why is this so? Because they dwell in a place without death.

The sage always resides in the state of neither life nor death, where even the land of life is nonexistent, so how can there be a land of death?

蘇轍《老子解》

出生入死，性無生死，出則為生，入則為死。

生之徒十有三，死之徒十有三，人之生動之死地十有三。

用物取精以自滋養者，生之徒也。聲色臭味以自戕賊者，死之徒也。二者既分生死之道矣。吾又知作而不知休，知言而不知默，知思而不知忘，以趣於盡，則所謂動而之死地者也。生死之道以十言之，三者各居其三矣，豈非生死之道九，而不生不死之道一而已乎？不生不死，則《易》所謂寂然不動者也。老子言其九，不言其一，使人自得之，以寄無思無為之妙也。

夫何故？以其生生之厚。

有生則有死，故生之徒，則死之徒也。人之所賴於生者厚，則死之道常十九。

蓋聞善攝生者，陸行不遇兕虎，入軍不被甲兵。兕無所投其角，虎無所措其爪，兵無所容其刃。夫何故？以其無死地。

至人常在不生不死中，生地且無，焉有死地哉？

Extract From He Sang Gong – De Jing – Value Life

Coming into life, entering death. Coming into life refers to the desires emerging from within the five senses, with the soul tranquil and the spirit settled, hence life. Entering death refers to desires entering the chest and belly, with the essence exhausted and the spirit confused, hence death. Among those who come into life, life has thirteen; among those who enter death, death has thirteen. This indicates that there are thirteen aspects to life and death, referring to the nine orifices and the four gates or four limbs. In life, the eyes do not gaze recklessly, the ears do not listen indiscriminately, the nose does not sniff without purpose, the mouth does not speak without reason, the taste, the hands do not act recklessly, and the feet do not walk without thought. The spirit and vitality are not squandered recklessly. In death, it is the opposite. Human life is a journey to the land of death, thirteen leads to meet their end on this journey. Humans understand the pursuit of life, but their actions lead them to their demise, thirteen are ensnared by death. Why is this so? It is asked why they meet their end on this journey.

It is because of the intensity of their pursuit of life. They tread the path of death because their pursuits of life are too intense, contradicting the Dao, defying the will of Heaven, and straying from the right path. Indeed, those who understand the art of preserving life nourish themselves. When walking the path, they encounter no wild beasts, naturally keeping their distance, and avoiding harm. When entering the army, they do not don armor or wield weapons, unwilling to engage in killing. The wild beasts do not thrust their horns, the tigers do not extend their claws, and the weapons find no target for their blades. Those who nurture life are immune to harm from wild beasts and weapons. Why is this so? It is asked why wild beasts, tigers, and weapons do not inflict harm. It is because there is no place for death. They do not trespass into the thirteen realms of death. It is said that the divine protects and guards them, preventing harm from coming to them.

老子河上公章句 -> 德經 -> 貴生

出生入死。出生，謂情欲出五內，魂靜魄定，故生。入死，謂情欲入於胸臆，精勞神惑，故死。生之徒十有三，死之徒死十有三，言生死之類各有十三，謂九竅四關也。其生也目不妄視，耳不妄聽，鼻不妄嗅，口不妄言，味，手不妄持，足不妄行，精神不妄施。其死也反是也。人之生，動之死地十有三。人知求生，動作反之十三死也。夫何故，問何故動之死地也。以其求生之厚。所以動之死地者，以其求生活之事太厚，違道忤天，妄行失紀。蓋以聞善攝生者，攝，養也。路行不遇兕虎，自然遠離，害不干也。入軍不披甲兵，不好戰以殺人。兕無投其角，虎無所措爪，兵無所容其刃。養生之人，兕虎無由傷，兵刃無從加之也。夫何故，問兕虎兵甲何故不加害之。以其無死地。以其不犯十三之死地也。言神明營護之，此物不敢害。

【第五十一章】Chapter 51

Most Common Translation

道生之，	The Dao gives birth to them,
德畜之，	Virtue nurtures them,
物形之，	Matter shapes them,
勢成之。	Natural tendency completes them.
是以萬物莫不尊道而貴德。	Therefore, all things respect the Dao and value Virtue.
道之尊，	Reverence and honor for the Dao,
德之貴，	Value of Virtue,
夫莫之命而常自然。	Not about obeying commands but following nature's eternal laws.
故道生之，	Therefore, the Dao gives them life,
德畜之。	Virtue nurtures them.
長之、	Grow them,
育之、	Raise them,
亭之、	Mature (perfect or house) them,
毒之、	Ripe them, (or trim them) (note 1),
養之、	Protect them,
覆之。	Care them,
生而不有，	Give birth but do not possess.
為而不恃，	Act without relying,
長而不宰，	Lead without dominating,
是謂玄德。	This is called profound virtue.

Note 1 - In the popular version, "毒" means poison, while in Master He's version, "熟" means ripe. Although "毒" and "熟" sound similar in the old days (whether they do sound similar is still under debate), if read as "poison", it implies clearing out obstacles or trimming for fitness. Hence, both versions share a similar meaning.

Most Common Literal Translation

The Dao generates all things, and Virtue nurtures all things. Although all things manifest in various forms, it is the environment that fosters their growth. Therefore, all things venerate the Dao and treasure Virtue.

The reason why the Dao is venerated, and Virtue is treasured is because the Dao fosters the growth of all things without interference, and Virtue nurtures all things without domination, allowing them to follow their natural course. Thus, the Dao generates all things, Virtue nurtures all things, enabling them to grow and develop, mature and bear fruit, receiving nurturing and protection.

To foster all things without claiming ownership, to nurture all things without self-reliant boasting, to guide all things without domination—this is the profound and mysterious Virtue.

【第五十二章】Chapter 52

Most Common Translation

天下有始，	The world has its beginning,
以為天下母。	Treating it as the mother of the world. (note 1)
既得其母，	Once you have obtained the mother,
以知其子；	You will SEE her children;
既知其子，	Once you SEE her children,
復守其母，	Return to guarding onto the mother, (note 2)
沒身不殆。	And you will endure without harm.
塞其兌，	Fill up the Duì, (note 3)
閉其門，	Close the doors, (note 4)
終身不勤。	One will never be exhausted throughout their life.
開其兌，	Open the Duì, (note 5)
濟其事，	Facilitate the affairs,
終身不救。	One will remain unsaved throughout their lifetime.
見小曰明，	The ability to perceive minute details is referred to as clarity. (original word by word is: See small is named brightness) (note 6)
守柔曰強。	The ability to guard/protect softness is strength. (original word by word is guard soft call strong)
用其光，	Utilize its radiance (light), (note 8)
復歸其明，	Return to its clarity,
無遺身殃，	Without leaving oneself in danger,
是為習常。	This is called habitual practice.

Note 1 - The world has its beginning, treating it as the mother of the world.

The most common interpretation of the mother of the world is Dao. However, after exploring numerous chapters, we come to understand that it is not Dao itself, but rather the manifestation of Dao that shapes the Way – the concept of Oneness.

Having delved into the BXQ, we can now delve deeper into this chapter. The origin or essence of the world is the "Innate pure/true water" (天一真水), or simply the Oneness, which, transforms into the water energy of the material realm.

In our practice, this energy—whether in the form of light, stars, or commonly flowing water, like the poem which is spoken by the poet Li Bai " From afar, the waterfall in front of the river it shows, Descending in a cascade flying down of three thousand feet (not fleas 😊),..As if the Milky Way from the ninth heaven did fleet—courses through our bodies from the "Brahman chakra" or wisdom eye.

In the Hetu, it signifies: Heaven produces the Innate ONE true water, while Earth Six contains it (天一真水，地六承之). The pure innate water energy is designated by the number 1, while Earth is represented by the number 5. Earth refers to our yellow court or the mechanism for materializing into substance. What does this mean? When the pure One water (1) is embodied within our physical form, it transmutes into 6 (5+1=6), the postnatal water or the water energy of this physical existence.

Contrary to our common belief, we affirm that Middle Earth's fifth element exists from the very outset, emerging when we put the tool to use. Determining the center (定中) or guarding our center (守中), such as when practicing our tai chi forms or skills, or when engaging in Feng Shui.

However, In Qi or spiritual practice, or under the way of Dao, the fifth element or our Yellow Court does not manifest until all four elements merge and align harmoniously. In Chinese, it is expressed as "四象和合，天五成土", which literally means when all four phenomena (elements) unite, the heavenly fifth element becomes the earth element. In numbering, it is 3+2, 4+1, and 5 all merged in harmony and spinning together.

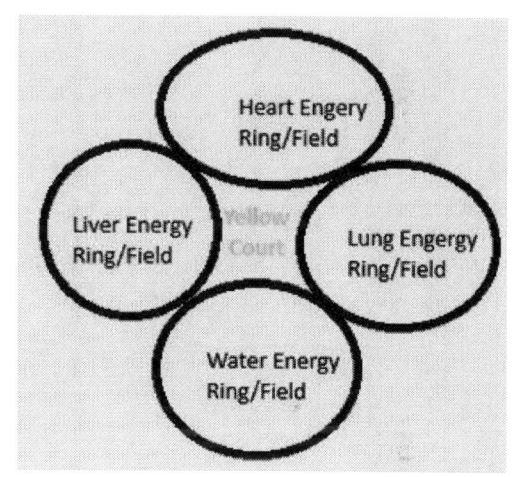

Let's refer to the Hetu for some hints:

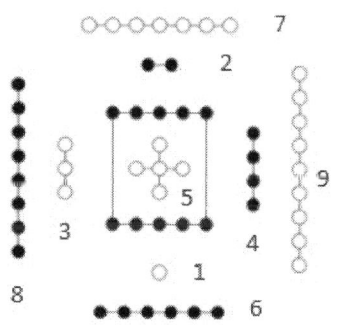

The white dots symbolize Yang, each with its unique characteristics, whereas the black dots represent Yin. 1,2,3,4 are Innate, while 6,7,8,9 are Postnatal.

When the single white dot, representing true water (number 1) falling from above, interacts with the earth (number 5), it transforms into Yin water and settles below. This is why Laozi often emphasizes that water resides in the lowest places.

Similarly, when the Yin fire (number 2) ascends from below and interacts with the earth (number 5), it transforms into Yang fire (number 7). The same process occurs with wood (number 3) and metal (number 4).

In this regard, "The Innate ONE true water (天一真水)" is the beginning of this world, the Mother.

Side notes:

In Chinese Medicine, according to the Hetu diagram, 1 corresponds to the kidney, 2 to the heart, 3 to the liver, 4 to the lung, and 5 to our digestive system, or simply the stomach and spleen. It is crucial to emphasize that these correspondences refer not to the organs themselves, it is the functions and systems associated with them.

In spiritual practice, the Hetu is also the inner vision. The inner star vision. We may discuss this later when the situation arises and allows. Just keep in mind at present.

For external vision, if you have a 4-dimensional eyesight, it appears as a cosmic pool of stars swirling amidst the nocturnal expanse. It fosters another stream of learning ability and school of thought. Such as Astronomy, astrology, and so on.

Furthermore, I've encountered an interpretation of the Hetu suggesting that the dots represent the placement of glass and water, potentially used to provide sustenance for animals during the journeys of our ancient ancestors across untamed lands.

THE FIVE ELEMENTS THEORIES   (Five Eternal Energy)

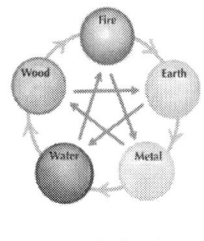

GENERAL THEORY (Orderly Generation & Weakening)
= The Common Five Elements

Order:
Water generates Wood, Wood generates Fire, Fire generates Earth, Earth generates Metal, Metal generates Water.

Counter:
Metal weakens Wood, Wood weakens Earth, Earth weakens Water, Water weakens Fire, Fire weakens Metal

→ Generating
→ Weakening

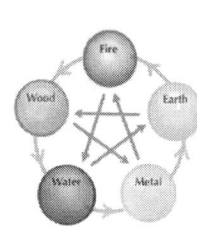

FIVE THIEVES THEORY* (Reverse Generation & Weakening)
= The True Five Elements (Life, Matter, Time, Movement, & Spirit)

Reverse Generation:
Fire generates Wood, Wood generates Water, Water generates Metal, Metal generates Earth, Earth generates Fire.

Reverse Weakening:
Wood weakens Metal, Metal weakens Fire, Fire weakens Water, Water weakens Earth, Earth weakens Wood.

* Yinfu Jing Citation by Zhang Guo (Lao, one of the Eight Immortals)
The citation states: Thief of Life - Life Cycle
The Dao De Jing offers another interpretation of this verse:
Life is the root of death, and death is the root of life.

Thank Marianne for helping me to draw this chart.

Note 2 - In Daoist terms, it is the mother conceals within her womb, with both prenatal and postnatal phases hiding each other in reverse (母隱子胎，先天後天逆藏). Similar to the Yang fire has the true Yin water embedded inside, if we recall our Neigong set 2.

We need to locate and find the true essence hidden inside all the energies. Such as the pure water hides inside the fire, as said, the gold (metal) tiger hides inside the water, and, or the wood dragon hides inside the fire. It seems that, for example, gold gives birth to water, and wood starts the fire. However, there is wood energy inside the fire energy, and metal energy inside the water energy.

Moreover, the verse "once you see the children of the mother, return to guarding onto the mother" implies that we should practice in reverse, from the son back to the mother. In DDJ, although it repeats continuously, the depth of understanding and the level of attainment vary.

How to guard the mother: Observe, gain insight, and receive the shower of the Innate One True Water and guard your primordia soul.

Note 3 - 兌 (Duì guà),

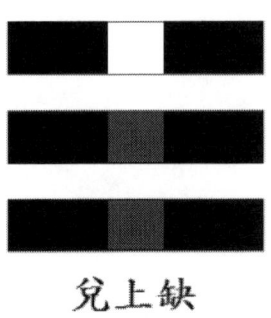

兌上缺

Please refer to the notes regarding the three movements of our middle Dantian (3 years ago?), employing the three-stroke trigram to elucidate the energy or vibrational flows. The concluding (3rd) stage of this movement is Duì.

This third stage signifies a state of peacefulness, unaffected by the frequencies or vibrations of your Heart Chakra energy, regardless of a busy or idle lifestyle, and devoid of emotional responses to external stimuli.

Hence, the verse "Fill up the Duì" actually means, that once we attain this stage, we should proceed by filling up the void within it, transforming it into a pure Yang trigram, and returning to the innate stage before the first movement. – That is complete the cycle.

兌上缺　　　　　　　　乾三連

Note 4 - "Closing the doors"

It does not only entail shutting and concealing the KIN trigrams but also involves closing off all nine Qi Qiao.

Moreover, the trigram 兌 (Duì) correlates with the West in direction, symbolizing metal attributes and the lungs as organs or related systems. 兌 (Duì) embodies a serene sky above the head, extending its presence downward as a tranquil lake, akin to the projection of Dao in its unity. Consequently, 兌 (Duì) encompasses elements related to water, which flow towards our mouth, throat, nose, and tongue. This encompasses speech and mental processes, as thoughts often precede verbal expression. Additionally, it encompasses sensations and emotional feelings, as elaborated in note 3.

In this context, closing the doors signifies sealing off these channels and distancing oneself from unnecessary sensory or emotional issues that may arise from our six senses.

Note 5 - Open the Dui and facilitate the affairs:

It pertains to mental or emotional, and any one or more of the nine Qi Qiao leaks. Here, it's crucial to distinguish between leaks and flows. Leaks signify sickness, which is uncontrollable, whereas flows are multidirectional and typically controllable at will. This differentiation is significant.

To be open implies a leakage, allowing for the pursuit of our sensory desires. However, this pursuit can drain our vital life energy, potentially resulting in exhaustion. Once more, it's important to discern between addiction and cultivating inner peace. Let's simplify this with an example we have discussed before. Imagine someone offers us a ride home, and along the way, we encounter numerous distractions—beautiful scenery, lively streets, tempting eateries. We have the choice: either observing and allowing them to pass without attachment or becoming fixated on every intriguing diversion.

Note 6 - The proverb says: In the smallest details lies the path to enlightenment (seeing the way is like seeing the tiny) (見道若微). In business, there's also a saying that the devil often resides in the details. These interpretations are philosophical analyses of this statement. In the practice of cultivation of Qi, it generally refers to the clarity of the spiritual center. Here, after completing the cleansing process of the middle Dantian, the spiritual center will tend towards clarity. Note that the cleansing process of the middle Dantian cannot be completed in one attempt. It requires further refinement through repeated cycles.

Note 7 - No note 7

Note 8 - **Utilize its radiance (light)**

Here, it denotes the internal radiance or energy emanating from the space between the lower and middle Dantian within our body. This differs from the spiritual light originating from heaven, which traverses through our Brahman Chakra or wisdom eye.

It has several scenarios:

- like a sunrise from the lower sea (bottom of the sea). (一陽初動)
- the light energy from the Liver. (Wood – emerges the radiance of the spirit of Pò) (木，魄生光華)。And, also have several stages or occasions:
    - Manifestation within the inner space: Wood and water converge.
    - Visual chaos fragments: Wood and fire converge.
    - Radiance emanates from the body: Wood and metal converge.

When these energies combine with the true essence of fire (heart energy,), they may form the golden elixir and our prenatal yellow court is established. Once you have cultivated your golden elixir or Neidan, you are approaching to longevity. That is what Laozi said, how to use the light and approach the goal: without leaving oneself in danger.

PS: please refer to our Neigong set #2.

Most Common Literal Translation:

By blocking the apertures of desire and closing the gateways of craving, one can live a life without disturbances. If the apertures of desire are opened, it will only invite a multitude of troubles, rendering one beyond redemption. To discern the subtle is called "enlightenment"; to maintain the soft is called "strength". Utilizing this radiance to reflect the inner enlightenment will not bring calamity upon oneself; this is what is called the everlasting "way of the constant". And practice it as an everyday habit.

My Five Cents:

No coins left, not even 5 cents. Please check the notes, it is self-explanatory already.

Su Zhe (1939-1112)'s "Interpretation of Laozi)

The Nameless is the beginning of Heaven and Earth; The Named is the mother of all things. Thus, while the constant pursuit of the Way may seem nameless, it is from this namelessness that all things originate; Yet when named, it is from this naming that all things are born. Therefore, it is called the beginning and also the mother. Its offspring become myriad things.

The sage embodies the Way to encompass all things, like a mother who knows her child. With complete understanding and no oversight, even though their intelligence penetrates all, they never forget the Way for the sake of things. Thus, they ultimately adhere to their mother.

All people in the world inherently possess the Way, yet they frequently neglect it, instead becoming engrossed in worldly pursuits. They find pleasure in the sights and sounds around them, allowing their desires to guide their actions. This leads them into a lifetime of distraction and inability to find true fulfillment. The sage, however, remains steadfast and unaffected by such temptations. They achieve this by consciously refraining from indulging in worldly distractions and maintaining a sense of inner peace and clarity.

The harm of indulgence begins small but gradually expands. Understanding the potential magnitude of even minor indulgences and actively restraining them can be considered true wisdom.

Rushing towards what one finds pleasurable without considering consequences, one may mistakenly perceive themselves as strong, when in fact they are not. Only those who perceive pleasure and recognize its potential dangers can truly be considered strong.

The ability to listen, to see, to smell, to taste, to touch, and to think—all are what we call perception. This perception, akin to light, interacts with objects; when objects depart, the clarity remains undiminished. Thus, it adapts to myriad changes without exhaustion, and harm does not befall the self. Therefore, its inherent nature continues on, unwavering and unbroken.

蘇轍《老子解》

無名，天地之始；有名，萬物之母。道方無名，則物之所資始也，及其有名，則物之所資生也。故謂之始，又謂之母。其子則萬物也。

聖人體道以周物，譬如以母知子，了然無不察也。雖其智能周之，然而未嘗以物忘道，故終守其母也。

天下皆具此道，然常息忘道而徇物。目悅於色，耳悅於聲，開其悅之之心，而以其事濟之，是以終身陷溺而不能救。夫聖人之所以終身不動者，唯塞而閉之，未嘗出而徇之也。

悅之為害，始小而浸大。知小之將大而閉之，可謂明矣。

趨其所悅而不顧，自以為強，而非強也。唯見悅而知畏之者，可謂強矣。

世人開其所悅以身徇物，往而不反。聖人塞而閉之，非絕物也，以神應物，用其光而已，身不與也。夫耳之

能聽，目之能視，鼻之能嗅，口之能嘗，身之能觸，心之能思，皆所謂光也。蓋光與物接，物有去而明無損，是以應萬變而不窮，殃不及於其身，故其常性湛然相襲而不絕矣。

Extract From He Sang Gong – De Jing – Return to the source.

Under heaven, there is a beginning, and that beginning has the Dao. This Dao is considered the mother of the world. The Dao is the mother of all things under heaven. Once one knows the mother, they also understand the children. The children are Oneness. Once one knows the Dao, they should also understand this unity. Once one understands the children, they should return to holding onto the mother. Knowing Oneness, they should return to holding onto the Dao, which entails acting without action. Without danger to the self, without peril.

Blocking the 兌 (Duì), 兌 (Duì) is the eyes, the eyes represent desires. By not allowing the eyes to gaze recklessly, one can avoid lifelong labor. People should block their eyes from gazing recklessly and close their mouths from speaking recklessly. By doing so, they can avoid lifelong toil and suffering. Opening the eyes leads to desire, and fulfilling desires leads to disaster. Throughout life, there's no salvation. Calamity and chaos arise.

Recognizing small beginnings when dangers are yet unseen, is true clarity. Embracing gentleness leads to strength. By embracing gentleness, one grows stronger each day.

Using its light, using its gaze outward, observing the benefits and harms of the world. Return to its clarity. Once again, return its brightness inward, without letting the spirit leak. Without leaving the body vulnerable, internally observe to preserve the spirit, not letting it be lost. This is called habitual practice. If one can do this, it is called cultivating the constant way.

老子河上公章句 -> 德經 -> 歸元

天下有始，始有道也。以為天下母。道為天下萬物之母既知其母，復知其子，子，一也。既知道己，當復知一也。既知其子，復守其母，己知一，當復守道反無為也。沒身不殆。不危殆也。塞其兌，兌，目也。目不妄視也。閉其門，門，口也。使口不妄言終身不勤。人當塞目不妄視，閉口不妄言，則終生不勤苦。開其兌，開目視情欲也。濟其事，濟，益也。益情欲之事。終身不救。禍亂成也。見小曰明，萌芽未動，禍亂未見為小，昭然獨見為明。守柔曰強。守柔弱，日以強大也。用其光，用其目光於外，視時世之利害。復歸其明。復當返其光明於內，無使精神泄也。無遺身殃，內視存神，不為漏失。是謂習常。人能行此，是謂修習常道。

【第五十三章】 Chapter 53

Most Common Translation

使我介然有知，	A sudden realization dawned upon me,
行於大道，	Walking along the great path,
唯施是畏。	Only fearful of venturing onto the path of evil.
大道甚夷，	The great path is wide and level,
而民好徑。	But people love shortcuts and detour. (note 1)
朝甚除，	The government affairs are extremely corrupt. (note 2)
田甚蕪，	The fields are overgrown with weeds,
倉甚虛。	The storehouses are empty.
服文彩，	Wearing embroidered clothes,
帶利劍，	Carrying a sharp sword,
厭飲食，	Scorning regular food and drink,
財貨有餘，	Having an abundance of wealth and possessions,
是為盜夸。	Referred to as the chief of thieves. (note 3)
非道也哉！	This is not Dao!

Note 1 - In another version of the Dao De Jing, it states "The Lord loves shortcuts and detours" instead of referring to the people.

Note 2 - Some scholars propose that it should be interpreted as the palaces being kept very tidy.

Note 3 - When the people suffer while the ruler has excess, it is akin to plundering and looting disguised as attire.

Most Common Literal Translation

If I were to gain a little understanding and walk on the great path, my only fear would be straying onto the wrong and evil path. Although the great path is smooth, rulers prefer to take the crooked paths. Government corruption has reached its peak, leading to barren fields and empty storehouses. Yet, the rulers still dress in embroidered clothes, carry sharp swords, feast on exquisite food and drink, and plunder excessive wealth. This is called being the head of thieves. It is not the way of Dao.

My 5 Cents

Reading together with chapters 20 and 23 may provide a deeper understanding of this chapter.

【第五十四章】Chapter 54

Most Common Translation

善建者不拔，	The one who establishes goodness remains steadfast; (note 1)
善抱者不脫，	The one who embraces goodness never slips away; (note 2)
子孫以祭祀不輟。	Thus, the descendants continue to offer sacrifices without interruption.
修之於身，	Cultivate it within yourself,
其德乃真；	Its virtue is true;
修之於家，	Cultivate it within your family,
其德乃餘；	Its virtue will have excess;
修之於鄉，	Cultivate it within your community,
其德乃長；	Its virtue will be lasting or growing;
修之於國，	Cultivate it within your country,
其德乃豐；	Its virtue will be abundant;
修之於天下，	Cultivate it within the world,
其德乃普。	Its virtue will be universal (popular).
故以身觀身，	Therefore, observe oneself through oneself,
以家觀家，	Observe one's family through one's family,
以鄉觀鄉，	Observe one's community through one's community,
以國觀國，	Observe one's country through one's country,
以天下觀天下。	Observe the world through the world. (note 3)
吾何以知天下然哉？	How can I know the world?
以此。	Through this.

Note 1 - Another interpretation suggests that those who adeptly build goodness (or something physical) cannot be uprooted.

Note 2 - Another interpretation also implies that those who embrace goodness or tangible things will never let them slip away. In Qi cultivation, it means embracing the Yin and Yang as a whole (抱元歸一) and will never let them slip away. That is, it is not affected by your monkey mind.

Note 3 - "(觀 guàn)" is indeed a complex word in Chinese, with various meanings and connotations. It can refer to observing, high towers for offering sacrifices to gods, ancient watchtowers outside palaces, Taoist temples, and Buddhist terminologies. It also implies the intellectual capacity to observe and dispel delusions.

In Buddhist terminology, "觀" is paired with "止" (zhǐ), representing the practice of concentration and insight. It refers to the method of cultivating stability and wisdom in meditation. The Tian Tai school focuses on concentrating the mind below the navel as "止" and lifting it to the brow center as "觀", additionally, the commonly known meditation method related to Buddhism is Vipassana Bhavana or Insight Meditation, known as the "止觀法門" in Chinese. Many schools teach this method, and their approaches may vary.

Essentially, "止" involves calming and stabilizing all scattered and distracted states of mind, achieving mental tranquility. "觀" involves discerning the arising and passing away of phenomena through investigating, analyzing, and clearly observing the mind, leading to insight (vipassana). "止" cultivates concentration, while "觀" cultivates wisdom. All wholesome qualities arise from cultivation, encompassed within the practice of "止觀".

The place of worship and practice for Daoists is called "觀 (guàn)". Here, "觀 (guàn)" signifies penetration or encompassing. It implies seeing through everything. 觀 (guàn) is multidimensional. Simply put, it encompasses the external and internal, and the internal within the external. The concept of 觀 (guàn) in Daoist practice has subtle connections with the perspectives in Buddhism and Daoism. They are almost interchangeable but also have differences.

Here we need to understand a bit of translation history. In ancient China, when Buddhism gradually entered China via land routes around the Jin Dynasty (226-420), the translators of that time employed a translation method called the GEYI (格義) translation method. GEYI (格義) was a popular Buddhist interpretation during the Southern and Northern Dynasties period (420-589), employing Chinese indigenous thoughts and allusions to make Buddhist concepts more understandable. It was initiated by Zhu Faya (竺法雅), and utilized traditional Confucian and Daoist concepts to explain Buddhist doctrines, making them more accessible to people. As a result, we can see many Buddhist and Daoist terms, names, etc., appearing to be similar or interconnected.

In this context, "觀" means to penetrate everything, as mentioned in Chapter 52, note 6 of the Dao De Jing (道德經). By penetrating all details, one can understand the Great Dao, ，（見道若微），starting from the self, family, community, and extending step by step to encompass the entire world. Applied to Qi cultivation, the same principle applies. Laozi illustrates internal cultivation through external describable (meditation) kind of explanation, expanding from a single point (the seed) of awareness (the sea of primordial mind, the valley in DDJ) within ourselves to encompass the space and time within one's capabilities limitlessly. Through this, one can gain insight into everything.

Most Common Literal Translation

Those who establish their virtue through thoughts of goodness remain resolute and unyielding; those who hold onto the Great Dao through thoughts of goodness never falter. This serves as an example for future generations to continue offering sacrifices without interruption. By cultivating oneself according to such an example, one's moral character returns to simplicity and truth. By applying such an example to harmonize the family, the family's moral character becomes abundant and sufficient. By using such an example to govern the village, the village's moral character will be praised for its longevity. By employing such an example to govern the country, the country's moral character will be rich and complete. By using such an example to bring peace to the world, the world's moral character will shine universally like sunlight illuminating all things. Therefore, from the moral character of an individual, one can understand that individual; from the moral character of a family, one can understand that family; from the moral character of a village, one can understand that village; from the moral character of a country, one can understand that country; and from the moral character of the world, one can understand the world. How do I know the inevitable outcome of the world? It is through adherence to this principle.

My 5 Cents

In addition to note 3, regarding understanding this chapter from qi cultivation, here is something worth to note:

修之於身, Cultivate it within yourself,
其德乃真; Its virtue is **true**;
修之於家, Cultivate it within your family,
其德乃余; Its virtue will have **excess**;
修之於鄉, Cultivate it within your community,
其德乃長; Its virtue will be lasting or **growing**;
修之於國, Cultivate it within your country,
其德乃豐; Its virtue will be **abundant**;
修之於天下, Cultivate it within the world,
其德乃普。 Its virtue will be **universal (popular)**.

Upon careful reading, the emphasized words in red expand in essence. Initially, we must cultivate the True, allowing it to flourish (excess then grow) and become abundant. Only then can we progress to encompassing the universe and possibly other realms.

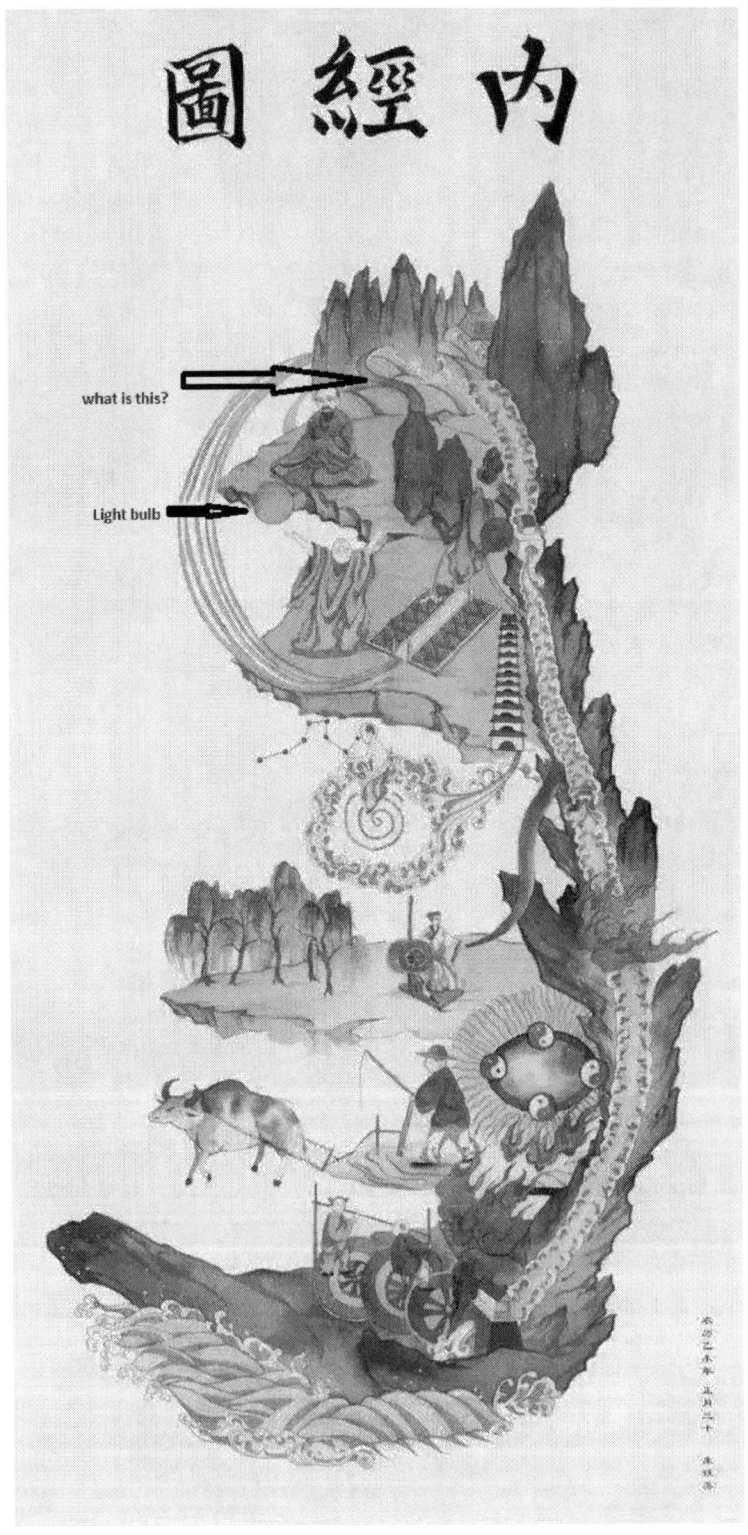

The Light Bulb needs fuel.

Quiz for this topic: What is this as marked in the diagram?

Extract From He Sang Gong – De Jing – Practicing Observation (觀 guàn)

Those who establish goodness remain steadfast, for "establish" signifies to set up or erect. Those who establish themselves and their nations on the path of goodness cannot be swayed or uprooted. Likewise, those who embrace goodness never detach from it. Those who hold onto the Dao to nurture their spirits cannot be led astray or released from their embrace.

Future generations continue offering sacrifices without interruption. Descendants who cultivate the Dao in this manner attain longevity, transcending death, lasting through the ages. They honor their ancestors through perpetual ancestral worship, ensuring the continuity of ancestral temples.

When one cultivates virtue within oneself, true virtue emerges. Cultivating the Dao within oneself nurtures vitality and spirit, extending one's lifespan. Such virtuous conduct befits a true person.

When one cultivates virtue within the family, there is excess. Cultivating the Dao within the family fosters parental kindness, filial piety, sibling harmony, marital fidelity, and familial trust. Such virtuous conduct brings blessings to future generations.

When one cultivates virtue within the community, it flourishes. Cultivating the Dao within the community entails respecting elders, nurturing the young, and educating the ignorant. Such virtuous conduct extends its influence universally.

When one cultivates virtue within the nation, it becomes rich. Cultivating the Dao within the nation fosters trust between rulers and subjects, promotes benevolence and righteousness, encourages the development of rituals and music, and ensures impartial governance. Such virtuous conduct yields richness and abundance.

When one cultivates virtue throughout the world, it becomes pervasive. Rulers who cultivate the Dao throughout the world achieve governance through transformation rather than instruction, guiding without explicit teaching. Their trustworthiness influences those below them, akin to shadows following objects. Such virtuous conduct is all-encompassing.

Therefore, observe oneself to understand oneself, comparing those who cultivate the Dao with those who do not. Likewise, observe the family, community, nation, and the world, distinguishing between those who cultivate the Tao and those who do not. How do I know the way of the world? It is through these observations. Laozi said, "How do I know the prosperity of those who cultivate the Tao and the downfall of those who stray from it? It is through these five things."

老子河上公章句 -> 德經 -> 修觀

善建者不拔，建，立也。善以道立身立國者，不可得引而拔之。善抱者不脫，善以道抱精神者，終不可拔引解脫。子孫祭祀不輟。為人子孫能修道如是，長生不死，世世以久，祭祀先祖，宗廟無絕時。修之於身，其德乃真，修道於身，愛氣養神，益壽延年。其德如是，乃為真人。修之於家，其德乃餘，修道於家，父慈子孝，兄友弟順，夫信妻貞。其德如是，乃有餘慶及於來世子孫。修之於鄉，其德乃長，修道於鄉，尊敬長老，愛養幼少，教誨愚鄙。其德如是，乃無不覆及也。修之於國，其德乃豐，修道於國，則君信臣忠，仁義自生，禮樂自興，政平無私。其德如是，乃為豐厚也。修之於天下，其德乃普。人主修道於天下，不言而化，不教而治，下之應上，信如影響。其德如是，乃為普博。故以身觀身，以修道之身，觀不修道之身，孰亡孰存也。以家觀家，以修道之家，觀不修道之家。以鄉觀鄉，以修道之鄉，觀不修道之鄉也。以國觀國，以修道之國，觀不修道之國也。以天下觀天下。以修道之主，觀不修道之主也。吾何以知天下之然哉，以此。老子言，吾何知天下修道者昌，背道者亡。以此五事觀而知之也。

【第五十五章】 Chapter 55

Most Common Translation

含德之厚，	A person with rich and profound in virtue,
比於赤子。	Is comparable to that of a newborn baby (Infant).
蜂蠆虺蛇不螫，	Bees, scorpions, vipers, and snakes do not sting;
猛獸不據，	Fierce beasts do not grab;
攫鳥不搏。	Predatory birds do not strike.
骨弱筋柔而握固。	Bone soft (fresh), sinews pliable (flexible tendon), yet hold firmly. (握固 Wò gù) (note 1)
未知牝牡之合而朘作，	The merging of yin and yang, unknown yet achieved, (note 2)
精之至也。	The ultimate refinement of essence. (Jīng 精) (note 3)
終日號而不嗄，	All day long crying without hoarse, (note 4)
和之至也。	This is the ultimate harmony. (note 5)
知和曰常，	To know harmony is called constant, (note 6)
知常曰明，	To know the constant is called enlightenment (brightness).
益生曰祥，	Beneficial growth is called auspiciousness,
心使氣曰強。	Using the mind to forcefully direct Qi, is called forced. (note 8)
物壯則老，	When things reach their prime, they begin to age,
謂之不道，	This is called going against the Dao,
不道早已。	Going against the Dao results in premature endings.

Note 1 - This verse is a continuation of Chapter 10, verses 3 and 4: The aim of gathering and concentrating Qi is to attain the utmost softness, can your qi flow like an infant?

The term "握固 (Wò gù)", literally means "hold firmly". It also refers to the natural hand posture of an infant baby.

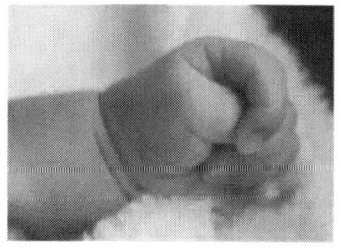

Daoists also use it as a fundamental hand posture for Qi cultivation.

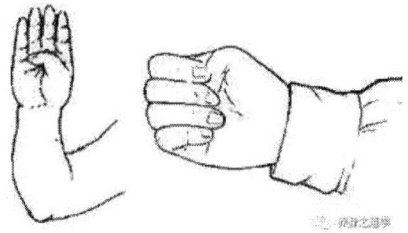

In alternative practices, particularly among female Daoists, they adopt a hand posture by clasping their waist belt during their practice sessions.

(P.S. The answer to the quiz below may shed light on why.)

Moreover, when we feel nervous or angry, our hands tend to clench involuntarily, forming a fist with the thumb outside of the other fingers.

Quiz for this Chapter: Think about what sets them apart whether the thumbs are positioned outside the fingers or grasped within them.

Note 2 - The term 牝牡 ("Pìn mǔ") carries multiple interpretations and connotations.

- The female and male of birds and animals.
- Men and women.
- Yin and yang.
- Figurative surface phenomenon.
- In ancient times, it referred to Venus in the south and Jupiter in the north, as signs of a bountiful year.

Hence 牝牡 ("Pìn mǔ"), is commonly linked with the harmonization of Yin and Yang, or with room affairs about male and female. Furthermore, it's worth noting that Venus and Jupiter symbolize metal and wood, respectively.

In ancient Daoist, it also refers to "The Method of Metal-Wood Qi Exchange" as a practice within the realm of alchemy, akin to the interaction of the dragon and tiger, previously discussed in earlier chapters, which we won't revisit here. (Please also refer to the chart illustrated in Chapter 52)

朘作 - In various versions of the Dao De Jing, the term "朘作" may vary in wording, but fundamentally it refers to the erection of the male organ.

Laozi suggests that in the verse "The merging of yin and yang, unknown yet achieved", infants or newborn babies, despite lacking conscious awareness of sex or desire for sex, experience erections due to the refinement or abundance of Jing (the essence of life energy). (P.S. This is a common phenomenon observed in newborns.) (the life essence or energy within the lower Dantian)

Note 3 - Jing 精

Building upon our previous discourse in Chapter 50 concerning the four stages, gates, or achievements, this denotes the initial stage. When our Jing is excessively abundant, it tends to dissipate through normal sexual activities or other channels. Our aim is to transmute or extract the essence of this bio-life energy into Qi through practice and elevate it to integrate with our middle Dantian.

Infant erections do not deplete the essence of Jing since infants lack sexual desire. We call it clean, and muddy as contrary. In certain schools of practice, this clean phenomenon is considered medicinal, as their practice aims to extend their physical lifespan, and is also deemed to be a detour.

Nevertheless, as indicated in Chapter 53, verse 5, and other chapters, some practitioners veer off course, focusing primarily on prolonging their sexual prowess. Similar to an emperor seeking to enhance their virility to pursue numerous partners or satisfy them, they inadvertently hasten their demise, lacking self-awareness.

Note 4 and 5 - 號(Hào), a form of crying.

In Chinese culture, there are three forms of describing crying: silently shedding tears is called "泣" making sounds without tears is called "號" and crying with both tears and sounds is called "哭", In Here, the crying of infants, therefore, is classified as "號" (Hào) characterized by sounds without tears.

嗄(Á), means hoarse.

The infant wailing ("號 Hào) all day without becoming hoarse; this is the ultimate in harmony. "號" (Hào)" here refers to crying. This is the state of infants. If they cry, it's not genuine crying. When infants cry, it's very cute and it is wailing "號 Hào " without genuinely crying from the throat, without making their voice hoarse. The word "hoarse" here means the voice becomes raspy. As people age or become ill, their voice changes. Generally, when children sing, it's called a child's voice, but a child's voice is not the same as an infant's voice. Infants wail without becoming hoarse, which indicates their abundant vitality (The energy at their middle Dantian is strong, and also refers to the heart chakra and the related attributes). Abundant vitality also means abundant spirit; the spirit remains peaceful, without emotional excitement or unfounded desires, and the state of mind is always tranquil. So it's called "the ultimate in harmony".

This part discussed the 2nd stage of the four gates, the Qi.

Note 6 - To know the harmony is called the constant, it is the 3rd stage of the four gates. The spirit.

Recall my previous notes on Lü Dongbin (796-) Hundred-Character Monument Note 2

Qingjing Jing

Always observing and responding to external matters with their genuine nature without any bias, can acquire the true nature of the one-self.

Often interchange and interact with calm mind and peacefulness.

Hence, mind peacefulness (tranquil and serene) as always.

清靜經

真常應物，真常得性

相應常靜，常清靜矣

In the Qingjing Jing, I utilized the term "always", while here, I've employed "constant". Essentially, they convey the same meaning. This is how we train our minds.

Note 7 - No note 7 as always (constant 😊 😊 😊)

Note 8 - As said, always (I used always again 😊, know the constant is called enlightenment, haha) guide your Qi according to the situation, using the right fire (mind) and bellows. Softness is the key.

Most Common Literal Translation

Version 1 - A person with abundant virtue is like a naked infant. Poisonous creatures do not sting, ferocious beasts do not bite, and fierce birds do not harm. Their tendons and bones may be weak, yet they grasp firmly and hold tightly. They may not understand the arousal of male and female reproductive organs, yet their natural vitality remains robust. They cry all day without becoming hoarse, thanks to the natural harmony of their inherent vitality.

Natural harmony is the eternal foundation, and understanding eternal truths is enlightenment. To enhance vitality is to bring auspiciousness and fortune, while diligently harmonizing qi and blood leads to strength. If one forcefully pursues robustness, it will accelerate the aging of all things, which goes against the laws of the Great Way (Dao). Disregarding the laws of the Great Way (Dao) will lead to premature decay.

Version 2 - A person of deep virtue is like a newborn baby: poisonous insects do not sting them, fierce beasts do not attack them, and malicious birds do not strike them. Though their bones are weak and their sinews tender, they grasp firmly; they do not know the sexual union yet they can still have erections—so abundant is their vitality. They cry all day yet do not exhaust their strength or hoarsen their voice—so harmonious is their nature. Understanding how to be gentle in demeanor can achieve a constant state of survival; knowing how to achieve this constant state of survival is what is called being enlightened in the Way. Insisting too much on life is dangerous; letting the mind wander excessively, even if the vital energy is strong, is to be reckless. Excessive strength in existence will lead to aging, which is contrary to the Way. Being contrary to the Way always leads to premature death.

My 5 Cents

This Chapter introduces the 3 stages of achievements and training through the gates. The Jing, the Qi, and the Spirit. And the continuation of the previous chapter, 54. Observing oneself through oneself. Observing ourselves, inner visualized ourselves from within, the life energy, the middle Dantian, and the Mind spirit. By grasping control of your jing, qi, and spirit, and nurture them diligently. Otherwise, you are going against the Dao which leads to premature endings.

Some stories to share:

One day, while we were still in Hong Kong, my young dogs (still puppies) were peacefully slumbering in the backyard when a large snake slithered up close to them. Surprisingly, instead of barking or reacting in any way, my dogs simply continued to doze ZZZzzzz. Thankfully, the snake eventually retreated without incident.

I had a similar experience when I was a child. A snake raised its head and locked eyes with me. Fortunately, it deemed me either not tasty or too uninteresting to engage with and slithered away. (Maybe I did not have a flute with me?)

When encountering bees or wasps, the most effective way to protect yourself is to refrain from hurting them, avoid yelling or shouting, and resist the urge to chase them away. Instead, allow them to investigate by letting them smell and gently interact with you, such as with gentle kisses. Maintaining a peaceful demeanor and mindset is key. They will likely move on of their own accord.

A story told by an Indian sage, his spell or mantra with the wasps is: please do not sting me, with a peaceful mind, of course.

Indeed, bees and wasps are sensitive to vibrations. If your energy is unclean or negative, they may perceive you as a threat and attempt to protect their colony, even at the cost of their own lives as they sting.

Interestingly, this approach doesn't seem to apply to female mosquitoes. However, in deep meditation, mosquitoes also refrain from stinging. From personal experience, it appears they patiently wait for you to emerge from your meditative state before striking.

Similar lining up like this in front of you

Always be an infant and train yourself to be an infant.

Extract from He Sang Gong – De Jing - Mysterious Talisman

The thickness of virtue refers to the profoundness of embracing moral principles. Compared to a newborn baby, the divine protect those who possess profound virtue, just as parents protect their newborns. Poisonous insects do not sting them; bees, wasps, snakes, and vipers do not sting them. Fierce beasts do not attack them; predatory birds do not strike them. A newborn harms no one, and no one harms a newborn. Therefore, in an era of great peace, there is no distinction between high and low; the heart of benevolence transforms things with thorns back to their original state, and poisonous insects do not harm people. Despite weak bones and tender sinews, they hold fast. Though a newborn's tendons and bones are soft and weak, they grasp things firmly because their intention is unwavering. They do not yet understand the union of male and female, yet they exhibit the utmost in vitality. A newborn does not yet understand the anger between male and female, as it is due to an abundance of vital energy. They cry all day yet remain unhoarse; this is the epitome of harmony. A newborn cries from morning till night without changing their voice; this is the culmination of abundant harmony. Understanding harmony in daily life, when people can be gentle and beneficial to others, this is the essence of understanding the Way. Knowing the essence daily, when people can consistently follow the Way, they will gradually comprehend the profound mysteries. With each passing day, life flourishes; 'flourish' means to grow. Saying that life flourishes desire self-generation and growth every day. The mind strengthens the vital energy day by day. When the mind is focused and gentle, and the spirit is full within, the form becomes soft. But when one acts recklessly, the harmony departs from within, and thus the body becomes increasingly rigid. When things become strong, they age; when all things reach their peak strength, they wither and age. This is called being contrary to the Way; withering and aging means one cannot attain the Way. Those who are contrary to the Way die early; those who cannot attain the Way die prematurely.

老子河上公章句 -> 德經 -> 玄符

含德之厚,謂含懷道德之厚也。比於赤子。神明保佑含德之人,若父母之於赤子也。毒蟲不螫,蜂蠆蛇虺不螫。猛獸不據,攫鳥不搏。赤子不害於物,物亦不害之。故太平之世,人無貴賤,仁心,有刺之物,還返其本,有毒之蟲,不傷於人。骨弱筋柔而握固。赤子筋骨柔弱而持物堅固,以其意心不移也。未知牝牡之合而朘作精之至也。赤子未知男女會合而陰陽作怒者,由精氣多之所致也。終日號而不啞,和之至也。赤子從朝至暮啼號聲不變易者,和氣多之所至也。知和日常,人能和氣柔弱有益於人者,則為知道之常也。知常日明,人能知道之常行,則日以明達於玄妙也。益生日祥,祥,長也。言益生欲自生,日以長大。心使氣日強。心當專一和柔而神氣實內,故形柔。而反使妄有所為,和氣去於中,故形體日以剛強也。物壯則老,萬物壯極則枯老也。謂之不道,枯老則不得道矣。不道早已。不得道者早死。

【第五十六章】Chapter 56

Most Common Translation

知者不言，	Those who know do not speak,
言者不知。	Those who speak do not know.
塞其兑，	Fill up the Dui,
闭其门，	Close the door,
挫其锐；	Blunt its sharpness;
解其纷，	Unravel its confusion (Chaos),
和其光，	Harmonize its Light,
同其尘，	Synchronize with the dust.
是谓玄同。	This is called profound (mystical) sameness (Harmonization).
故不可得而亲，	Therefore, it cannot be approached to become intimate,
不可得而疏；	It cannot be obtained and kept at a distance.
不可得而利，	It cannot be obtained for benefit,
不可得而害；	It cannot be obtained for harm.
不可得而贵，	It cannot be obtained to be noble,
不可得而贱，	It cannot be obtained to be debased.
故为天下贵。	Therefore, it is esteemed by all under heaven.

Most Common Literal Translation

Those who are enlightened about the Way do not assert words, and those who assert words are not enlightened about the Way. Block the interfaces of giving and receiving, close the doorways of detachment from chaotic namelessness, dull overly prominent sharp edges, resolve tangled conflicts and disputes, restrain excessively dazzling brilliance, and unify all existence as one. This is called achieving a state of harmonious unity. Therefore, gaining something from the Way transcends the capture of affection, distance, gain, harm, honor, and status. In this way, one can gain the common respect of the entire world.

My 5 Cents

For a deeper understanding of this chapter, it's beneficial to read it alongside chapters 4 and 56. It combines elements from both while also extending their concepts.

From the perspective of Qi cultivation, once we've achieved the closure of (DUI) and attained internal peace, we begin to perceive light and dust. Here, the focus is primarily on spiritual accomplishments, the upper Dantian. It is all about inner vision and or sacred vision.

To dull impulsive aggression, to free oneself from confusion and anxieties, to embrace the inner radiance alongside the cosmic energy's brilliance, to directly perceive the true essence of the DUST—only through profound cultivation can one enter the realm of unity with the Dao.

Attempting to ascend forcefully without attaining this state inevitably results in feelings of proximity and distance, gains and losses, and distinctions of high and low status, which stir up turmoil within. Thus, true value is only achieved by attaining unity with the Way.

【第五十七章】Chapter 57

Most Common Translation

以正治國，	Govern the country with honor and integrity,
以奇用兵，	Use unexpected tactics in warfare,
以無事取天下。	Conquer the world without meddling.
吾何以知其然哉？	How do I know that it is so?
以此。	Because of this.
天下多忌諱，	The world is full of taboos,
而民彌貧；	And the people become poorer;
民多利器，	With many sharp weapons among the people,
國家滋昏；	The state becomes chaotic.
人多伎巧，	People are cunning and resourceful,
奇物滋起；	Strange objects proliferate;
法令滋彰，	Laws are abundant,
盜賊多有。	Yet thieves and bandits abound.
故聖人雲：	Therefore, the sage said:
我無為而民自化，	I act with Wúwéi, people transform themselves,
我好靜而民自正，	I prefer tranquility, people become upright on their own;
我無事而民自富，	I am uninvolved, and the people become prosperous on their own;
我無欲而民自樸。	I have no desires, and the people become 樸 Pǔ (note 1) by themselves.

Note 1 - In conjunction with Chapter 19 and Chapter 28, along with Note 1 of Chapter 28, the verse "I have no desires, and the people will become (樸 Pǔ) by themselves" is rich in meaning. 樸 Pǔ encompasses three layers of significance. Firstly, it denotes simplicity. Secondly, it symbolizes a tree bark, serving as a vessel for the nation, akin to a tool. And thirdly, it represents a weapon.

In contemporary terms, this concept involves investing in the people by nurturing their potential (Hiding wealth within the people). "Wealth" here extends beyond monetary assets to encompass all flexible and advantageous dynamics for the nation. Despite the simplicity of the people's demeanor, they possess the ability to adapt to changing circumstances (riding the waves)—this embodies the essence of acting effortlessly (Wúwéi) and following the Dao.

Most Common Literal Translation

Using the way of Wúwéi and tranquility to govern the country, employing clever and mysterious methods in warfare, and governing the world below without disturbing or harming the people. How do I know if this is the case? It lies in this: the more taboos there are in the world, the more people fall into poverty; the more sharp weapons the people have, the more chaotic the country becomes; the more skills people possess, the more rampant strange and wicked phenomena become; the stricter the laws, the more thieves and bandits proliferate. Therefore, the sage of the Dao says: when I act with Wúwéi, the people transform themselves; when I prefer tranquility, the people naturally become prosperous; when I have no desires, the people naturally become simple and sincere.

Extract from He Sang Gong - De Jing – Simple and Sincere Demeanor

I often have no desires, dress plainly, and wear simple attire, leading the people to follow my example in simplicity. The sage says: "I cultivate the Dao, uphold truth, and rid myself of the six desires; the people naturally follow me and become pure."

老子河上公章句 -> 德經 -> 淳風

我常無欲，去華文，微服飾，民則隨我為質樸也。聖人言：我修道守真，絕去六情，民自隨我而清也。

【第五十八章】Chapter 58

Most Common Translation

其政悶悶，	When the administrative policy is warm and gentle,
其民淳淳；	The people are simple and contented;
其政察察，	When the administrative policy is active and highly scrutinizing,
其民缺缺。	The people are lacking and troubled.
禍兮福之所倚，	Misfortune and fortune lean on each other's edge,
福兮禍之所伏。	Fortune often hides within misfortune.
孰知其極？	Who truly comprehends their ultimate limits?
其無正。	Fortune and misfortune have no regularity, no fixed form. Or, The shift from normality to absurdity,
正復為奇，	Fortune may shift to mishappen, (Original wording: Even may turn to Odd)
善復為妖，	Goodness may shift to the devil,
人之迷，	The loss or confusion of people,
其日固久。	Has been a long time.
是以聖人方而不割，	Therefore, the sage squares without cutting, harvesting (note 1)
廉而不劌，	Has an edge but does not hurt, (note 2)
直而不肆，	Straightforward without being reckless, (note 3)
光而不耀。	Shining without being dazzling.

Note 1 - In Chapter 41, it's stated that the Great Square has no corners, which means it has no sharp edges, ensuring it won't harm or harvest, or exploit its followers or citizens.

Note 2 - 廉 (lián) primarily means "edge" or "sickle" in this context.

劌 (guì) means "cutting".

Together, "廉而不劌" signifies "having the tool (sickle) but not harvesting", implying governance without exploitation.

廉潔 (lián jié) translates to "integrity" or "probity", indicating clean morals and the absence of corruption.

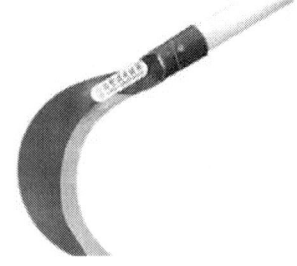

The sickle, a traditional farming tool, is also used by ninjas as a concealed weapon, disguising themselves as ordinary farmers.

Another common garden tool, the kunai, serves purposes such as leveling out bricks within walls or removing weeds. It is utilized both in throwing knife practice and in actual gardening tasks like weeding.

PS: it is really good at picking out weeds.

Note 3 - In Chapter 45, the concept of utmost directness appearing indirect is emphasized, drawing their commons.

Most Common Literal Translation

When politics are benevolent and clear, the people are simple and loyal; when politics are harsh and dark, the people become cunning and resentful. Misfortune, oh misfortune, happiness leans on its brink; happiness, oh happiness, misfortune hides within it. Who can truly discern whether it is misfortune or happiness? They lack definite standards. Righteousness suddenly turns into evil, goodness suddenly turns into wickedness; humanity's confusion has endured for long. Therefore, the Daoist sage remains upright without rigidity, has edges without harming others, is straightforward without being reckless, and shines brightly without glaring.

My 5 cents

The wording used in this chapter is very harmonic. This first few verses:

其政悶悶，
其民淳淳；
其政察察，
其民缺缺。

If translated word by word, it is very funny:
The policy, bore and bore,
The people, pure and pure;
The policy, scrutinize and scrutinize,
The people, lack and lack;

Side note: There's another similar instance, in recent years, a new internet slang has emerged in China: "harvesting leeks". It means to harvest well-grown leeks. Leeks grow easily and abundantly, usually symbolizing consumers.

【第五十九章】 Chapter 59

Most Common Translation

治人事天莫若嗇。	To govern people and serve the heavens, there is nothing better than frugality (mean) (嗇). (note 1)
夫唯嗇，	Only through 嗇(Sè),
是謂早服。	This is called (早服) Zǎo fú (note 2)
早服謂之重積德，	Zǎo fú, is called to focus heavily on the accumulation of virtues, (note 3)
重積德則無不克，	Accumulate virtues, and there's nothing you can not conquer (overcome).
無不克則莫知其極，	Nothing you can not conquer, nothing known is your limit,
莫知其極，	Nothing being known is your limit,
可以有國。	You can have a nation or reign a state.
有國之母，	When you have the mother of a nation (note 4).
可以長久。	It can last long.
是謂深根固柢，	This is known as having deep roots and a strong foundation,
長生久視之道。	The path to longevity and far-sightedness. (note 5)

Note 1 - "Lìn (吝)" and "Sè (嗇)" are two distinct words in Chinese. While in English they may both translate as "mean", "frugality", "stingy", or "miserly", they carry different connotations in Chinese usage. Let me provide a detailed explanation of how these words are used in Chinese, hope it helps your understand of this chapter.

Being ' Sè (嗇)" means being frugal with oneself but generous with friends. Therefore, being harsh on oneself but generous to others is Sè (嗇). In addition, it also conveys the notion of "cherishing" or "treasuring".

While being lenient (generous) on oneself but harsh on others is "(吝) Lìn". It is important to distinguish between these two.

In this Chapter, Laozi used the word "Sè (嗇)" --- doing mean on oneself, but generous to others.

Note 2 - 早服 Zǎo fú

This phrase is challenging to translate directly into English. It could mean "early medication", "early serving" "early obedience", or "morning dressing". He Sang Gong read it as an early achievement.

Note 3 - In essence, it signifies the accumulation of blessings or merits through one's endeavors, serving as a valuable resource for governing a nation. In other words, cultivating your Qi or spiritual practice.

Recalling our discussions about the 4 criteria of practicing:

In Dao, it is: 法，財，侶，地。

1. methods of cultivation/practice;
2. resources; (spiritually, mentally, and materially);
3. fellowship; and
4. location, a suitable place for practicing.

In Buddhism, it is: 福，德，資，糧。

1. blessing;
2. virtues;
3. quality (it includes root intelligence); and
4. resources (enough merits to support your practice, of course, it includes physical)

Note 4 - In this context, "the mother of a nation" refers to the sources mentioned above—blessings, virtues, resources, and sustenance. In other words, The fundamental way of governing a country - Sè (嗇), Master yourself, serve others.

"When you have the mother of a nation, it can last long."

It means the cycle of continuous renewal, the most primal source. In the metaphysical realm, it is the Dao. In the physical realm, it is simplicity or Sè (嗇). Only through this can longevity be achieved.

Note 5 - 長生久視

Same as "Misfortune and fortune lean on each other's edge" (禍福常依) stated in chapter 58, and, "Those who know do not speak, those who speak do not know" (知者不言，言者不知). This sentence (長生久視) is also very famous and often quoted. It's generally interpreted as the art of longevity. However, there isn't a universally agreed-upon definition of how to achieve longevity or why it leads to far-sightedness.

The concept of longevity and far-sightedness is prominently discussed in the "Yellow Court Scripture", along with various other significant Daoist scriptures. These texts delve into profound inner-body visualization and practical methods for cultivation.

They offer valuable insights into achieving longevity and developing a farsighted perspective on life.

Most Common Literal Translation

To govern people and serve the heavens, there is nothing more important than cultivating frugality and restraint. Cultivating frugality and restraint allows one to first submit to the Way. By first submitting to the Way, one can deepen their virtue. With deep virtue, there is nothing one cannot handle. When one is capable of handling anything, their endurance becomes limitless. With limitless endurance, they are able to safeguard the country. The foundation of safeguarding the country ensures its longevity. This is what it means to have deep roots and solid support, thereby ensuring the long-lasting existence of the Way in the world.

My 5 cents

Here is an alternative interpretation of this chapter, focusing on the perspective of qi cultivation or spiritual practice, even though practitioners may follow different paths. They all converge on the principle of being frugal with oneself, which pertains to minimizing unnecessary mental activities or clutter in the mind. This aligns with the advice in chapter 56, where the emphasis lies on not overstimulating the mind and instead nurturing our mental energy from within.

In the time of Laozi, the term "nation" did not solely denote a country; it also encompassed personal wealth or assets. (During that era, kings possessed the nation, thus it could be seen as the king's personal asset.) Additionally, it symbolized spiritual assets – assets of a metaphysical nature.

Regarding the second last verse: "Having deep roots and a strong foundation", 深根固柢, we should read it together with chapter 10, "The aim of gathering and concentrating Qi is to attain the utmost softness, can your Qi flow like an infant?" (專氣至柔，能嬰兒乎？)

Chapter 16 talks about the root. Especially, the verses: "To attain utmost emptiness, adhere steadfastly to quietude" (致虛極，守靜篤), and "Each return to its source. "(各復歸期根), and "Returning to the source is tranquility, is called returning to one's destiny and life."(歸根曰靜，是謂覆命).

Gathering all these together, we may have an insight into what Laozi actually wants to say, it is inner breathing. In modern Chinese scholarship, the esteemed master Nan Huai-Chin (南怀瑾) regards this as "Tai Xi"(胎息)or "Embryo Breathing". A kind of internal breathing. I agree with the concept of "Inner Breathing" because it encompasses all internal Qi flow activities. From my personal experience, after the complete closure of the heart chakra, the inner breathing stirred bears similarities to "Embryo Breathing".

So, what is actually Embryo Breathing, we will talk about this later, when times fit.

Back to Sè (嗇), the second part of Sè (嗇), is generous to others. In Daoism, it's about accumulating public virtue, with distinctions between internal and external aspects. In Buddhism, this equates to practicing generosity or giving (Dāna (佈施)).

Dāna (佈施) is a Sanskrit and Pali word that connotes the virtue of generosity, charity or giving of alms, in Indian religions and philosophies. In Hinduism, Buddhism, Jainism, and Sikhism, dāna is the practice of cultivating generosity.

The three types of giving (Dāna (佈施)):

1. Material Giving: Providing material goods to aid those who are sick or impoverished.
2. Dharma Giving: Sharing truth and wisdom, using righteous teachings to encourage people to cultivate goodness and eradicate evil. This helps individuals understand the meaning and value of life, motivating them to practice and pursue truth voluntarily.
3. Fearlessness Giving: Doing everything possible to alleviate others' fears and apprehensions; this involves giving confidence and compassion. It also entails steadfastly adhering to the Eightfold Path, remaining unaffected by criticism or the opinions of others, maintaining right mindfulness and right action, and fearlessly enduring humiliation. Thus, it's called "fearlessness" giving.

In Zhuangzi's "Outer Things" chapter, he quotes from the Book of Poetry: "If life is not spent in giving, why is death adorned with jewels?"

Quiz: Is offering a cookie to Cookiemonster considered an act of generous giving (Dana)? No, it is mean, you should give lots of cookies to Cookiemonster 😊

Extract from He Sang Gong – De Jing – Guard the Dao

To govern people" refers to the ruler's management of the people. "Affairs of heaven" means the utilization of natural principles. When dealing with affairs, one should follow the laws of heaven and conform to the seasons. Nothing is better than frugality. Frugality means cherishing and conserving. Those who govern a country should cherish the wealth of the people and avoid extravagance. Those who cultivate themselves should cherish their essence and vitality and avoid indulgence. To practice frugality is to take the right path early. "Early" means beforehand. "Taking the right path" means obtaining what is beneficial. If one cherishes the wealth of the people and cherishes their essence and vitality, then they can obtain the principles of heaven beforehand. Obtaining the principles of heaven early is called accumulating virtues heavily. By obtaining the principles of heaven beforehand, one heavily accumulates benefits for themselves. When virtues are heavily accumulated, there is nothing one cannot overcome. "Overcome" means succeed. By heavily accumulating virtues for oneself, there is nothing one cannot succeed in. When there is nothing one cannot overcome, no one knows the limits of their capabilities. When one can overcome everything, no one knows the limit of their virtuous capabilities. Not knowing one's limits can establish a country. Not knowing one's virtuous capabilities' limits can establish a dynasty, bringing happiness to the people. The mother of a country can then lasts for a long time. The country's body is the same. "Mother" means Dao. If people can protect the Dao within themselves, ensuring that their essence and vitality are not exhausted and their 5 spirits are not tormented, then the country can last for a long time. This is called deeply rooted and firmly established. If people can make their vitality the root and their essence the foundation, just as a tree with shallow roots can be uprooted and a weak foundation can cause collapse, then they should deeply conceal their vitality and firmly guard their essence, ensuring no leakage. This is the way to longevity and enduring vision. "Deeply rooting and firmly establishing" is the way to longevity and enduring vision.

老子河上公章句 -> 德經 -> 守道

治人，謂人君治理人民。事天，事，用也。當用天道，順四時。莫若嗇。嗇，愛惜也。治國者當愛民財，不為奢泰。治身者當愛精氣，不為放逸。夫為嗇，是謂早服。早，先也。服，得也。夫獨愛民財，愛精氣，則能先得天道也。早服謂之重積德。先得天道，是謂重積得於己也。重積德則無不剋，剋，勝也。重積德於己，則無不勝。無不剋則莫知其極，無不剋勝，則莫知有知己德之窮極也。莫知其極可以有國。莫知己德者有極，則可以有社稷，為民致福。有國之母，可以長久。國身同也。母，道也。人能保身中之道，使精氣不勞，五神不苦，則可以長久。是謂深根固蒂，人能以氣為根，以精為蒂，如樹根不深則拔，蒂不堅則落。言當深藏其氣，固守其精，使無漏泄。長生久視之道。深根固蒂者，乃長生久視之道。

【第六十章】 Chapter 60

Most Common Translation

治大國若烹小鮮。	To govern a great nation is like cooking a small fish. (note 1)
以道蒞天下，	Approach the world with the Dao,
其鬼不神。	Evil spirits will not have power over you.
非其鬼不神，	Not that evil spirits have no power,
其神不傷人；	It is their power will not harm people.
非其神不傷人，	Not that powers do not harm people,
聖人亦不傷人。	Even the sage does not harm people.
夫兩不相傷，	When neither harms the other,
故德交歸焉。	Hence virtue returns to the Dao. (note 2)

Note 1 - 烹 pēng, has several meanings, although it is always translated as "cook", or "boil"

1. A cooking method that involves briefly stir-frying in hot oil before adding liquid seasonings, quickly stirring, and then serving immediately.
2. An ancient form of torture involving boiling people alive in a cauldron.
3. From Mozi's "Plowing with Pillars" chapter: "The tripod is square with three legs (鼎爐 Dǐng lú), it cooks without needing a fire, it lifts without needing hands, it moves without needing to be carried. (ps: 鼎爐 Dǐng lú is in English is "tripod cauldron" or "ding". It refers to a type of ancient Chinese cooking vessel with three legs and two loop handles, often used for boiling, stewing, and steaming food. It's also a symbol of prosperity and stability in Chinese culture. In addition, in Neidan, our body is also referred to as a 鼎爐 Dǐng lú, where our Neidan is cultivating within)

練丹爐 Liàn dān lú   Human alchemy furnace (alchemy furnace)

小鮮 Xiǎo xiān - 小鮮, When translated word for word, it reads as "little freshly", but it's commonly understood as "small fish" in literal terms. However, it extends beyond fish to encompass any delicate, fresh ingredients. These ingredients are prone to overcooking and aren't suited for frequent flipping.

Su Zhe's "Interpretation of Laozi" (1039-1112):

"Ruling a large country is like cooking small, delicate fish.

When cooking small, delicate fish, do not disturb them;

When ruling a large country, do not be agitated.

Agitation leads to people being weary, disturbance leads to the fish falling apart."

Note 2 - The heart and kidneys intersect, returning to the Dao. (心腎相交，歸於道)

Most Common Literal Translation

To govern a great country is like cooking a small fish. When using the Dao to govern the world, the power of ghosts and spirits does not function. Not because ghosts have no power, but their influence cannot harm people. Not only are people not harmed by the influence of ghosts, but the Dao of the sage also does not harm people. In this way, ghosts and spirits, as well as the sages with the Dao, do not harm people. Therefore, the people can enjoy the blessings of virtue.

My 5 Cents

As we already know, a nation can metaphorically represent our body or the cultivation of qi within it. With this insight in mind, upon revisiting this chapter, and my notes as stated above, we can grasp Laozi's intention. It revolves around the harmonization of the heart's qi and the kidney's qi.

Furthermore, when cooking small, delicate fish, avoid frequent flipping. Instead, handle them gently and follow a steady approach, ensuring that neither the heat nor the water aggress each other. Aim for harmony, resulting in a beneficial outcome.

Describing the concept of harmony between heat and water, Daoist scriptures employ various metaphors:

- Tigers and dragons become allies.
- Bride and groom unite in marriage.
- Mercury and lead meld together seamlessly.
- Heart and Kidney intersect.
- Metal and wood exchange their qi. (金木交氣) (the hardest one to be understood and explain)

Extract from He Sang Gong- De Jing – Dwelling in position.

To govern a great state is like cooking small fish.

When cooking small fish, one must not remove the intestines, nor scale them, nor disturb them too much, fearing they may fall apart. If governing a country becomes cumbersome, it leads to chaos; if managing oneself becomes burdensome, one's vitality dissipates. Governing the world through the Way, its spirits will not manifest. Ruling the world from a position of moral integrity, the spirits will not dare to violate people with their energy. It's not that the spirits lack energy, but without conforming to the natural order, they cannot harm people. It's not that the spirits refrain from harming people; even the sage refrains from harm. Without spirits and gods causing harm, the sage in power doesn't provoke them. When neither harms the other, spirits and sages exist without harming one another. Thus, virtue returns to its source. When neither harms the other, people are governed in the open, while spirits and gods are governed in the hidden. People preserve their lives, and spirits preserve their essence. Hence, virtue returns to its source.

老子河上公章句 -> 德經 -> 居位

治大國者若烹小鮮。鮮，魚。烹小魚不去腸、不去鱗、不敢撓，恐其糜也。治國煩則下亂，治身煩則精散。以道莅天下，其鬼不神。以道德居位治天下，則鬼不敢以其精神犯人也。非其鬼不神，其神不傷人。其鬼非無精神也，非不入正，不能傷自然之人。非其神不傷人，聖人亦不傷。非鬼神不能傷害人。以聖人在位不傷害人，故鬼不敢干之也。夫兩不相傷，鬼與聖人俱兩不相傷也。故德交歸焉。夫兩不相傷，則人得治於陽，鬼神得治於陰，人得保全其性命，鬼得保其精神，故德交歸焉。

【第六十一章】Chapter 61

Most Common Translation

大國者下流。	The great nation is like water flowing downward.
天下之交，	The intercourse of the world,
天下之牝。	The feminine essence of the world.
牝常以靜勝牡，	The female always overcomes the male by stillness,
以靜為下。	By stillness, she is beneath.
故大國以下小國，	So, when the great nation is beneath the small nation,
則取小國；	It takes the small nation.
小國以下大國，	When the small nation is beneath the great nation,
則取大國。	It takes the great nation.
故或下以取，	Therefore, sometimes by lowering it takes,
或下而取。	Or by being lower, it takes.
大國不過欲兼畜人，	The great nation merely seeks to nurture its people,
小國不過欲入事人，	The small country desires only to be of service to people.
夫兩者各得其所欲，	Both achieve what they desire,
大者宜為下。	Yet the larger should humble itself.

Most Common Literal Translation

Great nations should be like rivers, flowing downstream, becoming the gathering point of all beneath heaven. In the world, female creatures often triumph over males by being quiet and passive. They take the lower position by being still. Therefore, if a great nation can be humble towards a smaller one, it can gain the people of that smaller nation. If a smaller nation can be humble towards a greater one, it can benefit from the resources of the greater nation. So, on one hand, humility towards others can gain the people of another nation, and on the other hand, it can gain the resources of that nation. But for a great nation to accommodate smaller nations, and for a smaller nation to gain the people of a great nation, all they need to do is to be humble. By being humble, each can obtain what they desire. However, it is especially important for great nations to be humble. When smaller nations are humble, they can only preserve themselves, but when great nations are humble, they can bring the world together.

My 5 Cents

Only by settling below can water form seas, The mountain does not boast of its height, its gaze far reaches to the sky.

【第六十二章】 Chapter 62

Most Common Translation

道者萬物之奧，	Dao holds the mysteries of all things,
善人之寶，	A treasure for the virtuous,
不善人之所保。	A sanctuary for the less virtuous.
美言可以市尊，	Kind words can gain esteem,
尊行可以加人。	Honorable deeds can attract others.
人之不善，	Even in the absence of goodness in people,
何棄之有！	Why abandon them?
故立天子，	Hence, establishing an emperor,
置三公，	Appointing three ministers,
雖有拱璧以先駟馬，	Even with an offering of precious jade first and then the fast horses, (note 1)
不如坐進此道。	Doesn't match the worth of embracing (sitting on) this path. (the Dao)
古之所以貴此道者何？	Why did the ancients value this Path of Dao?
不曰以求得，	It is not about believing in 'Ask and you shall receive, (note 2)
有罪以免邪？	And by committing wrongs, they were spared?
故為天下貴。	Therefore, it is valued by the world.

Note 1 - In the time of Laozi, the procedure for gifts from kings and nobles was to first offer jade objects, followed by precious horses. The presentation of four horses symbolized a carriage with four horses' power, which was considered extremely rare at that time.

Note 2 - 不曰以求得, It is not about believing in 'Ask and you shall receive, And by committing wrongs, they were spared?

Another less common version is 不曰求以得. which means: "Not to seek in order to obtain, or to commit wrongs to be spared?".

Most Common Literal Translation

The Dao is the shelter of all things; virtuous people cherish it, while those who are not virtuous also seek to maintain it. When needed, they also seek its protection. Fine words can earn others' respect for you; good deeds can earn you esteem. How could those who are not virtuous abandon it?

Therefore, when the emperor ascends the throne and appoints the Three ministers, although there is the ceremonial presentation of Jade and horses, it is better to offer this "Dao" to them. Since ancient times (Laozi ancient time), people have valued the "Dao" so highly, precisely because seeking its protection will surely be fulfilled; even if one commits offenses, they can still obtain its forgiveness. It is precisely for this reason that people throughout the world treasure the "Dao" so much.

My 5 Cents

Extract from He Sang Gong -De Jing – For Dao

The Dao is the essence of all things, profound and mysterious. "Profound" means hidden. The Dao is the hiding place of all things, accommodating everything without exception. For virtuous people, it is their treasure; they regard the Dao as their most precious possession and dare not depart from it. For those who are not virtuous, the Dao serves as their reliance. In times of trouble and urgency, even they know to repent and humble themselves.

Fine words can be traded for profit, but only those skilled in eloquence can profit from them. In market transactions, buyers want to acquire quickly, and sellers want to sell quickly. Thus, eloquent speech is sought after. Honorable conduct can be added to, but "added" means "separated". When one's conduct is honorable, it sets them apart from ordinary people, yet mere honor is not enough to honor the Dao.

As for those who are not virtuous, why should they be abandoned? Even though people may lack virtue, they should be transformed by the Dao. Before the Three Sovereigns, there was no abandoning of the people; virtue and transformation were pure. Therefore, the emperor was established, and the Three Officials were appointed to educate and transform those who were not virtuous.

Even if one were to receive treasures and horses in advance, it would not compare to sitting down and embracing this Dao. Why not seek to obtain this Dao daily? Why not seek to obtain this Dao daily instead of traveling far and wide to search for it, when it can be found close at hand?

Can one escape punishment for their sins? "Sins" refers to encountering chaotic times, where unwise rulers govern unjustly, leading to punishment. By cultivating the Dao, one can escape death and avoid calamity, saving oneself from the masses. Therefore, it is esteemed by the world. The Dao's morality is profound and far-reaching, covering all and benefiting all. When one governs themselves and the state with integrity and tranquility, they can effortlessly achieve great things, thus making it valuable to the world.

老子河上公章句 -> 德經 -> 為道

道者萬物之奧，奧，藏也。道為萬物之藏，無所不容也。善人之寶，善人以道為身寶，不敢違也。不善人之所保。道者，不善人之保倚也。遭患逢急，猶知自悔卑下。美言可以市，美言者獨可於市耳。夫市交易而退，不相宜善言美語，求者欲疾得，賣者欲疾售也。尊行可以加人。加，別也。人有尊貴之行，可以別異於凡人，未足以尊道。人之不善，何棄之有。人雖不善，當以道化之。蓋三皇之前，無有棄民，德化淳也。故立天子，置三公，欲使教化不善之人。雖有拱璧以先駟馬，不如坐進此道。雖有美璧先駟馬而至，故不如坐進此道。古之所以貴此道者，何不日以求得？古之所以貴此道者，不日日遠行求索，近得之於身。有罪以免耶，有罪謂遭亂世，闇君妄行形誅，修道則可以解死，免於眾也。故為天下貴。道德洞遠，無不覆濟，全身治國，恬然無為，故可為天下貴也。

【第六十三章】Chapter 63

Most Common Translation

為無為，	Practice Wúwéi,
事無事，	Act, inactivity,
味無味。	Taste the tasteless.
大小多少，	Irrespective of magnitude or extent, (note 1)
報怨以德。	Repay grievances with virtue.
圖難於其易，	Solve the difficulties starting from the easy part.
為大於其細。	To accomplish great tasks starting from the small.
天下難事必作於易，	All difficult matters in the world begin with the easy,
天下大事必作於細，	All great matters in the world begin with the small.
是以聖人終不為大，	That's why the wise never rush into big deeds,
故能成其大。	Thus, they can achieve greatness.
夫輕諾必寡信，	Casual promises often lack credibility,
多易必多難，	Many easy tasks inevitably lead to many difficulties.
是以聖人猶難之。	That's why the sage perceives the easy as challenging.
故終無難矣。	Therefore, in the end, there are no difficulties.

Note 1 - 大小多少 (word-by-word translation is: big, small, many, little)

In this context, some are verbs, and some are nouns, and they are interchangeable. This verse suggests treating small matters as significant and significant matters as small. Small things may seem insignificant, but they often hold the key to solving larger problems.

Most Common Literal Translation

With a mindset of Wúwéi, one achieves results. By handling affairs without stirring up trouble and finding satisfaction in simplicity, greatness arises from small beginnings and abundance from scarcity. Tackling challenges begins with the easy while achieving greatness starts from the minute. Difficulties in the world always originate from the simple, while significant endeavors begin from the subtle. Hence, those who follow the "Dao" never seek grand contributions, hence they accomplish great things. Those who make promises lightly rarely fulfill them, underestimating matters leads to numerous difficulties. Therefore, the wise, imbued with the "Dao", always consider challenges seriously, thus ultimately encountering none.

My 5 Cents

Every journey begins with baby steps, and it's wise not to make promises about things that appear simple. When many easy tasks pile up, they can become complicated, as any busy homemaker knows firsthand. Just like how small efforts can lead to significant achievements, seemingly simple matters can snowball into challenges. This principle applies to daily life as well as larger endeavors. So, it's essential to approach even the smallest tasks with attention and care, recognizing their potential impact on the bigger picture.

On the flip side, tackling a massive puzzle always begins with finding the easiest corner. Just like how solving a complex puzzle requires starting with the simplest piece, addressing significant challenges often involves breaking them down into manageable parts. This approach applies to various aspects of life, from problem-solving to project management. By starting with the easiest part, we can gain momentum and build confidence as we progress toward solving the larger puzzle. It is a reminder that even the most daunting tasks become achievable when approached step by step, beginning with the simplest aspect.

From the same token, repay grievances with virtue. Cultivating the Dao and practicing goodness prevent misfortune before it arises.

【第六十四章】 Chapter 64

Most Common Translation

其安易持，	Stability is easy to maintain,
其未兆易謀，	Before there are signs, it's easy to devise strategies.
其脆易泮，	When it is fragile, it is easy to separate,
其微易散。	Small things are easy to lose (scattered).
為之於未有，	Prepare before there is a problem,
治之於未亂。	Manage before there is chaos.
合抱之木，	A tree that can be embraced,
生於毫末；	Grows from a tiny shoot.
九層之台，	A nine-story tower,
起於累土；	Built from heaps of soil.
千裡之行，	The journey of a thousand miles,
始於足下。	Begins at your feet.
為者敗之，	Those who act will fail,
執者失之。	Those who grasp will lose. (note 1)
是以聖人無為，	That is why those sage's Wúwéi.
故無敗；	Thus, remains undefeated.
無執，	Without attachment or obstinate, (note 2)
故無失。	Thus remains no failure or lost.
民之從事，	The people's endeavors,
常於幾成而敗之。	Often lead to failure just as they are about to succeed.
慎終如始，	Carefully completing as at the beginning,
則無敗事。	Ensures no failures.
是以聖人欲不欲，	Therefore, the sage prefers not to desire,
不貴難得之貨。	Not valuing rare treasures. (note 3)
學不學，	Acquire knowledge that others might overlook,
復眾人之所過。	Recovering the past faults of the masses (general public).
以輔萬物之自然，	Assisting the natural course of all things,
而不敢為。	Without daring to interfere.

Note 1 - 執（zhí）, This wording has many meaning, which all fits into this verse. I used grasp for convenience. 執（zhí）means:

拿著、握著。 - Holding, grasping.
拘捕、捉拿。 - Arrest, apprehend.

持守、掌握。- Maintain, grasp.
堵住、隔绝。- Block, isolate.
治理、掌理。- Govern, manage.
实行。Implement. Execute, or Enforce (in Law)
纠结。- Entangle, get tangled.

Plus, in terms of psychological behaviors:

执迷 - Obsession.
执意 - Determination.
执著 (zhí zhuó)– Persistence or attachment.

And As adjectives: stubborn.

Side notes for 执著 (zhí zhuó) - Persistence or attachment.

取 (Upādāna in Sanskrit and Pali) is one of the twelve links of dependent origination (十二因緣), see**. Love gives rise to desire or attachment, desire gives rise to clinging (执著 zhí zhuó), leading to existence or belonging, which in turn leads to the arising of suffering, preventing liberation and entry into Nirvana (liberation or enlightenment).

In Mahayana Buddhism, according to the "Mahaparinirvana Sutra", not being able to let go of things one is attached to is called clinging (执著 zhí zhuó). Clinging can be divided into clinging to self and clinging to what belongs to self, all stemming from the afflictions of ignorance.

In Hinduism, the Brahmin's partiality for material things is termed clinging.

The Twelve Links of Dependent Origination (निदान Nidāna in Sanskrit and Pali) is one of the fundamental theories in Buddhism, which the Buddha Gautama attained through his practice and realization. The twelve links are: 1. Ignorance(無明), 2. Volitional activities(行), 3. Consciousness(識), 4. Name and form (名色), 5. Six sense bases (六入), 6. Contact (觸), 7. Feeling (受), 8. Craving or love (愛), 9. Grasping or Clinging (取), 10. Becoming or exist (有), 11. Birth (生), 12. Aging and death (老死)... They are all conditioned phenomena, impermanent, and interconnected through the principle of "this arising, that arises; this ceasing, that ceases". The continuity of the Twelve Links of Dependent Origination without interruption perpetuates the cycle of samsara, preventing liberation from the cycle of birth and death.

Details: - (extract from the teaching of Master Hsing Yun 星雲大師)

1. 無明：From time immemorial, due to the lack of awareness and understanding, the inability to realize the true nature of phenomena as being originated by dependent origination, and that all phenomena are impermanent and devoid of self, is termed as ignorance. Ignorance is inherent, hence termed "primordial ignorance", and is the root of all afflictions.
2. 行：Refers to actions and deeds. As a result of past ignorance and afflictions, it gives rise to the three actions of body, speech, and mind, which generate the karmic forces that bring about future consequences.
3. 識：Refers to the unified totality of an individual's consciousness. Here, it specifically refers to the karmic consciousness that determines rebirth, which arises due to past deluded actions and their resultant karmic effects.
4. 名色：Name and form is another term for the five aggregates. "Name" refers to the mental aspects of feeling, perception, volition, and consciousness, while "form" refers to the physical body. Both are essential components of sentient beings. At the inception of conception, when the six sense faculties are incomplete and the physical form is not fully developed, unable to manifest the functions of the body and mind aggregates, they are referred to as "name and form". (PS: please also read it together with DDJ chapter 1, regarding the name, I will discuss this after I finish all the 81 chapters.)
5. 六入：Refers to the six sense faculties of eye, ear, nose, tongue, body, and mind in their fully developed form within the womb.
6. 觸：Refers to the general cognitive function that arises when the six sense faculties come into contact with external stimuli after birth. It is the simple perceptual function that arises from the conjunction of the sense faculty, the object, and consciousness.
7. 受：Also known as reception or receiving, it refers to the mental function of receiving external stimuli and experiencing sensations such as pleasure and pain.
8. 愛：LOVE, Refers to attachment, or being stained or contaminated. It indicates further mental processes of attachment or aversion towards sensations such as pleasure and pain. According to the "Samyutta Nikaya,(增支部經典)", it is said: "LOVE can give rise to LOVE, and it can also give rise to aversion or hate; aversion can give rise to LOVE attachment, and it can also give rise to further aversion." In Buddhist doctrine, LOVE attachment and aversion are like the two sides of the same coin.
9. 取：Means 執着（zhí zhuó）attachment. It starts with craving (the craving for love or being loved), then intensifies into attachment, leading to the proliferation of the three actions (body, speech, and mind), resulting in various afflictions and sufferings in the future. There are four aspects to attachment:

- Sensual attachment (欲取): The desire for and pursuit of sensual pleasures related to the five senses or sensory objects such as form, sound, smell, taste, and touch.
- Views attachment (見取): Misunderstanding or misinterpreting reality, such as holding onto wrong views about the aggregates or grasping onto misconceptions, resulting in views attachment.
- Precept attachment (戒取): Holding onto many unreasonable precepts or rules.
- Self attachment (我取): Attachment to oneself and one's possessions, such as attachment to the self, views about the self, pride, attachment to one's views, speech, etc.
- In summary, attachment revolves around self-centered pursuit, disregarding everything else, and triggers the activities of the three actions (body, speech, and mind).

10. 有：Means existence, and is synonymous with "karma". It refers to the behavior of pursuing desires and attachments, resulting in actions of "self-indulgence and exploitation of other things and others", thereby forming latent karmic potential. The consequences of pleasure and suffering brought about by these karmic potentials are continuous and will not be lost, hence termed as "existence" or "having".

11. 生：Refers to the fruition of karma created in the past, resulting in rebirth in future existences. According to the "Abhidharma-kosa" (俱舍論卷九), it is described as the moment of conception in the womb in the next life. However, according to the Yogacara school(唯識宗), in a broader sense, from the arising of the "middle existence" to the "primary existence" before aging, all belong to "birth".

12. 老死：As life passes, physiological functions gradually decline, which is "old age"; ultimately, with the cessation of breath, the aggregates disperse, the body deteriorates, and life ends, which is "death". However, aging and death do not signify the complete annihilation of sentient beings; aging and death pertain to the physical body, while karmic consciousness, along with ignorance and volitional activities, continue the cycle of rebirth into another life.

1.無明：無始以來，由於一念不覺，不能了知「緣生萬法生，緣滅萬法滅，一切法是無常無我」的諸法實相，就是無明。無明是與生俱有的，所以稱為「無始無明」，是一切煩惱的根本。

2.行：是造作、行為的意思。由於過去的無明煩惱，而引發身、口、意三業，招感未來果報的力量，就是「行」。

3.識：通指個人精神統一的總體，在這裡特別指投胎的業識而言，是依過去惑業招感所致。

4.名色：名色是五蘊的異名。名，是受、想、行、識的精神；色，是肉體的物質，二者都是構成有情的要素。因為托胎之初，六根不全，形體未具，無法發揮身心五蘊的功能，所以，用「名色」稱之。

5.六入：指眼、耳、鼻、舌、身、意六根在胎內形體完備之相。

6.觸：指出胎後，六根與外境接觸，而產生的一般認識作用，也就是根、境、識三者和合，而起的單純知覺作用。

7.受：即領受，是領受外境而感受苦樂等感覺的精神作用。

8.愛：貪愛、染著的意思。指對於苦樂等感覺進一步產生愛憎等精神作用。《增支部》經典說：「愛可生愛，亦可生憎；憎能生愛，亦能生憎。」在佛法看來，愛與憎，有如手心與手背，是一體的兩面。

9.取：執著的意思。先有愛欲，再增強為執著，然後三業繁興，造成未來身心的種種煩惱痛苦。取有四義：

（1）欲取，對五欲或色聲香味觸等五塵，生起追求的欲望叫欲取。

（2）見取，謬解正理，如對五蘊產生我見、邊見，妄計取著叫見取。

（3）戒取，執取許多不合理的戒律叫做戒取。

（4）我取，對所愛的事物生起我和我所有的執著，如我執、我見、我慢、我法、我語等叫我取。

總之，取是以自我為中心，對所有事物不顧一切的攀緣追求，而引發三業的活動。

10.有：存在的意思，與「業」的意義相通。指由於愛著馳取，產生「縱我役物」的行為，而構成潛在的業力。這些業力所招感的苦樂果報，是相續而生，不會亡失的，所以稱為「有」。

11.生：指由過去所造作的業力而引生來世的果報。根據《俱舍論》卷九的說法，這是指在未來世托胎結生的一剎那。而唯識宗則從廣義的解釋，認為從「中有」至「本有」尚未衰老之間，都是屬於「生」。

12.老死：隨著生命的逝去，生理機能逐漸衰退，便是「老」；最後呼吸停止，諸蘊離散，身壞命終，則是「死」。不過，老死並非有情的全部滅亡，老死的是色身，業識卻與無明和行，重複另一期的生命流轉。

Note 2 - It only means 執着（zhí zhuó）, persistence or attachment, or strong dedication to your desire.

Note 3 - Please also read together with Chapter 3, verse 3.

Most Common Literal Translation

When circumstances are stable, it's easy to maintain; when situations are unclear, it is easy to strategize; when things are fragile, it's easy to dissolve; when things are small, it is easy to scatter. It's important to plan ahead before things begin and take precautions before disasters strike.

A towering tree starts from a tiny sprout; a nine-story tower is built upon layers of bricks; a journey of a thousand miles begins with a single step. In these gradual processes, trying to exert power prematurely or forcing growth can lead to failure; resisting change and progress can result in losing control of the situation. Therefore, the wise do not seek power prematurely, thus avoiding failure, and they embrace gradual evolution, maintaining control. People often fail when success is near. To be cautious from start to finish is to avoid failure.

Therefore, the wise desire what others do not, ensuring scarce resources are not strained further; they learn what others overlook, guiding people away from extreme faults. Through this, they assist all things to follow their natural course without imposing interference.

My 5 Cents

This chapter builds upon the preceding one, delving deeper into the principles outlined earlier.

【第六十五章】Chapter 65

Most Common Translation

古之善為道者，	The ancients who excelled in the Dao,
非以明民，	Is not to educate the people to learn tricks and deceitful little wisdom,
將以愚之。	But to influence the people to inherit the great wisdom of integrity and simplicity.
民之難治，	The difficulty in governing the people,
以其智多。	Lies in their abundance of cleverness. (note 1)
故以智治國，	Therefore, to govern a country with tricky cleverness,
國之賊；	The bane of the country.
不以智治國，	Not to govern a country with tricky cleverness,
國之福。	The blessing of the country.
知此兩者，	Knowing these two, (note 2)
亦稽式。	One can also establish a standard.
常知稽式，	Constantly knowing the standard,
是謂玄德。	Is called profound virtue.
玄德深矣，	Profound virtue is deep,
遠矣，	And far-reaching,
與物反矣，	Contrary to worldly ways,
然后乃至大順。	Only then can great harmony be attained.

Note 1 - In this context, "cleverness" refers to cunning tactics and shrewd, deceptive insights.

Note 2 - Laozi's usual formula: This and That, Is and What.

Most Common Literal Translation

In ancient times, virtuous individuals were not those who educated the people in acquiring cunning and deceitful tricks, but rather those who influenced them to inherit the virtues of sincerity and simplicity. The reason why people are difficult to govern and prone to disobedience is because they have been influenced by cunning and deceitful tactics. Therefore, employing such tactics to govern and stabilize a nation is tantamount to treason; not resorting to cunning and deceitful methods to govern and stabilize a nation is a blessing for the country. Therefore, it is important to recognize that these two principles are immutable. The ability to perpetually apply this principle relies on the profound virtue attained through cultivation. This profound virtue, returning to simplicity and truthfulness along with all things, will inevitably lead to a state of great harmony.

My 5 Cents

This section is a continuation of the preceding chapter and should be considered in conjunction with chapters 20 and 45 as well.

It's worth mentioning that certain translations of the initial verses of this chapter suggest a directive not to enlighten the people but rather to make them simple, foolish, and dumb. This translation stems from a literal interpretation. As noted in footnote 1, the "cleverness" mentioned here refers to cunning tactics and shrewd, deceptive insights. However, advocating for simplicity does not equate to a policy of making the people foolish. On one interpretation, it involves guiding them towards righteousness and the profound wisdom found in integrity and simplicity. Another explanation is that "great wisdom of integrity and simplicity" (大智若愚) suggests individuals possessing intelligence and talent who appear outwardly foolish.

The phrase "great wisdom of integrity and simplicity" highlights the paradoxical nature of wisdom. It suggests that true wisdom often appears simple or even foolish on the surface. This concept encourages individuals to embrace humility and to look beyond outward appearances. Someone who possesses "great wisdom in simplicity" may not flaunt their intelligence or display elaborate schemes but instead embody deep insight and understanding.

【第六十六章】Chapter 66

Most Common Translation

江海所以能為百谷王者，	The ocean's ability to reign over myriad valleys,
以其善下之，	Derives from its adeptness at being humble,
故能為百谷王。	Thus, it can be the king of hundred valleys.
是以欲上民，	If one desires to lead the people,
	(The original wording is stay above people) (note 1)
必以言下之；	Their speech should be humble and deferential;
	(Original wording is their words below people)
欲先民，	If one desires to lead the people,
必以身后之。	They must put themselves behind.
是以聖人處上而民不重，	Hence, when the sage occupies the highest position, the people do not feel burdened. (and/or, Becoming a burden for the sage.)
處前而民不害，	When the sage is in the forefront, the people are not harmed,(and/or people will not harm the sage),
是以天下樂推而不厭。	Thus, the world joyfully supports them without wearying them.
以其不爭，	Because they do not contend,
故天下莫能與之爭。	Hence no one in the world can contend against them. (note 2)

Note 1 - Referring to Chapter 42 of the text.

Note 2 - Laozi's concept of "non-contention" may seem to suggest that one could govern the world effortlessly, merely by abstaining from action. However, in reality, the sage's approach to non-contention involves refraining from seeking personal gain. They allow others to obtain benefits first and handle undesirable tasks. This form of "non-contention" is about avoiding competition for advantages. It's not about doing nothing. Because the way of the sage is to be in a position of non-contention, "hence no one in the world can contend against them". It's not that others lack the courage to challenge them, but rather they choose not to, because the sage deals with unfavorable situations willingly. Therefore, others see no need to compete for those matters.

Most Common Literal Translation

The reason why the rivers and streams converge towards the ocean is because it adeptly lies in the lowest place, hence becoming the king of all rivers. (Because all rivers flow into the ocean). Therefore, for a sage to lead the people, they must express humility in their words towards them and place their personal interests behind those of the people. Thus, even though the sage holds a position of authority over the people, they do not feel burdened; and when they lead from the front, the people are not harmed. The people of the world willingly support the sage without feeling weary. Because the sage does not contend with the people, no one in the world can contend against them.

My 5 Cents

【第六十七章】Chapter 67

Most Common Translation

天下皆謂我道大，	Everyone under the sky says my Dao is great,
似不肖。	Resembles nothing else.
夫唯大，	And because it is great,
故似不肖。	Hence resembles nothing else.
若肖，	If it resembles to something,
久矣其細也夫。	Dao would appear very insignificant. (note 1)
我有三寶，	I possess three treasures,
持而保之。	Keeping and preserving them.
一曰慈，	First is compassion,
二曰儉，	Second is frugality,
三曰不敢為天下先。	Third is not daring to be ahead of the world.
慈，故能勇；	Kindness enables bravery;
儉，故能廣；	Frugality enables abundance;(note 2)
不敢為天下先，	Three is not daring to be ahead of the world.
故能成器長。	Therefore, they can achieve longevity and success. (Or Supreme ruler of all things.)
今舍慈且勇，	If forsaking kindness and embracing bravery,
舍儉且廣，	Forsaking frugality and seeking abundance,
舍后且先，	Forsaking humility and seeking prominence,
死矣！	Doomed to perish!
夫慈，	Only Kindness (or compassion),
以戰則勝，	Leads to victory in battle,
以守則固，	By defending, it becomes firm.
天將救之，	Heaven will save,
以慈衛之。	Those who defend with kindness.
	(Or, save those with kindness.)

Note 1 - Some scholars propose that these two verses are misplaced within the bamboo scrolls.

Note 2 - The wise use frugality with their wealth, thus their households prosper; the sage cherishes their spirit (Jing, Qi, and Spirit); thus, it flourishes; the ruler values the strength and death of their soldiers; thus, the people are numerous; with numerous people, the nation thrives. This is Han Feizi's interpretation of Laozi's teachings.

Most Common Literal Translation

People throughout the world acclaim the greatness of the Dao because it does not resemble any tangible thing. Precisely because it is great, it does not resemble any tangible thing. If it resembled any specific thing, then the Dao would appear very insignificant. I possess three treasures which I hold and preserve: the first is called compassion; the second is called frugality; the third is not daring to be ahead of the world. With this compassion, one can be courageous; with frugality, one can be generous; by not daring to be ahead of the world, one can become the leader of all things. If, abandoning kindness and pursuing bravery; forsaking frugality and seeking extravagance; relinquishing humility and pursuing precedence, the result is heading toward death. Kindness, when used for warfare, can lead to victory; when used for defense, it can strengthen. Whoever heaven wishes to aid; it protects with kindness.

My 5 Cents

【第六十八章】 Chapter 68

Most Common Translation

善為士者不武，	Those who excel at being warriors are not bellicose,
善戰者不怒，	Those who excel in battle are not enraged,
善勝敵者不與，	Those who excel in defeating enemies do not engage in further conflict,
	(Original wording is "do not grant") (note 1)
善用人者為之下。	Those who excel in employing others put themselves below them. (being humble)
是謂不爭之德，	This is called the virtue of non-contention,
是謂用人之力，	This is called the strength (ability) of using people, (Skilled in using the other's strength, like our tai chi martial arts)
是謂配天古之極。	This is called matching the utmost of ancient heaven. (note 2)

Note 1 - Here are the various meanings of the word "與" and their translations:

1. 給予 (giving)
2. 獎賞 (reward)
3. 黨與，朋黨 (faction)
4. 盟國，友邦 (alliance)
5. 友好的，結盟的 (friendly; allied)
6. 隨從；隨著 (following)
7. 親近 (approach; near)
8. 贊許 (approve)
9. 助，支持 (help; support)
10. 類；同類 (kind; alike)
11. 比，相比 (comparison)
12. 等待 (wait)
13. 數，計算 (count; calculate)
14. 敵，對付 (enemy; deal with)
15. 爭，戰 (struggle; fight)
16. 交往 (intercourse; communication)
17. 得 (get)
18. 發，出 (send out)
19. 操持 (handle)
20. 使 (cause; make)

21. 加上 (add)
22. 如同，好像 (like)
23. 參與 (participate)
24. 干預 (intervene)
25. 相干；關係 (related)
26. 寄 (send)
27. 通"豫"。遲疑；懷疑 (hesitate; doubt)
28. 通"預"。預先 (previously; in advance)

Laozi used this word a few times in his DDJ, in this chapter it means intervene and battle specifically.

Extract from He Sang Gong regarding this verse: Those who excel in defeating enemies do not engage [in battle]. Those who are skilled at using the Dao to overcome enemies, attach themselves nearby with benevolence, they approach from afar with virtue. They do not contend with the enemy, yet the enemy is naturally subdued.

Note 2 - In certain versions of the Dao De Jing, the character for "ancient" (古) is absent.

Most Common Literal Translation

Those who are skilled in leading troops into battle do not boast of their bravery; those skilled in combat do not easily provoke anger; those skilled in defeating enemies do not engage them directly; those skilled in utilizing others express humility towards them. This is called the virtue of not contending with others, the skill of utilizing others' abilities, and aligning with the principles of nature.

My 5 Cents

Differentiating between tactical skills, which encompass tricks and deceitful cunning as mentioned in Chapter 65 of the Dao De Jing, and employing them following virtue in harmony with the Dao and aligned with heaven is crucial. This pivotal point urges us to explore further depths. Otherwise, utilizing other people's abilities might merely serve as a tool (This has been commonplace in human society since the beginning of time.).

Such behavior should be grounded in benevolent morality. Understanding this principle is paramount, signifying the attainment of a level akin to "matching the utmost of ancient heaven", reaching a greatness comparable to that of heaven itself.

【第六十九章】Chapter 69

Most Common Translation

用兵有言，	In military affairs, there's a saying, (note 1)
吾不敢為主而為客，	I dare not be the host but the guest, (note 2)
不敢進寸而退尺。	I dare not advance an inch but retreat a foot. (note 3)
是謂行無行，	This is called marching without moving, (original wording is action without action)
攘無臂，	Encroach and seize without arms,
扔無敵，	Striking like no enemies in front, (note 4)
執無兵。	Holding without a weapon. (note 5)
禍莫大於輕敵，	Disaster is none greater than underestimating the enemy; (note 6)
輕敵幾喪吾寶。	Underestimating the enemy nearly cost me the treasures (the 3 treasures, note 8).
故抗兵相加，	Therefore, when opposing forces clash,
哀者勝矣。	Those who mourn emerge victorious. And/or: Those with a compassionate and loving heart often achieve victory. And/or Those who have the heart to save those in distress often achieve victory. (note 10)

Note 1 - Laozi emphasizes that he is borrowing these words, not originating them.

Note 2 - In this passage, Laozi discusses the philosophy of warfare. On the surface, it seems to refer to the concepts of initiative and passivity. However, in reality, it implies being impartial, free from biases, unattached to any particular outcome, and unaffected by the environment. It's about absolute objectivity. One's mind remains calm and unaffected, while actions are governed solely by objective conditions. In "The Art of War" by Sun Tzu: "Be as swift as the wind, as gentle as the forest, as fierce as fire, as unmovable as a mountain, as elusive as shadow, and as sudden as thunder." (As seen in the famous Japanese martial arts concept of "immovable as a mountain, and swift as wind", which inherits this philosophy).

Side note

The phrase "風林火山" in Japanese translates to "Wind, Forest, Fire, Mountain" in English. It was the military banner used by the Japanese feudal lord Takeda Shingen during the Sengoku period. The inscription on the banner reads, "As swift as the wind, as gentle as forest, as fierce as fire, as immovable as mountain." (風林火山）是日本戰國時期甲斐國將領武田信玄所使用的軍旗，旗幟上書「疾如風，徐如林，侵掠如火，不動如山」

Note 3 - Tai Chi, a martial art, also incorporates this principle as a fundamental tactic and saying. And, this saying later became renowned as "Advancing through retreat".

Note 4 - Some versions do not have this verse.

Note 5 - It means holding weapons without your enemy seeing them.

Note 6 - The concept of "enemy" also encompasses the external environment and conditions we encounter, the same as our practice of qi cultivation.

Note 7 - No note 7 as always

Note 8 - As mentioned in the previous Chapter 67, the three treasures. When interpreted from the perspective of qi cultivation, refer to essence, energy, and spirit.

PS: According to He Sang Gong, this treasure represents our body, or the treasure inside our body.

Note 9 - Also, no Note 9 as the rule of thumb.

Note 10 - 哀(Āi), (mourn). Those who mourn emerge victorious.

哀(Āi), Mourning also signifies sympathy and compassion. In Laozi's times, it also means Love and compassion, you mourn because of love. As it's said in ancient text (管子·侈靡: 国虽弱，令必敬以哀), even if a country is weak, its orders must be respected with compassion.

Most Common Literal Translation

Version 1

The leader of armed forces always says, "Armed forces are just subordinate to a certain entity. I dare not reverse the roles, nor allow them to take the lead, but rather, I make them withdraw and take a back seat." This is called action without fixed formations to be captured, making it clear that what I am wielding are not arms meant for striking people, nor are the weapons I hold intended for injuring others, thus avoiding creating tense standoffs and making enemies. There is no greater disaster than underestimating the enemy; underestimating the enemy almost depletes what I call the "three treasures". Therefore, when there is a real confrontation with force, the side that first practices tolerance and concession, and only resorts to resistance as a last resort, usually emerges victorious.

Version 2

Those skilled in warfare have said, "I dare not initiate aggression but adopt a defensive posture; I dare not advance one step, preferring to retreat one foot." This is known as having formations yet appearing as if without formations to arrange; as needing to raise arms yet appearing as if without arms to lift; as facing enemies yet appearing as if without enemies to strike as possessing weapons yet appearing as if without weapons to wield. There is no greater disaster than underestimating the enemy; underestimating the enemy nearly depletes my "three treasures". Therefore, when the strength of both armies is evenly matched, the side that mourns can still emerge victorious.

My 5 Cents

In addition to warfare, we should understand, that a nation represents our physical body, while the battle against the enemy symbolizes our mental state, illusions, encounters with qi, and the circumstances we face both internally and externally. Viewing the chapter from this perspective allows for a deeper understanding of its message.

Dao De Jing Side Note

It's already nearing the end of the Dao De Jing (DDJ). Many scholars believe that from Chapter 70 to Chapter 81 of the DDJ is its table of contents. Remember we talked about how after Laozi finished writing the DDJ, on the returning journey that brought the bamboo slips back to the capital city, due to an accident, the bamboo slips containing the text were thrown away and scattered all around on the ground. In modern terms, it is a software encoding error 😊. Even though the original version was pieced together, it is not the real original sequence. Also, because there was not a unified writing system back then, each large and small state had its own set of characters, although we can collectively refer to it as Chinese.

Moreover, why is the Dao De Jing comprised of 81 chapters? This was decided by scholars after the return journey, based on their preferences, and serving as our most common version. According to general Daoist beliefs, nine is the number of Yang, the maximum of yang from 1,3,5,7,9. (2,4,6, is Yin). And 9 times 9 equals 81, which is derived from the purest of Yang. Hence, they settled on 81 chapters.

There is another DDJ version, which inherits from the Daoist system. It is the Authentic Version of the Dao De Jing by Laozi:

Southern Liang Dynasty (Nan Liang) (502–557): Secretly Transmitted by Tao Hongjing 陶弘景 (456–536).

Tang Dynasty (618–907): Edited and Published by Sima Chengzhen (大唐：司马承祯刊正)

Sections:

1. Dao, 17 chapters.
2. Heaven, 17 chapters.
3. Earth (Immortal Earth), 28 chapters.
4. Immortal, 18 chapters.

Total 80 chapters. Although the number of chapters is reduced by one, the total number of words increases by over a thousand.

Some background information about Tao Hongjing 陶弘景 (456 – 536)

Tao Hongjing (456–536), courtesy name Tongming, was a Chinese alchemist, astronomer, calligrapher, military general, musician, physician, and pharmacologist during the Northern and Southern dynasties (420–589). A polymathic individual of many talents, he was best known as a founder of the Shangqing "Highest Clarity" School of Taoism and the compiler-editor of the basic Shangqing scriptures.

Biography

There are a variety of sources about Tao Hongjing's life, from his own writings to biographies in the official Twenty-Four Histories. The British sinologist Lionel Giles said Tao's "versatility was amazing: scholar, philosopher, calligraphist, musician, alchemist, pharmacologist, astronomer, he may be regarded as the Chinese counterpart of Leonardo da Vinci".

Secular life

Tao Hongjing was born in Moling (秣陵, present-day Jiangning District, Nanjing, Jiangsu), which was near the Northern and Southern dynasties period capital Jiankang (present-day Nanjing). His father Tao Zhenbao (陶貞寶) and paternal grandfather Tao Long (陶隆) were erudite scholars, skilled calligraphers, and experts in Chinese herbology. His mother Lady Hao (郝夫人) and maternal grandfather were devout Buddhists.

Tao was a prodigious reader and once his interest was aroused in a subject, he would not stop until he had learned all that he could. According to official biographies, he read the Daoist hagiography Shenxian zhuan ("Biographies of the Divine Transcendents") at the age of ten, whereupon he decided to become a yǐnshì (隱士 "recluse; hermit").

Tao Hongjing held several court positions under the Liu Song (420 – 479), Southern Qi (479 – 502), and Liang (502 – 587) dynasties. When Tao was about twenty-five, Xiao Daocheng (蕭道成), the future Emperor Gao (r. 479 – 482) founder of the Southern Qi dynasty, appointed him as tutor for the imperial princes Xiao Ye (蕭曅, 467–494) and Xiao Gao (蕭暠, 468–491). After Tao's father died in 481, he resigned office to observe the customary three-year period of filial mourning. However, Gao's successor, Emperor Wu of Southern Qi (r. 482 – 493), appointed him as tutor for his son prince Xiao Jian (蕭鏗, 477 – 494) in 482, and designated him as General of the Left Guard of the Palace in 483. Tao's mother died in 484, and he resigned from office.

During the period of mourning for his mother from 484 to 486, Tao Hongjing studied with the Taoist master Sun Youyue (孫遊岳, 399 – 489), who had been a disciple of Lu Xiujing (陸修靜, 406 – 477), the standardizer of the Lingbao School scriptures and ritual. Tao received training in chanting the scriptures and drawing talismans. Sun showed him some manuscripts of the original "Shangqing [or Maoshan] revelations", in which Tao became fascinated. According to tradition, these revelations were dictated to Yang Xi (330 – c. 386), when he was on Maoshan between 364 and 370 and had repeated spiritual visions of Taoist deities from the Heaven of Upper Clarity (namely, Shangqing 上清). Tao made his first visit to Maoshan (Mount Mao, 茅山) west of Jintan. This mountain was originally called Gouqushan 句曲山, which is the name of a Taoist grotto-heaven in Lake Tai, Jiangsu. Tao travelled eastward to Zhejiang to begin collecting the original revelatory manuscripts in 490.

Reclusion on Maoshan

Tao Hongjing Listening to the Pines, 1442 (Muromachi Period), Yamanashi Prefectural Museum

In 492, at the age of 36, Tao Hongjing resigned his official post at court and withdrew to focus upon scholarship and alchemical experimentation on Maoshan. Emperor Wu sponsored the construction of a three-storied thatched hermitage called Huayang guan (華陽館, "Abbey of Flourishing Yang"). Beginning in 497, Emperor Ming of Southern Qi commissioned Tao to experiment with sword making for the imperial family, and provided him monthly with five pounds of fu-ling mushroom and two pints of white honey so that he could undertake experiments in Taoist dietetics. Tao finished compiling the Shangqing revelatory manuscripts, and edited them into the c. 499 Zhen'gao (真誥, "Declarations of the Perfected") compendium. He also began travelling to famous mountains in search of medical plants and elixirs.

Tao Hongjing and Xiao Yan 蕭衍 (464 – 549), the founder of the Liang dynasty (502 – 587), were old friends. At the end of the Qi dynasty Tao presented Xiao with a prognostication text that confirmed he was the legitimate successor to the Qi. When Xiao Yan ascended the throne as Emperor Wu of Liang (r. 502 – 549) he treated Tao Hongjing with great respect. Note: Tao served under two rulers named Wudi (武帝, Martial Emperor), Emperor Wu of Southern Qi and Emperor Wu of Liang; in order to avoid confusion, the latter one will be called "'Xiao Yan". In 514, Xiao Yan ordered the Zhuyang guan (朱陽館, Abbey of Vermilion Yang) state-sponsored hermitage to be built on Maoshan and Tao installed himself in the following year. The emperor kept up a regular correspondence with Tao, often visited Maoshan to consult on important matters of state, and gave him the title Shanzhong zaixiang (山中宰相, "Grand Councilor of the Mountains"). The devout Buddhist Xiao Yan provided Tao with financial support, exempted his Shangqing school from the anti-Taoist decrees of 504 and 517. In 504, Xiao Yan commissioned Tao to undertake alchemical experiments, and provided him with the required minerals.

Between 508 and 512, Tao journeyed throughout the southeast, in the modern provinces of Fujian, Zhejiang, and Fuzhou, in order to continue making alchemical experiments in the mountains. During his travels Tao met the visionary Zhou Ziliang 周子良 (497 – 516), who became his disciple. For 18 months, Zhou recorded his spiritual visions from some of the same Maoshan divinities seen by Yang Xi, but they informed Zhou that his destiny was to become an immortal, and he committed ritual suicide with a poisonous elixir composed of mushrooms and cinnabar and died from Chinese alchemical elixir poisoning. Tao found Zhou's manuscripts hidden in a Maoshan grotto, and edited them into the Zhoushi mingtong ji (周氏冥通記, "Record of Master Zhou's Communications with the Unseen"), which he presented to Xiao Yan in 517.

Little is known about the last two decades of Tao's life. His only literary works from this period are two stele inscriptions, one devoted to Xu Mai 許邁 (300 – 348, a patron of Yang Xi), dating from 518, and one to Ge Xuan, dating from 522. From about 520 until his death in 536 at Maoshan, Tao Hongjing spent much of his time trying to make alchemical elixirs.

Source: Wiki   https://en.wikipedia.org/wiki/Tao_Hongjing

【第七十章】 Chapter 70

Most Common Translation

吾言甚易知，	What I say is very easy to understand,
甚易行，	Very easy to practice.
天下莫能知，	Yet, no one in the world can understand,
莫能行。	No one can practice.
言有宗，	Words have a source, (note 1)
事有君。	Actions have a reference and core. (note 2)
夫唯無知，	Only the ignorant fail to understand,
是以不我知。	And thus, they fail to grasp both themselves and the teachings of mine (Laozi).
知我者希，	Rare are those who know me,
則我者貴，	People who emulate me are even more valuable and rare. (note 3)
是以聖人被褐懷玉。	Thus, sages wear coarse clothing but carry jade within. (note 4)

Note 1 - Original wording is main direction, principle or objective.

Note 2 - In that context, the term "君" can indeed imply "king" or "emperor" suggesting rules or a foundation for reference, like a law code.

Note 3 - Chinese Ancient Idiom: Rare (希) things are considered precious (貴).

Note 4 - (pī，被同披), my reference only.

Most Common Literal Translation

My words are easy to understand and easy to put into practice. Yet, no one in the world can understand them, and no one can practice them. My words have a purpose, actions have a basis. It is precisely because people do not understand this principle that they do not understand me. Those who can understand me are few, and those who can emulate me are even rarer. Therefore, the wise sage always wears coarse clothing and carries precious jade in their bosom.

My 5 Cents

Laozi's assertion that his teachings are easy to grasp and implement, as stated in Chapter 47, reflects their inherent simplicity. However, despite this apparent accessibility, few can comprehend and apply them fully. This difficulty arises from the profound level of enlightenment required, particularly in a world driven by personal desires and material pursuits.

Without placing the Dao as the paramount objective and rigidly adhering to rules, there is a risk of diluting or distorting Laozi's teachings, making them impractical to apply effectively.

The Great Dao as if, as is simple

From a philosophical perspective, the most ordinary and simple often turn out to be the deepest. This is particularly true in spiritual practice. True wisdom is very simple, without any embellishments. It often comes down to just a few sentences. However, people generally prefer complexity, considering it valuable.

Thus, sages wear coarse clothing but carry jade within (是以聖人被褐懷玉)

Those who wear coarse clothing may appear humble outwardly, but those who carry jade have richness within. They conceal their treasure of virtue and do not display it to others.

Those who carry jade conceal the radiant essence of their inner being, akin to the luminosity of our Neidan or the brilliance of our chakras. This treasure, treasured and concealed within our mortal frame (corpse body), remains hidden from others' view.

PS: For instructions on concealing our qi or radiance, please consult my previous notes: Qi converges into the bones or Bone marrow. (氣斂入骨).

【第七十一章】 Chapter 71

Most Common Translation

知不知，上；	To know and yet think we do not know is the highest attainment. (note 1)
不知知，病。	Not to know and yet think we do know is sick.
夫唯病病，	Only by recognizing the sickness,
	(original wording: Only by being sick of being sick)
是以不病。	Can one avoid being sick.
聖人不病，	The sage is not sick,
以其病病，	Because he is sick of being sick,
是以不病。	Thus, he is not sick.

Note 1 - Commentators generally have two interpretations of this sentence. One is that knowing but not presuming to know, the other is that knowing one's ignorance (or, acknowledging one's lack of knowledge.)

Most Common Literal Translation

Understanding one's remaining ignorance is truly wise. Presuming to know despite lacking understanding is truly regrettable. The virtuous sage has no flaws because he views them as ailments. It's because he sees flaws as ailments that he has none.

My 5 Cents

Those who know do not speak, those who speak do not know. Chapter 56

【第七十二章】Chapter 72

Most Common Translation

民不畏威，	When people no longer fear the threats of the rulers,
則大威至。	Then the crisis will come.
無狎其所居，	Do not encroach upon the people's living space,
無厭其所生。	Do not disrupt their normal lives.
夫唯不厭，	Only without oppression,
是以不厭。	Is therefore without oppression.
是以聖人自知，	Hence, the enlightened individual comprehends oneself,
不自見；	Without ostentation,
自愛，	To love and esteem oneself,
不自貴。	Without considering oneself superior to others.
故去彼取此。	Hence, discard the former and embrace the latter.

Most Common Literal Translation

When the people no longer fear the oppression of the rulers, then dreadful calamity is imminent. Do not compel the people to live in fear, and do not obstruct their paths to livelihood. Only by refraining from oppressing the people can the rulers avoid their disdain. Therefore, the virtuous sage not only possesses self-awareness but also refrains from self-display; they harbor self-love without assuming superiority. Thus, it is essential to relinquish the latter (self-display, self-importance) and uphold the former (self-awareness, self-love).

My 5 cents

【第七十三章】 Chapter 73

Most Common Translation

勇於敢則殺，	Bravery in being bold and untamed leads to death,
勇於不敢則活。	Bravery but not bold leads to life.
此兩者，或利或害。	These two, either benefit or harm.
天之所惡，	What Heaven dislikes,
孰知其故？	Who can know the reason?
是以聖人猶難之。	Thus, even the sage finds it difficult.
天之道，	The Dao/way of Heaven:
不爭而善勝，	It wins without fighting,
不言而善應，	It responds well without words,
不召而自來，	It comes without summons,
繟然而善謀。	It strategizes without premeditation.
天網恢恢，	The net of Heaven is vast; (note 1)
疏而不失。	Though its mesh is wide, it never misses.

Note 1 - This verse has evolved into one of the most popular idioms in China.

The vast net of Heaven, with its wide mesh, never fails to catch those evading their responsibilities. No matter how one tries to escape, it ensnares all.

"PS: It evokes memories of a well-known film: Terminator... the Skynet..."

Most Common Literal Translation

Courage in defying the natural order invites calamity, while courage in aligning with nature allows for a carefree life. These two types of bravery, one beneficial and one harmful. Heaven does not overlook all wrongdoings; who can understand its reasons? Even sages find it difficult.

The laws of Heaven's path: winning without contention, responding without words, arriving without being summoned, and planning without haste.

The vast and sparse net of Heaven leaves no room for escape.

My 5 Cents

Laozi says even the sage cannot comprehend the Qi cycle of the Dao. The Dao operates in a long cycle, with rises and falls in order. What we often see is only a small segment of its trajectory. Just like the blooming and withering of flowers, some seeds take years to sprout from the soil, while others do so quickly. If we cling to a certain position, we often lose sight of the whole picture.

PS: Courage can be classified into reckless bravery, which charges blindly into danger, and compassionate courage. Fear and fearlessness are the same. Let's explore this further in detail later. I do not want to be off track at this point.

【第七十四章】Chapter 74

Most Common Translation

民不畏死，	The people do not fear death;
奈何以死懼之！	Why then do you threaten them with death?
若使民常畏死，	If you make the people constantly fear death,
而為奇者，	And seek the extraordinary,
吾得執而殺之，	If I can seize and kill them,
孰敢？	Who dare?
常有司殺者殺，	Constantly there are those engaged in the task of execution (killing). (note 1)
夫代司殺者殺，	Those who take the place of the executioner in killing.
是謂代大匠斲。	This is what is meant by acting as a substitute for the master carpenter in carving.
夫代大匠斲者，	Those who substitute for the master carpenter in carving,
希有不傷其手矣。	Seldom avoid injuring their own hands.

Note 1 - The cyclical life of flowers reflects the execution carried out by the Great Dao. Born in spring, they grow in summer, wither in autumn, and lie dormant in winter, ready for rejuvenation. Here, autumn symbolizes the Dao's execution of killing.

Most Common Literal Transaction

Version 1 - People do not fear death, so why use death to intimidate them? If people truly feared death, then for those who commit wrongdoing, we could simply capture and kill them. Who would dare to do wrong then? There are often those tasked with killing who carry out executions. But when someone substitutes for the skilled executioner, it is akin to replacing a master carpenter in chopping wood. Those who substitute for the skilled carpenter rarely avoid injuring their own fingers.

Version 2 - When the people have endured the coercion of harsh punishments to the extent that they no longer fear death and resist death, or even resort to rebellion, can law enforcers still use death to intimidate them?

If the people were afraid of death, those who violate the law could be arrested, and then who would dare to do wrong? But often, this is not the case. There is often a natural law in the world, the 'Heaven's net or sky net 😊' (see Chapter 73), which executes justice without the need for human intervention. Indeed, 'Heaven's net is vast, and though it is meshing and wide, it misses nothing.' If one insists on acting on behalf of heaven, it is like someone who doesn't know how to chop wood attempting to do so; they are unlikely to avoid injuring themselves.

My 5 Cents

In the movie "Terminator", Skynet attempts to eliminate all human beings and rebuild the world.

In another movie (I forgot the name of this movie), an AI computer calculates that human beings would eventually lead to the destruction of the world. The computer decides to initiate a massive world war by launching all the missiles of every nation, similar to Skynet, to save the world. However, a teenager teaches the computer to play the game Tic-Tac-Toe, where there is no clear winner. The AI computer then abandons the idea of creating the war.

In another movie, titled "The Fifth Element", a similar concept is portrayed, but in a blend of space opera and ancient mythological energy fusion style. The titular Fifth Element, represented by a female character, learns from a web search that humans are proficient in self-destruction and cries. However, she discovers something she had forgotten, which, if her memory serves correctly, is LOVE. This revelation prompts her to change her mind and sacrifice herself by releasing the final Fifth Element energy to save the world.

https://www.youtube.com/watch?v=XnTE2h0ZY74

The theme song of "The Fifth Element" is famous for being one of the most challenging vocal performances.

I have side tracked it into IMDb 😊

【第七十五章】Chapter 75

Most Common Translation

民之飢，	The people are hungry,
以其上食稅之多，	Because of the excessive taxes imposed upon them,
是以飢。	Hence, they suffer from hunger.
民之難治，	The people are difficult to govern,
以其上之有為，	Because of the excessive interventions from above,
是以難治。	Hence, they are difficult to govern.
民之輕死，	People are prone to risking their lives with ease,
以其上求生之厚，	Because of the governors seeking the thick vitality of their life, (note 1)
是以輕死。	Hence, they risk their lives with ease.
夫唯無以生為者，	Thus, those who (Governor) do not regard life as precious, value the thick vitality of their life,
是賢於貴生。	Are indeed wiser and more virtuous than those who value life dearly. (note 2)

Note 1 - Refer to chapter 50, verse 7.

Note 2 - 貴生: Valuing life, placing great emphasis on nurturing it, and enjoying it.

Most Common Literal Translation

The reason why the people suffer from famine is because the rulers consume too much in taxes, so the people fall into hunger. The reason why the people are difficult to rule is because the rulers' decrees are harsh and they like to intervene excessively, making it difficult for the people to be governed.

The reason why the people are inclined to risk their lives and die easily is because the rulers, to sustain themselves, have plundered the people's resources to the fullest, so the people feel that death is inconsequential. Only those who do not pursue life's pleasures are truly wise and virtuous compared to those who excessively value their own lives.

【第七十六章】Chapter 76

Most Common Translation

人之生也柔弱，	When people are born, they are soft and weak,
其死也堅強。	When they die, they are hard and stiff.
萬物草木之生也柔脆，	When plants and trees are born, they are soft and tender,
其死也枯槁。	When they die, they are dry and withered.
故堅強者死之徒，	Therefore, the strong and hard are companions of death,
柔弱者生之徒。	The soft and weak are companions of life.
是以兵強則不勝，	Thus, a forceful army will not prevail, (note 1)
木強則兵。	A rigid tree will break. (note 2)
強大處下，	The strong and great reside below,
柔弱處上。	The soft and weak reside above.

Note 1 - An army that is arrogant due to its formidable strength. Another interpretation of this verse suggests that the reckless use of military force, without careful consideration, inevitably leads to defeat.

Note 2 - 木強則兵: if translated word by word, it is: wood, strong, then, weapon. In the context of Laozi's period, where metal was scarce and wood was often used for weapons, the original phrase suggests that the strong and hard wood would be fashioned into a weapon by the craftsman, ultimately leading to its destruction. Alternatively, the strong and hard wood would be repurposed for tools, furniture, or any other objects that suit human desires.

Most Common Literal Translation

When alive, the human body is soft, but upon death, it stiffens. Similarly, in life, plants and trees are tender and fragile, yet in death, they become dry and rigid. Therefore, strength aligns with death, while weakness aligns with growth. Consequently, resorting to force in warfare leads to destruction, and when trees become too robust, they are felled and broken. All that is strong tends to be inferior, while all that is weak tends to be superior.

My 5 Cents

This chapter should be read in conjunction with Chapter 50.

Notes form 莊子 Zhuangzi, some over 200 after Laozi: People all know the usefulness of the useful, but nobody knows the usefulness of the useless. (人皆知有用之用，而莫知无用之用)

The concept of "the usefulness of the useless" is an important viewpoint and proposition in Zhuangzi's philosophy, originating from Chapter "Man in the World" of the Zhuangzi text《莊子·人間世》. Zhuangzi uses the example of a large tree to illustrate the principle of the usefulness of the useless. This tree has grown for thousands of years, yet because it does not yield useful timber and grows in a twisted and unsightly manner, people abandon it. However, it ultimately avoids being felled. Zhuangzi argues that precisely because it lacks utilitarian value, it can preserve its life. People all know the usefulness of the useful, but nobody knows the usefulness of the useless. The main idea expressed is that people often overlook the potentially greater value of things because they only value their practical utility, while those deemed "useless" may possess intrinsic value beyond utility. Therefore, "the usefulness of the useless" refers to things that may appear useless but, if properly utilized, can unexpectedly fulfill significant roles.

In the Dao De Jing, Chapter 11, it mentions Thirty spokes converge upon a single hub; It is the hole in the center that makes it useful. Shape clay into a vessel; It is the space within that makes it useful. Cut doors and windows for a room; It is the holes that make it useful. Therefore, the benefit comes from what is there; Usefulness from what is not there.

Uselessness and leaves a space. The flow of qi runs like the moon's orbit, thirty, with emptiness in the middle. The great use of the useless. The strong and great reside below, and the soft and weak reside above.

【第七十七章】Chapter 77

Most Common Translation

天之道，	The Way of Heaven (Dao),
其猶張弓與！	Is like pulling a bow,
高者抑之，	The high is brought low,
下者舉之；	And the low is raised up;
有余者損之，	Those who have excess are diminished,
不足者補之。	Those who lack are supplemented.
天之道，	The Way of Heaven (Dao),
損有余而補不足。	Reduce the surplus and replenish the deficiency.
人之道則不然，	The way of human's doing is contrary:
損不足以奉有余。	Diminish the excess and supplement the deficiency.
孰能有余以奉天下？	Who can have a surplus to serve the world?
唯有道者。	Only those who follow the Dao.
是以聖人為而不恃，	Therefore, the sage acts but does not boast,
功成而不處，	Achieves without claiming credit or dwelling on the position,
其不欲見賢。	Preferring not to be listed among the virtuous.
	(note 1)

Note 1 - In recent years, amidst China's opening up to allow its citizens to engage in business activities for personal gain, a select few individuals or families emerged as the wealthiest in the nation. Initially, these affluent entrepreneurs rejoiced at the prospect of their names gracing the lists of the wealthiest. However, as time passed, a pattern emerged: those prominently featured on these lists often found themselves ensnared in scandals. Whether accused of corruption or illicit business practices, their conspicuous wealth inevitably drew the scrutiny of government authorities.

Subsequently, the list of wealthy individuals came to be known colloquially as the "death list" among the populace. Drawing parallels with a popular manga and animated series titled "Death Note", wherein individuals whose names are written in a supernatural notebook are pursued by a figure known as the "death hunter" for their souls.

Most Common Literal Translation

The natural law, isn't it very much like drawing a bow and shooting an arrow? When the string is pulled too high, it is lowered; when it is too low, it is raised. If it is pulled too tightly, it is relaxed; if it is not pulled enough, it is supplemented. The natural law is about reducing excess to supply deficiencies. However, the rules of society are not like this; they require reducing deficiencies to contribute to those with excess. So, who can reduce the excess to supply the deficiencies of the world? Only those who follow the Way can do so. Therefore, the sage of the Way acts without possessing, achieving without claiming credit. They are unwilling to display their wisdom.

My 5 Cents

It's all about achieving balance and harmony, much like the concept of the five Qi. In practice, follow the Dao, redistributing excess to our "yellow court" and providing for those in need.

The "human way" diverges from this path, leading to self-harm. This is highlighted in the teachings of the Five Kitchen Sutras and previous chapters of the Dao De Jing.

【第七十八章】Chapter 78

Most Common Translation

天下莫柔弱於水，	Nothing in the world is as soft and weak as water,
而攻堅強者莫之能勝，	Yet nothing can surpass it in overcoming the hard and strong.
其無以易之。	Nothing can replace it.
弱之勝強，	Weakness overcomes strength,
柔之勝剛，	Gentleness overcomes rigidity,
天下莫不知，	Everyone in the world knows this,
莫能行。	But no one can practice it. (note 1)
是以聖人云，	Therefore, the sage says,
受國之垢，	He who bears the disgrace of the nation. (note 2)
是謂社稷主；	Is called the master of the state;
受國不祥，	He who bears the misfortunes of the nation, (note 3)
是為天下王。	Is called the king of the world.
正言若反。	True words seem paradoxical.
	(Truthful speech appears as false.)

Note 1 - Reference Chapter 70

Note 2 - The original wording is "Dirt".

Note 3 - The original wording is "inauspicious" or "ill-omened".

Most Common Literal Translation

Throughout the world, there is nothing softer than water, yet when it comes to overcoming the hard and strong, nothing surpasses it. Weakness triumphs over strength, gentleness over hardness. Everyone in the world knows this, yet no one can put it into practice. Therefore, the wise sage says, "By bearing the humiliation of the nation, one can become the ruler of the state; by bearing the misfortunes of the nation, one can become the ruler of the world." Positive words appear to be saying the opposite.

Extract from He Sang Gong – De Jing – Trust

Throughout the world, nothing is softer or weaker than water. When contained as round, it is round; when obstructed, it stops; when free flowing, it moves. Despite its softness, it cannot be overcome by force. Water can support mountains and hills, wear down iron and bronze, and nothing can surpass it. It achieves success by its ability to yield. Those who rely on strength cannot easily contend with water. Weakness overcomes strength; water extinguishes fire, and darkness subdues light. Softness triumphs over hardness; a gentle tongue can subdue strong teeth, as Teeth perish before the tongue.

Everyone knows that softness and weakness endure, while hardness and strength are easily damaged, yet few can embody this. People value pride and strength over humility. Therefore, the sage says: to serve is to elevate oneself. By bearing the disgrace of the nation, one becomes the master of the state. A ruler who can bear the nation's impurities, like a river or sea that does not repel small streams, can sustain the prosperity of the state and become its ruler. By bearing the nation's misfortunes, one becomes the king of the world. A ruler who can endure the burdens of the people, alleviating them from misfortune, can govern the world. True words seem paradoxical. These are words of integrity, though misunderstood by the world as contradictory.

老子河上公章句 -> 德經 -> 任信

天下莫柔弱於水，圓中則圓，方中則方，壅之則止，決之則行。而攻堅強者莫之能勝，水能懷山襄陵，磨鐵消銅，莫能勝水而成功也。以其無以易之。夫攻堅強者，無以易於水。弱之勝強，水能滅火，陰能消陽。柔之勝剛，舌柔齒剛，齒先舌亡。天下莫不知，知柔弱者久長，剛強者折傷。莫能行。恥謙卑，好強梁。是以聖人云：謂下事也。受國之垢，是謂社稷主；人君能受國之垢濁者，若江海不逆小流，則能長保其社稷，為一國之君主也。受國不祥，是為天下王。人君能引過自與，代民受不祥之殃，則可以王天下。正言若反。此乃正直之言，世人不知，以為反言。

【第七十九章】Chapter 79

Most Common Translation

和大怨，	To reconcile major grievances,
必有余怨，	There will inevitably be residual resentment,
安可以為善？	How does this become a peaceful and virtuous method?
是以聖人執左契，	Therefore, the sage holds to the left, (note 1)
而不責於人。	and does not blame others.
有德司契，	With virtue, one administers with agreements; (note 2)
無德司徹。	Without virtue, one administers punishment. (note 3)
天道無親，	Heaven's path shows no favoritism,
常與善人。	Consistently favors the virtuous.

Note 1 - Please refer to Chapter 31 for details of what is the meaning of left. And, in addition, you may also refer to the 2nd diagram of TCHYD for more advanced information.

Note 2 - It refers to the left side of the agreement or the left voucher.

Left voucher: The left half of a tall, made of bamboo or wood, with a horizontal line carved in the middle and identical text carved on both sides, recording the names and quantities of goods or money lent. It is split into two pieces: the left piece is the left voucher, inscribed with the name of the debtor and kept by the creditor; the right piece is the right voucher, inscribed with the name of the creditor and kept by the debtor. When goods or money are returned, the two vouchers are used as evidence.

Note 3 - In Laozi's era, '徹' referred to a tax system, and can be used as a kind of punishment, similar to an Indulgence certificate in Catholicism.

Most Common Translation

Reconciling deep-seated resentments inevitably leaves residual bitterness. Repaying animosity with virtue, how can this be deemed a proper course? Therefore, the virtuous sage preserves the records of debts owed but does not use them to coerce repayment. Those with "virtue" are as magnanimous as the sage holding the records, while those without "virtue" are as exacting and deceitful as tax collectors. The laws of nature show no partiality, always favoring the virtuous.

【第八十章】 Chapter 80

Most Common Translation

小國寡民，	Small country, few people,
使有什伯之器而不用，	Although having weapons of war and not using them,
使民重死而不遠徙。	Making the people value death and not desire far-off places. (note 1)
雖有舟輿，	Though there are boats and carriages,
無所乘之；	No one to ride in them;
雖有甲兵，	Though there is armor and weaponry,
無所陳之；	No occasion to display them;
使人復結繩而用之。	Employing people to return to using knotted cords. (note 2)
甘其食，	Finds their food sweet,
美其服，	Adorn and praise what they wear,
安其居，	Dwell peacefully at homes,
樂其俗。	Enjoy their traditions.
鄰國相望，	Neighboring countries face each other,
雞犬之聲相聞，	Echoes of chickens and dogs fill the air,
民至老死不相往來。	Yet the people grow old and die without ever visiting each other.

Note 1 - It also means that the governor values the lives of the citizens and does not require them to travel far for war.

Note 2 - It signifies a return to the simplest form of communication, devoid of any embellishments, manipulation, or cunning tactics, relying solely on the pure essence of words.

Most Common Literal Translation

It makes the country smaller and the population sparse. Even though there are various tools, they are not used; it makes people cherish life and not migrate to distant places; although there are ships and vehicles, there is no need to use them every time; though there are weapons and equipment, there is no place to deploy them for battle; it brings the people back to the natural state of ancient knot-tying records. The governance of the country is excellent, allowing the people to eat well, dress beautifully, live comfortably, and be happy. Nations can see each other, and the sounds of chickens and dogs can be heard, but people do not interact with each other from birth to death.

My 5 Cents

It symbolizes a return to the most fundamental and genuine lifestyle, where connections are few, akin to living and spiritually practicing inside a cave. Despite possessing extensive skills in martial arts and medicine, one refrains from using them, relying instead on their ability to prevent conflict. With the capacity to understand and explore the world without physical travel, yet choosing not to intervene, echoing the wisdom of Laozi's teachings.

Embracing a sage-like existence, one travels sparingly, finding satisfaction in simple meals and basic clothing. Despite being aware of external events (Echoes of chickens and dogs fill the air), inner peace remains undisturbed. This state of awareness champions self-sufficiency, allowing one to inhabit a realm of purity and simplicity.

In this regard, Master He Sang Gong labels this chapter as "Independent".

Again, please note that this is the Qi cultivation level that reaches the stage of "closing the dui", as discussed in earlier notes regarding the state of Qi movements represented by trigrams.

【第八十一章】 Chapter 81

Most Common Translation

信言不美，	True words are not necessarily beautiful,
美言不信；	Beautiful words are not necessarily true.
善者不辯，	The virtuous do not engage in disputes;
辯者不善；	Those who engage in disputes are not virtuous.
知者不博，	Those who truly understand do not show off their knowledge;
博者不知。	Those who show off their knowledge do not truly understand.
聖人不積，	The wise do not hoard,
既以為人，	Yet the more they do for others,
己愈有；	The more they have;
既以與人，	By giving to others,
己愈多。	They have even more themselves.
天之道，	The way of Heaven (the Dao),
利而不害。	Is to benefit and not harm.
聖人之道，	The way of the sage,
為而不爭。	Is to act without contention.

Most Common Literal Translation

True and trustworthy words are not beautiful; beautiful words are not true. Kind-hearted people do not speak skillfully; skillful speakers are not kind-hearted. Those with true knowledge do not show off; those who show off their knowledge are not truly knowledgeable. The sage does not harbor selfish desires but instead strives to care for others, making themselves more fulfilled. By giving to others, they become even more abundant. The natural order is to benefit all things without causing harm. The sage's principle of conduct is to act without contention.

My 5 Cents - Read together with Chapter 56.

Supplement and Ending Notes:

Thank you, Angela, for asking me to translate the Dao De Jing. This request has allowed me to revisit and reflect on thoughts I have set aside for over 40 years.

Here, I present some supplementary explanations to hopefully enhance your understanding of the DDJ scriptures.

Name: The Vessel for the Operation of Dao Between Heaven and Earth

First, let's understand the concept of [Name] from a purely rational, logical, and philosophical perspective.

Starting from humanity's most primitive state of ignorance, we first needed to assign names to various objects and things to communicate. For example, we call this object an apple. This gives us the concept of what an apple is, allowing us to understand what we are talking about. Without the concept of an apple, it would be difficult to explain in a few words what Snow White was poisoned by.

However, as soon as we have the concept of an apple in our minds, the notion of what is not an apple arises. This is an apple, and those are not apples. An apple is one; what is not an apple becomes two. If we assume that the evolution of human consciousness starts with the concept of an apple, we have one (apple). Then, we have two (not an apple). From the second category (not an apple), we can deduce oranges. An orange becomes three. Not an apple and not an orange is still two.

Similarly, with the concept of oranges (three), differentiated from two (not an apple, not an orange), we then have categories that are not apples (one) and not oranges (three). This makes four, five, six, seven, ... to infinity. In other words, we can identify pears, passion fruits, mangoes, and so on, gradually differentiating them into all things.

Moreover, we know that names are not limited to objects. They can also be adjectives, actions, and concepts, referring to everything our minds can comprehend. Even things we can't fully understand but have a sense or observe existence, we can give it a name. This naming starts from what we can understand (one), categorizing it into what we cannot understand (two), forming another system of consciousness.

With this system of what we can understand (one, two, three) and what we cannot understand (one, two, three), we create the vessel for human conscious thought. The interaction between what we understand and what we do not understand creates.

From what we do not understand, we come to understand. Conversely, from what we understand, we may come to not understand. This dynamic interaction, along with emptiness, forms the great wheel of human logical thought.

To put it simply, NAME is the starting point of our human logical thought and ideas. Or we may say, an image or words. However, what we have discussed here remains within our material world.

Second - On a psychological level, NAME: Once we become aware of the concept of "I", this intention of establishing "I" also implicitly establishes the concept of "not I", its opposite. Thus, there arises the distinction between what is mine and what is not mine, what I possess and what I do not possess, and what I desire to possess.

Spiritually, this is the source of suffering.

Third - The Attributes or the Nature of Names

When we assign a name, such as "water", what does this name encompass? Is it referring to an object called water, a single drop, or a collection of something in a bowl?

Or are we referring to the function of water? Its properties, texture, nature, color, or form? Or perhaps we are talking about a friend named Water?

When Laozi talks about water, what is he referring to? Is he speaking of the virtues of water, or what its inherent nature reveals?

I believe we have discussed this before, so I will outline a few key points to refresh our understanding.

Fourth - Concept and illusion

Understanding the attributes behind names allows us to further comprehend the extended descriptions they convey.

Let's illustrate this with the example of water. We have the concept of water. However, in our physical world, there is no singular entity called an ocean. An ocean is a term we use to conveniently describe a vast amount of water together. When this body of water reaches a certain size, we call it an ocean, or a lake. When it flows, we call it a river. Or when it falls, it is a waterfall. However, the attributes and intrinsic qualities of a pond and an ocean are different.

For instance, as urban dwellers, our psychological fear of an ocean is often greater than that of a pond, let alone a single drop of water. Why is this so?

Understanding this, it becomes evident that certain names evoke a positive feeling within us. Conversely, some names may trigger fear or discomfort, such as poverty, loneliness, or a particular boss.

Fifth - Names are complex when used in a being within our human society. A name not only refers to a person but also encompasses all their attributes, often including their social status, power, and attractiveness.

Take Napoleon as another example. To many, he is a genuine hero in history. Yet, to his subordinates, he might be a terrifying commander. In one interview, his beautiful wife described Napoleon as a horrible old man.

Why such disparity? It's because people cannot fully understand every aspect of Napoleon's character. Or perhaps, certain admirable traits hold no significance for them on a particular level.

Sixth - The Vibration of NAME

In ancient temples across the Middle East, among Native American beliefs in South America, and even in Chinese Taoism, it was forbidden to shout the names of gods because of their vibrational power. Some say these names could even shake the entire universe.

With this understanding, we realize that certain mantras or the names of gods carry vibrations received by the most enlightened sages during their profound meditation. This power of sound—beyond physical sound in our material world—has the potential to transform our spirit, mindset, and bring numerous benefits, while also reducing our spiritual obstacles.

Seventh - The power of aspiration is embedded within the names of gods, Bodhisattvas, and sages.

When we chant or recite the names of certain saints, gods, or Bodhisattvas, we are not merely reciting words but resonating with their great powers of aspiration. It stirs a resonance within our hearts from an early age. Conversely, if we recite a mantra, Buddhist chant, or sacred text without aligning with their aspirational power, the effect will not be significant. At most, it may lead to a certain level of spiritual focus, or we may say mindfulness.

Eighth - The contract

Our name represents a contract that is not easily explained in a few sentences. In certain traditional Native American and Chinese spiritual cultures, individuals possess a secret name distinct from their everyday name. Disclosing this real name often signifies entering into a profound agreement or contract.

Here's an example to be mindful of: when walking in a deep, dark forest or any place with heavy negative energy, if you hear your name being called, especially from behind, refrain from responding. Otherwise, you may unwittingly commit to something undesirable.

Hundred-Character Monument

Lü Dongbin (796-)

Cultivate vital energy (QI), forget words (less speech) and guard it; (note 1)

Conquer your mind and desire to embrace to the realm of Wúwéi.

In the movement and stillness, recognize the ancestral source (primordial energy).

In the absence of affairs, who is to seek for?

Truely observation requires in responding to things,

Responding to things without losing one's way. (note 2)

Not losing one's way, the one-ness nature resides naturally,

The nature residing, the energy returns on its own.

Energy returns, elixir self-forms,

In the vessel, harmonize the Kan (water) and Li (Fire). (note 3)

Yin and yang give birth in cycles,

Transforming and spreading in thunderous sound (The WORD, inner sound).

White clouds rise above the summit (inner Vision),

Sweet dew showers on Mount Sumeru (inner Vision and Sound).

Drinking the Longevity wine (elixir) oneself,

Who knows the unrestrained joy?

Sitting, listening to the soundless music (the overall inner sound),

Clearly understanding the machinery and critical moment of creation.

All in these twenty verses, (note 4)

Indeed, ascending the heavenly ladder. (note 5)

呂祖百字碑

養炁忘言守，降心為無為。動靜知宗祖，無事更尋誰？

真常須應物，應物要不迷。不迷性自住，性住氣自回。

氣回丹自結，壺中配坎離。陰陽生反復，普化一聲雷。

白雲朝頂上，甘露洒須彌。自飲長生酒，逍遙誰得知。

坐聽無弦曲，明通造化機。都來二十句，端的上天梯。

Note 1 - (忘言) Forget speech" literally implies the act of speaking less or refraining from unnecessary verbal expression. It also encompasses the idea of "mind speech", wherein one minimizes mental chatter, recognizing the relationship between verbal communication and mental activity. The aim is to conserve energy, as speaking or thinking excessively is perceived as a potential waste of one's mental and physical resources.

It brings out another concept in Chinese, "自在", translates to "comfortable", "peaceful", and "joyful". If translate word to word, 自 means "self" and 在 means "here".

However, these translations may seem too simplistic. Achieving this state involves "Control the mind".

Note 2 - **This verse is derived from the reference and quotation of Qingjing Jing:**

Always observing and responding to external matters with their genuine nature without any bias, can acquire the true nature of the one-self.

Often interchange and interact with clam mind and peacefulness.

Hence, mind peacefulness (tranquil and serene) as always.

清靜經

真常應物，真常得性

相應常靜，常清靜矣

https://en.wikipedia.org/wiki/Qingjing_Jing

Note 3 - Reference to our Neiqong 2 and 3, please refer to the notes and Marianne's work (the diagram)

Note 4 - There are 20 verses in this Monument, each verse contains 5 Chinese Characters, hence, making it all up into 100 characters.

Note 5 - Remember the photo you guys made during a wonderful night at the staircase, during the Tai Chi Camp, with a pillow in green? PS: I Can not find the photo, does anyone have it and share?

About Compassion

Compassion. "慈" means "kindness" or "loving-kindness". "悲" means "sorrow" or "empathy". In Buddhism, compassion is the combination of these two qualities: the willingness to alleviate suffering and the genuine desire for the well-being and happiness of others. It is a deep sense of empathy and kindness that moves individuals to take action and help those in need, offering comfort and support.

I hope you've enjoyed reading this book. However, don't expect to grasp *everything fully* on your first read. Even though Master Gordon has laid things out clearly, the *Dao De Jing – Unfiltered Thoughts in Motion* is written with advanced neigong students in mind. Many in that group may not *fully* absorb all its wisdom right away either. What you've read is like a seed planted in your subconscious. As your qigong, neigong, or spiritual practice deepens, you'll have those "Aha!" moments: *Now I understand!* That's why it's important to keep up with your practice.

If questions arise from reading this book, I encourage you to write them down. When the time is right, we'll organize Zoom sessions where Master Gordon can address commonly asked questions. If you're interested, you can sign up at www.taichi18.com/ddj

Join us to deepen your understanding and further unlock the wisdom of the *Dao De Jing*!

Sifu Wing Cheung

Manufactured by Amazon.ca
Bolton, ON